*A Study in the
Theory of Investment*

STUDIES IN ECONOMICS

of the

ECONOMICS RESEARCH CENTER

of the

UNIVERSITY OF CHICAGO

A Study in the
Theory of Investment

By

TRYGVE HAAVELMO

THE UNIVERSITY OF CHICAGO PRESS

Library of Congress Catalog Number: 60-13057

THE UNIVERSITY OF CHICAGO PRESS, CHICAGO 37
The University of Toronto Press, Toronto 5, Canada

© *1960 by The University of Chicago. Published 1960. Composed and printed by* THE UNIVERSITY OF CHICAGO PRESS, *Chicago, Illinois, U.S.A.*

Preface

Dᴜʀɪɴɢ the past ten years or so I have tried, on various occasions, to speak and to write of the need for more axiomatic stringency in the field of investment theory. Economics can proudly exhibit a neat and elegant theory of "rational consumers' behavior." The gap between theory and reality may still be large even here, but we have at least a carefully built first approximation that helps us to approach the problems of consumers' demand in an orderly fashion. By comparison, the theory of the "demand for investment" shows a sad lag in this respect. True, there are enough writings on the subject. But my impression is that students of investment theory have proceeded somewhat like the busy typist who could never find the time to learn the touch system.

In order to make progress in the theory of investment, I think we should set out in a thorough and almost pedantic way to look for the relation between investment activity and the really fundamental laws of economic behavior. The findings of research in this direction may not be sufficient to enable us to predict the actual behavior of investors. But I tend to believe that such efforts represent one of the necessary steps toward a realistic theory.

In the chapters that follow I have tried my best to practice what I have preached above. Personally, I have found these exercises quite interesting and intriguing. But unfortunately, this experience of mine offers no guaranty against the final product being dull and tedious reading to others.

In writing this book I have met with some problems of references, which I should like to mention. One problem is, of course, that the literature is so enormous that it is very hard to give proper references and credits. But there is another problem that has seemed to me particularly difficult, namely, the question of how to deal with ideas, right or wrong, that we know are widespread and of considerable actuality, but for which it would be hard to find a representative statement in writing. I have met with many such instances in the present volume. This is the apology I have to offer for a rather frequent use of phrases like "it is often argued that," without reference to any particular book or paper.

As I have already indicated, this book is an outgrowth of many years of work. However, my first real opportunity of completing the manuscript came in 1957. In that year the University of Chicago honored me with an invitation to the Department of Economics as a Ford Foundation Visiting Professor of Economics for 1957/58. During my year at Chicago, I had the occasion to discuss the present research project with many outstanding scholars both at Chicago and at other American universities. In addition, I had enviable working conditions. For all this I should like to express my respectful gratitude to the University of Chicago and its staff.

I have received a great deal of help and encouragement from colleagues and friends. I do not know how I could fully thank them all. But I should like to mention some of those to whom my debt is particularly great.

First of all, I want to thank my students at the University of Oslo, who in 1953/54 listened patiently to my lectures on investment theory, and whose keen interest in the subject made me feel that further work might be worthwhile. I am likewise greatly in debt to students at the University of Chicago who, in the spring of 1958, followed my lectures on the topic of this book and taught me a great deal about how to distinguish between essentials and unessentials in this difficult part of economic theory.

Several of my colleagues have been kind enough to read first drafts of the chapters that follow. For invaluable service in this respect I owe sincere thanks to professors Yehuda Grunfeld of the Hebrew University, Jerusalem, formerly of the University of Chicago; Zvi Griliches of the University of Chicago; and to my colleagues at Oslo, Fritz C. Holte, Leif Johansen, Hans Jacob Kreyberg, and Bjørn Thalberg. The latter also prepared and edited mimeographed notes from my lectures at Oslo in 1953/54.

Among those who have otherwise helped me to complete the manuscript for this book I should like especially to mention Miss Marie Moe at the University of Chicago and Miss Inger Karlsen at the University of Oslo, Institute of Economics. I owe them my thanks for secretarial assistance and for efficient typing of a rather unwieldy manuscript.

It is almost certain that the reader will discover mistakes and shortcomings in the pages to follow. The blame for these things should, of course, be on the author alone. To the extent that errors have been happily avoided, the credit should go to those who generously gave me their help and advice.

Contents

vii

IV
Investment Behavior in a Market Economy

Index

PART I

Survey of Problems

1

Trends of Thought in the Theory of Investment

Economic theory can give a reasonably good account of how the level of investment activity influences effective demand and employment. If only we knew more about the determinants of investment! But, unfortunately, our knowledge in this direction is still very meager. One might well ask, What is wrong with the theory of investment? Or, perhaps, What is wrong with the subject matter itself! For one thing, this variable—the pivot of modern macroeconomics—has apparently lived a somewhat nomadic life among the various chapters of economic theory. Perhaps it has not stayed long enough in any one place. Perhaps it has been ill treated.

It may be worthwhile to examine these questions a little closer, before we set out to add more readings to an already voluminous literature.

I. INVESTMENT AND THE PURE THEORY OF CAPITAL

Some of the great "classical"[1] exponents of the pure theory of capital, notably Wicksell, have used the term "investment" in a manner which could easily confuse the modern student of economics. In this literature we frequently find such expressions as "the amount of capital invested," the "return on investment," the "period of investment." When we try to dig deeper into the meaning of these expressions, we find that they refer to one of two notions of "investment," neither of which corresponds to investment in the sense of the rate of growth of capital.

The first of these notions of investment is the transfer of a certain amount of wealth from one ownership, or employment, to another. In a closed economy it may be possible for single individuals or firms to carry out such "spot investment" operations. But for the economy as a whole it is obviously not possible to make any total *net addition* to any kind of capital equipment in this manner. In modern terminology the total net investment resulting from such operations is zero.

The second classical notion of investment is derived from the idea of capital as a revolving stock. If each capital item has a certain durability, or service life, a certain replacement per unit of time is required to maintain the total stock. A part of gross current output must be "invested" each year in order to keep the stock of capital constant. The capital is

1. I use the expressions "classical," "older," etc., to refer, somewhat loosely, to ideas and writings that belong to the pre-Keynesian era. But when I misuse the word "classical" in this way, I shall try to remember to use quotation marks.

3

"liberated" as it wears out, and is "reinvested." Under stationary conditions this means zero net investment. It is extremely important to be aware of this use of investment in the sense of replacement, e.g., when we consider older theories of the connection between investment and the rate of interest. The "classical" ideas on this point bear no direct relation to the "investment schedules" found in modern macrotheories of the Keynesian type. The "classical" reasoning is simply this: Assume that, at a lower rate of interest, it becomes profitable to apply more capital. When this larger amount of capital is somehow accumulated, it will require a larger annual rate of replacement. Consequently, if we compare various stationary conditions, each corresponding to a particular rate of interest, the annual gross investment (= replacement) will be the larger the lower is the rate of interest. This also means that a desire for more capital in any particular circumstance is, implicitly, the same as a desire for a higher rate of gross investment (= replacement). None of this has to do with the *dynamic process* of increasing (or decreasing) the amount of capital. In particular, *the speed of transition* from one amount of capital to another (i.e., net investment) is a question of an entirely different nature, as far as economic behavior is concerned. Wicksell, for one, is absolutely clear on this point.[2] His theory of the relation between capital and interest is a theory concerning alternative, stationary amounts of capital. The question of net investment is a separate, independent part of his *Lectures*, I, viz., Part III, "On the Accumulation of Capital." Surveying existing theory on this topic, he says that "the literature on this subject is very meagre," apparently in contrast to the state of affairs as far as pure theory of capital is concerned.

In the Böhm-Bawerk–Wicksellian theory and other "classical" theories, the problem of net investment, or formation of capital, is frequently dealt with under the heading of *Savings*. (Here again, however, we have to watch out, as the term "savings" is sometimes used for net capital accumulation, sometimes for reinvestment, sometimes for the non-consumption of a given amount of capital and sometimes for a spot transfer from cash to bank deposits or titles to real assets.)

Thus, the main body of the "classical" pure theory of capital is not concerned with the speed at which producers like to acquire new capital, once the desire is there, but only with the final amount of capital demanded, under alternative possibilities of yield. The parallel "theory of investment" is a theory of long-range accumulation of capital determined by society's willingness to refrain from consumption. In other words, the

2. K. Wicksell, *Lectures on Political Economy*, Eng. trans. E. Classen (New York: Macmillan Co., 1934), Vols. I, II. Hereafter referred to as *Lectures*, I, or *Lectures*, II.

"classical" theory of investment is one applicable to a full-employment society, where there is no question of not actually using available resources. It is a theory of growth in a society where effective demand is no limiting factor. Today these theories have, therefore, in a sense more actuality than the short-run macro theories developed during the great depression of the 1930's.

From the Böhm-Bawerk–Wicksellian theory of capital we have, however, inherited a class of unsolved problems which are fundamental to any theory of investment, viz., the problem of how to define capital as a *factor of production*. The essence of this problem is the relation between what might be termed the rate of saving, or net investment, in *value terms* and the expansion of capital as a *technical agent* of production.[3] The enormous amount of literature that exists on the—partly philosophical —question of the definition of capital has so far not been very comforting to those who have ambitions in the direction of econometric research upon the relation between investment and productivity growth (cf. chaps. xvii and xviii).

II. LONG-RANGE THEORIES OF CAPITAL FORMATION

As already has been mentioned, the Böhm-Bawerk–Wicksellian theory of capital formation was essentially a theory of savings, i.e., a theory of economic behavior aiming at explaining why people under certain circumstances do not consume their whole net income. The key variable in this theory was the rate of interest and one central problem was whether the rate of interest has to be positive in order that there should be a positive amount of savings.[4]

The classical economists, with Ricardo as the leading figure, had very definite ideas concerning the actual outlook for continued capital formation. Theirs was the idea of a high probability for eventual stagnation. Because of the tendency towards a falling rate of profit, capital formation would gradually dwindle. With wages at the subsistence level, population growth would also cease, and we would move towards a stationary economy. The possible objections to the realism of these forecasts are well known. One must distinguish between the possibility of a falling *rate* of profit and a falling *amount* of profit. The latter does not follow from the

3. See J. Robinson, *The Accumulation of Capital* (London: Macmillan Co., 1956). See also N. Kaldor, "Annual Survey of Economic Theory: The Recent Controversy on the Theory of Capital," *Econometrica*, V (1937), 201–33.

4. See, e.g., F. Hayek, *The Pure Theory of Capital* (University of Chicago Press, 1950), pp. 4–5.

former.[5] If the amount of profit is large, the question is what the recipients of this profit do with it. To assume that they could consume it all if the *rate* of profit is below a certain positive level is probably very unrealistic. If we consider capital and land as separate factors, it is possible that the rate of interest or yield on capital might gradually fall toward zero, while rent would increase (because of "land" being a constant factor). But there again it is a question of what the landowners would do with their growing amount of income. It would seem reasonable that they would choose a considerable amount of savings even at very low rates of return.

The classical idea of the tendency toward a zero-profit equilibrium had also another, entirely different, angle, viz., that competition would tend to eliminate pure profits in industrial enterprise. The reasoning was that the yield of capital in a firm could not for long remain above the general level of the rate of interest in the market, because such net differentials would result in entry of new firms. Here we meet a very complicated aspect of the rate of investment: the rate of growth of the number of firms in the various industries. In order to establish new enterprises, the capital equipment of these enterprises would have to be produced. This process would certainly have a profound effect upon the profitability of already existing firms. It is by no means obvious that such a process would converge to a stationary situation with zero net profit. The question of the determinants of the size, and the number, of firms in an economy is probably one of the most complicated problems of economic dynamics.

The long-range development of capital formation is, of course, closely related to the development of production technology. It is extremely difficult to distinguish between increased productive capacity as a result of an increase in the "physical amount" of capital and increases in capacity due to new techniques. There are here some formidable problems of theory as well as of practical statistics. These problems we meet in full force when we try to measure the "amount of capital" as a factor of production. This means that we may expect real trouble when we try to establish a correspondence between the rate of "real saving," in the sense of non-consumed income, and the growth of capital as a factor of production.[6]

More recent theories of economic growth have developed along two

5. Cf., e.g., the author's *A Study in the Theory of Economic Evolution* (Amsterdam: North-Holland Publishing Co., 1954), pp. 9–12.

6. See, e.g., J. Robinson, "The Production Function and the Theory of Capital," *Review of Economic Studies*, XXI (1953–54), 81–106.

somewhat different lines. One could perhaps describe the difference by saying that one approach is concerned with the problem of a society's ability to *utilize* the real possibilities of growth, whereas the other is concerned with a society's capacity to *produce* growth.

The first type of problem is concerned with the question of whether the economic organization of society is such that the demand for investment is sufficient to bring about the "desired" rate of growth in the society. This problem seems to have its root in the depression mentality of the 1930's and is essentially a problem of rich and unplanned societies.

The second type of problem is, in a sense, the opposite of the first, viz., the question of *willingness to save* in order to meet as much as possible of an almost unlimited demand for capital accumulation. This is a main problem in many underdeveloped countries. It includes also such more technical problems as the problems of adequate financial institutions to organize the accumulation process and to promote savings. The problem is also met in the richer "planned" societies, but there as a problem of how to strike a reasonable balance between the desire for high, current consumption and the desire for economic progress.

The amount of literature dealing with these two kinds of problems is already quite extensive and is growing very rapidly.[7]

III. A Central Variable in Business Cycle Theories

The Theory of the Business Cycle may be gradually dying out as a separate branch of economics. Most of the subject matter has been incorporated in the field of general short-run macrodynamics. But when the interest in "looking for cycles" was at its height, investment was among the strategic variables.[8] We may, perhaps, distinguish between two different roles that investment has played in these theories.

The first role (although not historically so) is that of an external disturbance. Since investment is an important part of total economic activity, variations in the rate of investment would naturally affect other variables such as consumption, employment, wages, etc. The result could be cyclical in various ways. Irregular bursts of investment could be transformed into serial correlation patterns of other economic time series through various lag relations among these other variables. But investment could also conceivably have some serial correlation of its own due

7. See, e.g., the references in Harvey Leibenstein, *Economic Backwardness and Economic Growth* (New York: John Wiley & Sons, 1958).

8. Cf. G. v. Haberler, *Prosperity and Depression* (Geneva, 1939).

to a dynamic behavior pattern connecting investment with a more or less random sequence of innovations.[9]

In the historically more important business cycle theories, investment, and investment behavior, are important also as *endogenous* elements of a complete theory. One important branch of such theories was based on the phenomenon that variations in the rate of new investment may set in motion a pattern of repetitions through the recurrent need for replacements. Another branch of theories has been built on the fact that there is a considerable lag between the "starting" of work on a new capital item and the time of completion (at least in the case of large units, such as railroads, ships, large plants, etc.). If there are many independent investors, it may not be obvious to any one of them what the future total effect of their activities will be, as far as total productive capacity is concerned.[10]

A more recent development along ideas similar to the one last indicated is the theory of a relaxation process in investment activity. The basic hypothesis is that investment may, for a while, be "high because it is high," or "low because it is low." These statements are not as empty as they sound, because of the fact that the economy tends to produce some kind of automatic switching back and forth between the two types of situations. This switching system operates via the gradual effects of investment on the amount of capital. Each of the two trivial explanations mentioned above remain true only for a certain length of time, viz., as long as the amount of capital is not "high enough" or "low enough."[11]

This latter idea on business cycles is actually an outgrowth of an older line of thought, known as the "acceleration principle." This principle has often been misstated. It is actually not a theory of investment. It is a theory of alternative desired levels of capital stock. The theory needs an essential additional element to become an investment theory, namely, some hypothesis of a given *speed of adjustment*. But one could perhaps say that the acceleration principle indicates one kind of driving force in the dynamics of investment.

9. The basic ideas in this field go back to J. Schumpeter's work, *The Theory of Economic Development* (Harvard University Press, 1949). See also Haberler, *op. cit.*, pp. 81–83.

10. See Aftalion, *Les Crises periodiques de surproduction* (Paris, 1913); also J. Einarsen, *Reinvestment Cycles and Their Manifestation in the Norwegian Shipbuilding Industry* (Oslo, 1938).

11. See P. M. Goodwin, "The Non-Linear Accelerator and the Persistence of Business Cycles," *Econometrica*, XIX (1951), 1–17; J. R. Hicks, *A Contribution to the Theory of the Trade Cycle* (Oxford, 1950).

IV. The Role of Investment in Keynesian Theories of Employment

In the macroeconomic models that grew out of the experience of the great depression a remarkable change in view took place on the welfare implications of a given rate of investment. Its role as a growth factor was pushed almost entirely out of the picture and replaced by that of determining the current level of employment. This change in view is, of course, quite understandable. Why should one be concerned about the creation of more production capacity when so many developed economies could not even manage to put existing productive resources to work? In fact, one could even argue that increasing the capacity to produce by means of investment would gradually counteract the effects of investment itself as an employment-creating factor.

In these macromodels of employment the elements that represent investment theory may be subdivided into (1) theories of the *effects* of the rate of investment, (2) theories of the determinants of the level of investment activity, and (3) theories of the determinants of *variations* in this level. Perhaps one could add a fourth category: theories analyzing the effects and the desirability of autonomous public investment.

The macrotheories concerning the effect of the level of investment upon output and employment centered around the idea of "multipliers," of various kinds. These theories assumed, in essence, that investment was the active element determining the total amount of savings that the economy was capable of offsetting. Given the behavior patterns of consumers (or savers), the demand for, and the output of, consumer goods would be determined, the *producers* being rather passive agents in the whole game. Since the real difficulty of the situation was seen as that of a limited level of investment activity, the interest centered around the problem of how the economy could make the most out of a given level of investment, insofar as total employment was concerned. This led to such problems as that of the effects of redistributing income, the effects of cash reserves upon the propensity to consume, etc.

A much more difficult chapter was the theory of the *determinants* of private investment. The classical theories of capital and of capital accumulation could not answer the question of "insufficient demand for investment." A good deal of confusion seems to have arisen in the attempts to derive the demand for investment as a function of the profitability of employing capital in production. The difficulty here is that the existence of a possibility for increased earnings by using more capital does not by itself determine the *speed* at which the amount of capital will actually be increased. A good part of the following study will be devoted to efforts toward clearing up this point.

In the host of Keynesian models that we now have, it is not at all clear whether the term "investment opportunities" means an existing "fund" of unused opportunities, or a more or less regular flow of new opportunities over time. It makes a great deal of difference for the interpretation of "demand for investment" which one of these interpretations one has in mind.

The list of factors that influence investment can be made very extensive. The factors most frequently mentioned are, of course, the rate of interest, the existing amount of capital, and the current level of economic activity. But even if the main factors and their specific influence on the average level of investment were clarified, there remains the problem of the short-run variations in investment activity. In this connection, the importance of *expectations* has been strongly emphasized by nearly all the model-makers. It is, however, probably fair to say that the constant reference to the importance of expectations has served more as an excuse for the fact that we know so little about investment behavior than as the foundation of explicit theories that could make predictions possible. Expectations have to have a known relation to something that is itself known or predictable. Otherwise, the emphasis upon the importance of expectations will serve as a proof of hopelessness for the theory that we are concerned with.

The doctrines of deficit government spending are related to the theory of investment in various ways. The most direct relation is, of course, that growth of capital can be brought about as a result of public investment activity as well as by private investment. Some of those who advocate public investment see the purpose of it as that of creating capital. Since this is presumably a desirable thing, the government ought to do this to the extent that private initiative fails. Other doctrines of deficit spending stem from almost the opposite point of view, viz., that government deficit spending may be needed in order to create purchasing power, and that it is all right, or even desirable, that such spending be as useless as possible, since the problem in an unemployment situation is one of excess capacity. In the case where deficit spending takes the form of doles, etc., or expenditure on useless projects, it represents investment in a rather peculiar sense: It is investment in hoarded purchasing power. If the government borrows money for this purpose, national bookkeeping would show that the resulting net "real" investment would be zero, the government debt being balanced by the increase in private financial assets. However, if the private sector always wants to see its assets grow, that is, if it never wants to "use up" its financial wealth, the deficit spending operation does in fact create something which is in a sense real, viz., hoarded private wealth. The "yield" of this "capital" is a feeling of security, which undoubtedly is real enough in the sense that it satisfies a real demand. If this demand is not satisfied, the private sector will *try* to increase its wealth by not spending, with the result that it reduces its income. If this kind of "investment" is included in the annual net investment of an economy, the connection between investment and the increase in capital as a factor of production becomes even more problematic than when investment is only real investment in the usual sense.

The fact that man could ever think of investment for other purposes than to increase capacity or to store real values must certainly be considered a result of organizational defects in the economic system. It cannot be a basic problem of man in relation to his real economic resources.

V. "Excess Demand" and Inflation

When World War II changed the depression milieu of the 1930's into an economy of shortages and rising prices, there were many economists who felt that the "unemployment theories" also could serve to explain inflation. If too little investment could cause unemployment, too much investment demand could be a cause of rising prices when the economy hit the ceiling of output capacity. The old quantity theory of money was replaced by a theory of "excess demand."[12] Actually, this was a revival of the ideas of the famous Wicksellian cumulative process.[13] In fact, it is probably doubtful whether modern theories of inflation have as yet reached much beyond the profoundness and elegance of the Wicksellian price dynamics.

It could be argued that the notion of excess demand is applicable to any element of total demand, not merely to the demand for investment. Thus, in a situation where the public sector has to use a large share of the national product for defense, etc., in competition with private investment and private consumption, it may be difficult to say which of the two latter is "too high."

One reason why excess demand is often attributed specifically to private investment may be that the desired economic policy actually is to substitute public disposal of goods and services for private investment; that "the future has to wait until the war is over."

The main reason for identifying excess demand with too high demand for investment is, however, that the "budgetary constraints" upon in-

12. See, e.g., Bent Hansen, *A Study in the Theory of Inflation* (London, 1951).
13. Wicksell, *Lectures*, II, sec. IV. 9.

vestment demand are quite different from—and in a sense much more loose than—those of consumers' demand. While consumers' demand, for most people, is a question of disposable income, the demand for capital goods is largely a question of how much money the investors want to, or are able to, borrow. Therefore, when the line of policy is that of using general monetary measures to curtail demand, the most relevant sector of demand is often that of private investment. Thus, the perpetual debate on the efficiency of the rate of interest as a parameter for stabilizing prices is essentially a debate on the effects of the rate of interest on investment.

In the vast amount of literature that now exists on the problems of stability under full employment, the instability of the demand for investment is the key problem. In this field the economist probably has to admit that he knows relatively little. Existing theory may give us some idea of the factors which *on the average* determine the propensity to invest. But the problems of finding general policy parameters that would harness the short-run fluctuation due to, e.g., changing price expectation have proved exceedingly difficult. Here may lie one of the strongest justifications for direct controls, or at least for the use of a large variety of selective policy parameters, even in a "free" economy.

2

The Scope of This Study

THE brief survey in the preceding chapter is probably sufficient to show that the subject matter of a general theory of investment could be wide indeed. There are many unsolved problems. It is clear that if one were to present a really comprehensive treatise on this subject it would mean that one would have to rewrite—or simply reproduce—a substantial part of central economic theory. I do not have such an extensive treatise as the objective for what follows. The present study has in fact grown out of a rather narrow interest in the theory of investment, viz., an interest in the concept of the *demand for net investment* as a behavior relation in macroeconomic models. As I tried to dig deeper into this problem, seeking to clarify the implications of the *per-unit-of-time dimension* of investment, I found that the problem was intimately tangled up with the notion of capital as a factor of production, and, in a more general way, with the field of *dynamic production theory*. Here I found myself involved in a section of economic theory where it seems that the literature is very scarce.

As I worked my way through the problems of the determinants of investment, I became more and more aware of the extreme narrowness of the market framework within which the bulk of modern macrotheories have been conceived. The distinction between the more basic economic data (such as technological constraints, the nature of human wants, etc.) and the institutional, man-made "data" of a particular market form often becomes blurred or is lost altogether. Thus, for example, a theory, or model, that seems to explain why we get the investment that we do get in our particular society tends to become *the* theory of investment, a finished chapter of economic theory. Regardless of political views as to how the economy ought to be organized, the a priori elimination of other forms of economic organizations than the one in operation is certainly a bad way of teaching economics. It is as bad as if chemistry would never look at anything but what one could see on a Sunday hike.

It is with these problems in mind that I have found it justified, and to some extent necessary in this study, to include a few considerations of the more basic elements of the process of capital accumulation.

This was a broad outline of my interests in the subject at hand. But let me try to be more systematic about what is to be dealt with in the following chapters.

I. Capital as a Factor of Production

I have already indicated the reason why this subject became a part of the present study. The most immediate reason is the intricate connection that exists between additions to the stock of capital as a store of wealth and the corresponding addition to output capacity in the more technological sense. To illustrate, if one builds two houses that differ only with respect to durability, they may represent different stocks of value, but their annual output capacity (i.e., "housing") could be the same.

If we want to use a notion of investment that corresponds to the usual notion of produced non-consumed income, and if we want to connect this rate of investment with such parameters as the marginal productivity of capital, it is quite obvious that we must at least try to make our bookkeeping straight, both in the sector of technology as well as in the sector of financial transactions.

The problems of defining capital as a factor of production are, of course, old acquaintances from classical economic theory. We have, e.g., the old question of whether "capital" is in fact a separate factor of production or whether it is simply stored-up labor and land services which take a round-about route toward final consumption. It might seem cruel to awaken these dead or at least slumbering ghosts. But anybody who has tried an econometric attack on the problem of production functions will know that the problems of how to deal with capital remain as formidable and challenging as ever. Thus, to illustrate: Is it meaningful at all to use such concepts as the marginal productivity of capital? Should warehouse stocks be considered as productive capital, and if so, in what sense are they "productive"? Should we include durable consumer goods? Or land improvements? Goods in process? Public buildings and constructions? How do we add up machines and tools of widely different qualities and technological properties?

One type of problem met in all these cases is the ever-present problem of aggregation. Not much can be said on this problem except to express the warning that one must judge the degree of approximation that can be expected in relation to the questions asked. Serious as this problem of aggregation may be, it is, nevertheless, perhaps not the most fundamental problem that we face in the theory of capital.

The fundamental problem is to decide in what sense the physical quantity of capital can be regarded as a factor of production. In trying to clarify this question we are automatically led into a nearly empty box of economic theory, that of time-consuming production processes.

II. Dynamics of Production

I think it is fair to say that economic theory has, on the whole, dealt rather lightly with the subject of dynamic production functions. We know, of course, that production takes time. However, when there is actually the question of expressing this in the production functions considered, the textbook theory usually does not go far beyond the introduction of some sort of lag between input and output. But the serious problem in this connection is that these lags, in most cases, cannot be regarded simply as technological data. Such parameters as the "period of construction" are in fact, to a large extent, a result of *producers' behavior*, e.g., some scheme of profit maximization. The choice of lag between input and output may be of great significance to the quantity of goods in process. Lags of this kind are evidently also of great importance for the relation between investment activity, or "income-generating investment," and the output of finished capital goods. There is also the question of the essential difference between "desired" or "optimal" *amounts* of input (e.g., of capital) and the *speed* with which such optima are approached.

I have found that these problems are so closely related to the process of capital accumulation that any serious study of the latter demands that we give serious attention to the dynamics of production. The results of my attempts to do so, as well as my conclusions concerning the nature of capital as a factor of production, are given in Part II of this study.

III. The "Real" Economics of Growth

We have already mentioned the desirability of making a distinction between the more fundamental problems of capital accumulation as a problem of scarcity in relation to human wants, and the problem of what kind of growth we actually get in a particular market economy. The most clear-cut model to explain the fundamentals is, of course, the traditional Robinson Crusoe economy. It is quite irrelevant to criticize this model on the ground that it only represents the economy of a hermit. The relevant analogy is that of a completely centralized economy. Even if the economy is not completely centralized, a reasoning "as if it were" may be very instructive in order to clarify which constraints are given by nature and which are man-made.

It is, however, by no means simple to draw a line of demarcation between the natural constraints and the man-made constraints of a particular market form. There is the problem of the distribution of income and economic power or, more generally, the role of individual differences within society. There is the problem of changing preferences over time, both for particular individuals and for successive generations. And there is the question of whether it is possible to separate the strictly technological conditions from methods and skills in organizing production.

In spite of these difficulties it seems, however, desirable to try to distinguish between some sort of optimal rate of capital accumulation and the kind of growth which may result from the failure of a particular market economy to function properly. In the opinion of the present writer economic theory could be more useful to practical economic policy if we could learn to look upon parameters characterizing the organization of the economy as the *quaesita* of our models and the desired economic results as the *data*, rather than the other way around. Of course, if there were only a limited number of organizational forms, or frameworks, that had practical feasibility, it could be more or less arbitrary whether we work out the models "backward" or "forward." The fact that is important is, however, that it is possible to *discover* methods of organizing the economy in order to produce desired economic results. To look for a workable organizational procedure that could produce a prescribed result does not mean that we have to like this procedure. The final choice of organizational framework is a political matter. But it could probably be agreed that we do not want to base this choice on ignorance concerning feasible alternatives.

With these views in mind, I have tried to make a distinction between the more fundamental problems of an optimal or desired rate of growth, and the problems of investment behavior in a market economy. The former type of problems are dealt with in Part III, the latter in Part IV.

IV. The Functioning of Investment Demand and Investment Supply in a Market Economy

One of the first things that we try to impress upon freshman students of economics is the fundamental distinction between demand and supply. These are the key concepts upon which we base our understanding of the functioning of any market. They help us to organize the factors that together determine output and disposal of goods and services in a non-centralized economy. Regardless of the commodities or services considered, our analysis follows a more or less standardized pattern: We try to *derive* demand on the basis of (*a*) certain basic preferences or purposes of the group who want to acquire the economic objects considered and (*b*) the constraints under which this acquisition must take place. We try to *derive* supply on the basis of (*a*) certain preferences or purposes of the group who want to acquire the right to obtain other economic objects by disposing of some economic objects which they own or command, and (*b*) the constraints under which this disposal must take place. The stability, or the degree of permanence, of the "laws" of demand and supply depend on the degree of constancy of the underlying preferences, or "purpose structures," and the degree of permanence of the constraints.

The fundamental problem of a market theory of investment is to find out what the nature of the relevant preference structures are, and, in particular, whether these structures could be expected to yield to econometric efforts. The fundamental difficulty about investment behavior is not only that its purpose is indirect in satisfying human wants, but that investment represents only the *speed of adjustment* from one economic situation to another. To illustrate by an analogy, suppose that a person wants to move from one city to another. It is obviously much too simple to say that the more he wants to move the faster he will choose to travel. And even if this were the case, his choice would depend on the cost of various means of transportation. If transportation did not cost him anything he might say, "as quickly as possible," regardless of the intensity of his desire to move. But this statement alone is certaintly very insufficient to determine the moving time that would result.

Let me stretch this analogy a little further. One could perhaps ask: Why bother with something as unimportant as whether it takes the person one, or two, or three days to move? The answer is that it may make an enormous difference to the *transportation industry*. Even if the number of man-hours required for the operation were the same, regardless of speed, the level of employment (while it lasts) may be about twice as high for the one-day alternative as for the two-day alternative.

Analogies are deceitful, but I think that ours may serve to emphasize the following point, which I believe is a rather fundamental one. If a producer, or society as a whole, wants more output capacity in the future by increasing the amount of capital, it may not be of decisive importance whether the goal is reached next year or the following year. But if the investment goods industry is a going concern, the difference to it may be tremendous.

This kind of problem might be irrelevant in a perfectly rational economy that did not waste manpower or resources, but it has at certain times been the nightmare of "free market" economies.

The problems of discovering the laws of investment behavior in a market economy have proved exceedingly complicated. Some people have concluded that this is in itself a proof that the free market economy is no good. Others have the hope that if we could discover the laws of investment behavior, we could make the market economy work with a minimum of regulations. The present study does not aim at voting in this debate. Our task in what follows will be a purely theoretical one, to try to find out how far the behavior of investors can be brought under the command of familiar concepts and methods of economic theory. We want, if possible, to indicate more explicitly the reasons for the volatile nature of this particular economic variable. These problems will be examined in the fourth and last part of the present study.

3

Justification of a Non-Stochastic Theory

THE theories and models examined in this study are of a non-stochastic, or so-called "exact," nature. This means that the theories do not have the final form which is desirable, or perhaps necessary, for the purpose of statistical testing. It could be argued that this is a particularly serious shortcoming in the present case, as the introduction of stochastic elements perhaps is the key to clearer understanding of the investment process. Before trying to justify restricting ourselves to "exact" theories let us, therefore, survey briefly some of the stochastic elements which could be said to be essential in the theory of investment.

I. Probabilistic Nature of Investment Behavior

One could think of a whole hierarchy of random elements that could influence total net investment of an economy.

First, there are the various types of risk elements that are relevant to the behavior of the individual investor. Among these elements we have those that are associated with future values of prices, with outputs resulting from given inputs, and with other variables which are *data* in the calculations of the individual investor. These are the kind of risk elements most frequently dealt with in the literature. If the information about the future values of the data is given in the form of certain probability distributions, it is possible to develop a probability calculus for prospective yields, etc. The usual procedure in specifying the nature of the relevant probability distributions is to start from the assumption that there is some dependence, in the probabilistic sense, between the past and the future, in such a way that the investor's data of the past become parameters of the probability distributions of the future data. Here a distinction must be made between such stochastic schemes as the individual investor has knowledge of, believes in, or actually uses and the more complete, or "true," schemes that would represent "all that anybody could know" about the future. The fundamental econometric problem in this connection is not so much that of setting up a fine probability calculus and a technique of estimation. The fundamental problem is what we can actually find out, by empirical experience or informed guesswork, concerning the nature of the basic probability distributions involved. In addition, we also have to find out something about how the investor uses his probabilistic information concerning the future. Does he look at expected values in the statistical sense or does he use some other kind of "personal" average? What role do the higher moments of the probability distributions play in his calculations, i.e., what kind of gambling does he prefer? And so on.

A second category of error elements has to do with behavior itself. The probability calculus that we mentioned above is based, more or less, on the assumption of a systematic and rational behavior of the investor in response to uncertainty. But, if we make the individual investor our object of observation, we may find it relevant to assume that the way he behaves is itself, to some extent, a random process. We may find it necessary to introduce random elements to explain changes in behavior of the individual investor over time, as well as differences in behavior in a cross-section of simultaneously operating investors.

Third, if we think of the volume of net investment for the economy as a whole, we shall find that the final result is influenced by random elements from many other behavioral sectors of the economy. Even in a very simple complete dynamic model it would not take particularly unreasonable assumptions concerning stochastic elements to explain the most violent fluctuations in investment. But if we do not want these explanations to be merely scientific expressions for the fact that we know very little about the determinants of investment, the real task is to look for as many *constant* elements as possible in investment behavior, rather than to be satisfied with large, unexplained residuals.

Stochastic models have one very dangerous property which we must watch out for: They are in a sense too difficult to reject on the basis of empirical observations. What we really want is not just *a* theory that fits the facts. Among the many different theories with stochastic elements that are compatible with our observations, we want one which is in some sense as interesting and useful as possible. That is, we want to be able to *predict*. Now it is probably true that we can hardly even hope for exact predictions. On the other hand, from the point of view of a stochastic scheme, we can always predict in the sense of making true statements about the future, provided that we make the predictions uninteresting enough!

II. The Use of "Exact" Models

Granted that realistic theories concerning economic phenomena would require a stochastic formulation, there is the question what role, if any, an exercise in various "exact" models could play in the search for empirically significant theories.

I think most of us feel, in some vague sense perhaps, that the study of exact models is a means of *gaining insight* into the way in which an economy works. We experiment in our mind with a large variety of exact schemes before we pick out one or more alternatives which we think are worthwhile to formulate into a final, meaningful shape for statistical testing. Some people are of the opinion that it is the task of pure theory to work with exact models, and that the stochastic embroidery can be left to the statisticians. The present writer thinks that this is a very dubious division of labor. Some simple "errors-of-measurement" scheme loosely added to an exact theory is very far from representing a satisfactory procedure. The stochastic nature of economic behavior is certainly something that the economist has to take very seriously. But even so, it would be silly to deny the enormous practical importance that the intellectual play with exact theories has had. It is no simple task to give a rational explanation for this curious phenomenon, nor would it be in place here to elaborate very much upon this philosophical subject. But a few comments may perhaps serve as an excuse for our procedure in what follows.

One view that can often serve as a justification for studying exact models is this: We want to see how a certain type of economy would operate under ideal conditions. For example, we might like to know what the result would be if a producer accurately maximized his profit under strictly given prices and an explicitly known technology. This may sometimes be no mean problem, even from a purely mathematical point of view, and we may take a good deal of pleasure in solving the problem for its own sake. What is more important, however, is the possibility of drawing useful *negative* conclusions from such mental experiments. It may sometimes be intuitively obvious that if a certain proposition does not hold even under ideal conditions it would not hold in the real world.

Another type of justification, closely related to the one above, lies in the fact that we have inherited a great many exact models as part of the general body of economic theory. It is both educational and intriguing to try to follow the logical reasoning involved.

Then there is the view that exact theories could be some sort of first approximations to more realistic theories. If the expression "first approximation" is not taken too literally, we have no difficulty in underwriting this idea. That is, the possibility of reaching reasonably realistic, explanatory models by the mental process of working from the simple to the more complex is unquestionable (although most of us will have a difficult task explaining why). On the other hand, if we take the idea of a first approximation more literally, as a model where we simply have omitted random elements that we must expect to find in the real world, the approximation may become problematic. First of all, there is the question of knowing at least something about what we have omitted! Without some idea in this respect it is, indeed, difficult to interpret the meaning of a "first approximation." In this respect there are at least two different possible interpretations of an exact model. We could think of it as what would be if certain realistic elements of disturbance were totally inactive. Or we could consider the exact model as including the "expected values" of certain disturbing elements. These two types of exact models could be very different. Thus, for example, we could consider the behavior of an investor under the assumption that future yields are exactly known to him. Or we could consider his average behavior if the expected yield were the same as in the first case while the actual yield has a certain variance. These models could both be called "exact" but they might give very different results. We also have to be aware of the high degree of relativity that is attached to the notion of a first approximation. The same kind of approximation may be sensible and useful for one purpose while completely wild for another purpose.

In the theory of investment we do not as yet have anything that could be called *the* theory. We have a long way to go before we can even think of applying refined concepts and tools of modern econometric analysis. In the theory of investment we are, I think, very far from having exhausted the amount of clarification and insight that can be gained from the study of exact models. We shall find more than enough to do even in a hypothetical world of non-stochastic models.

4

Problems of Terminology, Definitions, and Symbols

I‍T has often been said that economics will not become a respectable science until we reach a fairly widespread agreement on the precise meaning of the things that we talk about. The ideal would seem to be to have some kind of intellectual dictionary naming all the objects and phenomena that should somehow be reserved for the science of economics. A "Linnean" system for economics!

But there are some good reasons why we cannot very easily copy the procedure of the botanist or the zoölogist. First of all, the objects that we try to handle in economics are nearly always some kind of aggregates. And we concern ourselves with many different kinds of overlapping classifications. In fact, the kind of aggregative variables that we work with often grow out of theory itself instead of being preconceived objects of analysis. Second, not only does the economist study existing economies, he "creates" new kinds of economies, mostly in his own mind perhaps, but sometimes even in the direct sense of influencing economic structure or policy. Third, there is the fundamental difference between the implicit meaning, or content, of the named "objects" we talk about in pure economic theory and the alleged counterparts of these objects in the world of practical statistics (cf. the concept of "income").

For these reasons economics shall probably never be able to rid itself of the less interesting controversies on terminology. Perhaps more progress could be made on this point if we tried to think a little more soberly about what we are actually asking for when we require precise definitions of economic concepts. As we are about to concern ourselves with a field of economics where the problem of terminology has proved particularly tricky, it may perhaps be permissible to add a few philosophical thoughts on this subject.

I. Relativity of the Meaning of Theoretical Concepts

The concept of capital is a good illustration of the kind of definitional problems that worry the economist. In the vocabulary of reviewers dealing with contributions to the theory of capital we find some familiar phrases: "The author has a misleading capital concept." "He has confused 'capital' in sense A with capital in sense B." "His capital concept is not precise." "How could we ever hope to measure capital in this sense?" "The author has misunderstood Prof. N. N.'s concept of capital." "The logical consequence is that man himself is capital, which is ridiculous!" etc., etc.

In controversies of this kind there are in fact, implicitly, two very different ideas involved, as far as the meaning of a would-be precise definition is concerned. A great deal of confusion is caused by mixing these ideas.

One idea is this: Suppose that if theorist A is pressed for an answer as to what his concrete recipe is for measuring capital, he would give a list of inclusions and exclusions which would not coincide with theorist B's list. Hence, it is concluded, one of them or both must be wrong.

The other idea is something like this: If the author wants to define capital as he does on page x, then his conclusion on page y is wrong, unless in the latter case "capital" means something else.

The first kind of criticism has many sides. The least interesting of these, although the literature dealing with it is enormous, is based on the idea that there exists one "correct" measure of capital, and that a given theoretical framework may be bad in relation to this particular way of measuring capital. Another, more important, side of the problem is that not all capital concepts are equally interesting and that a theory is bad if it does not apply to what most people like to include under capital. A third side is that there may be disagreement as to whether a particular theorist has good judgment in suggesting practical measurements that he thinks would match his theoretical capital concept. Or, conversely, that he has set out committing himself more or less explicitly to explain a reasonably well-measured thing and that his theory is bad for this purpose. A fourth side of the problem may be that a particular theorist simply does not have a very clear notion about what kind of measurements should be made in order to get something that would correspond to the capital concept he is thinking of.

Now, all discussions along such lines have one thing in common: The discussions are concerned with various kinds of *empirical* capital concepts: how to observe, which is the better or more interesting, and so on. In other words, such discussions are concerned with the *applicability* of a theoretical framework and not with its logical consistency! The question of whether or not a theory is any good when applied is, of course, of unquestionable importance. In fact, this ought to be the only thing worth discussing, whereas the question of logical consistency ought to be trivial. It is not logically inconsistent to consider alternative theoretical frameworks as possible explanations of what we think of as one and the same, reasonably well-described, real phenomenon. Nor is it inconsistent to consider one and the same particular theoretical framework as a possible explanatory model for different things in the real world.

The second kind of controversy mentioned above has to do with logical consistency. There may be misuse of the rules of operations that have been laid down as valid for the particular model considered. Or, one may have had the misfortune of mixing up conclusions drawn from different models. The question of avoiding such logical inconsistencies is not, as some people think, that of describing exactly what each variable means. It is the *rules of operations* within the model considered that need to be precisely described and adhered to. The economic interpretation of the variables in a theoretical model matters a great deal for the *kind* of model that we choose, but it does not matter in the least as far as drawing logically valid conclusions is concerned.

From the remarks above we can get some idea of what we are up against if we look for a foolproof economic terminology. First, we should have a separate name for every empirically distinct phenomenon in the real economic world. Second, we should have a corresponding set of "theoretical" concepts. These latter ones would have to be distinct in two directions as follows: Each theoretical concept would have to be labeled according to which theoretical model it appears in. And at the same time it would have to have a separate label according to the particular concrete object or phenomenon it is supposed to imitate.

I do not mean to use these considerations as a *reductio ad absurdum;* I do not want to conclude that we might as well forget about precise terminology. The conclusion that I think should be drawn is, however, that we must not introduce so many terms and symbols that they become a veritable burden to a reader or listener. To this end we must rely to a large extent on additional explanatory remarks on what a particular term or symbol means when used in a particular line of thought. Nevertheless, a certain standardization of terms and symbols can certainly be of great help in conveying ideas and in avoiding misunderstanding. Thus, for example, it is certainly of some convenience if we agree to use a particular symbol, say K, whenever we talk about "capital" in some sense or other. It helps in directing our thoughts toward a particular category of things. But we must try to find a convenient balance between the use of subscripts, superscripts, etc., to distinguish between the various uses of "capital" and the use of explanatory remarks such as "in this connection K means ———."

II. Remarks on Terms and Notations Used in This Study

We have dealt at some length with the problem of symbols and terminology because these problems are particularly difficult in a study containing many different or alternative theoretical models. In such a study it would be very problematic to begin by giving a complete list of variables to be considered. We shall, instead, have to rely on defining and redefining variables as needed in each particular model. But it may still be helpful to indicate, in somewhat general terms, the kind of notations that we intend to use.

We shall use K exclusively to denote a stock of capital measured in some physical units, or an index to this effect. The money value of capital will be indicated by multiplying K with a price or by using a separate symbol. We shall use k to denote flows of physical capital per unit of time.

The letters x, y, z will be used more generally to indicate physical *flows* per unit of time, while X, Y, Z will denote corresponding *stock* concepts.

We shall use p, P, and q to denote *prices*, with appropriate subscripts, etc. *Rates of interest* and similar rates of growth will be denoted by ρ. R and r will be used for income concepts.

As far as the timing of variables is concerned, we shall make some effort to write $x(t)$ when the functional form of a time function x is to be emphasized. Otherwise we may write x_t, or omit t altogether. Expressions like

$$\frac{\partial \phi \, [y\,(t), \, x\,(t)]}{\partial x\,(t)}$$

will be written simply as $\partial \phi / \partial x$, where there is no chance of confusion. We shall use $\dot{x}(t)$, or simply $\dot{x}$, to indicate the derivative dx/dt.

Otherwise there is no need to burden the reader with "definitions" until we get to their place of use.

PART II

Capital as a Factor of Production

In this part of our study we shall be concerned with some technological aspects of time-consuming production processes. When we say "technological" we do not mean that we intend to trespass upon the field of engineering. What we mean is that we shall try to keep problems of economic choice out of the picture, as far as possible. Admittedly, the distinction between the purely technological aspects of production and the economic behavior of producers is a problematic one. It may be nearly impossible to conceive of production functions that are not, to some extent, a mixed result of purely technological relations and organizational procedure. This fact has been brought very sharply to light in modern theories of programing for efficient use of resources. However, our view will be a technological one in the sense that we shall, in general, leave out the problems of adaptation to cost, prices, or general welfare criteria, except when needed to illustrate certain ideas in the history of capital theory. Furthermore, when we say time-consuming production processes we realize, of course, that this category actually could cover almost all kinds of production processes. What we mean is that we shall consider such aspects of the theory of production where it is *essential* to make explicit allowance for the fact that production takes time. The purpose of entering into this more technological field here is to clarify the role of capital in production.

5

The Böhm-Bawerk–Wicksellian Approach

We shall begin our analysis by surveying some of the ideas that these early masters of economic theory had on the problems of capital as a factor of production. One reason for not going farther back in the history of economic thought is that a full-fledged historical review is not our objective. Moreover, it seems that Böhm-Bawerk has managed to sum up pretty well what were the controversial issues in the theory of capital up to his time.[1] It seems that the fundamental problems of capital theory

1. Böhm-Bawerk, *Positive Theory of Capital*, trans. W. Smart (New York, 1923), chap. iii.

that worry us today are either those where we are not satisfied with the solution which Böhm-Bawerk offered or problems that he mentioned but left unsolved.

As has been pointed out by Hayek,[2] the theory of capital has long suffered from the fact that the chief objective of this part of economic theory seems to have been that of explaining the rate of interest, and not so much that of analyzing the technology of capitalistic production. This is true of Böhm-Bawerk and, I think, also of Wicksell. On the other hand, what little these writers had to say on the more technical aspects of capitalistic production is in many ways stronger and more clear than their arguments to establish a logically consistent theory of interest.

Whatever we may think of Böhm-Bawerk's various "grounds" for the existence of interest or of his more explicitly formulated rule of roundaboutness, there is certainly not much to be said against his general description of what capital *is* and how it functions. His analysis[3] of this subject is clear and convincing. He points out the indisputable fact that man can get more out of nature, in the economic sense, by a technology which brings into existence certain tools and products that are not in themselves consumer goods. That such roundabout procedures are productive he considers an empirical fact, which it would be silly to deny. He is very emphatic on this point, which he considers fundamental to the understanding of the role of capital in production. At the same time he is somewhat apologetic for dwelling at some length upon a subject that belongs to the natural sciences.

I. Capital Not a Factor of Production

After such a start it may seem surprising that Böhm-Bawerk most emphatically wants to deny that capital is a factor of production.[4] Capital is useful, productive, even absolutely necessary in some cases, for the output of consumer goods. It is an "instrument" of production, but not a factor of production! At first sight this might look like hair-splitting. But he has reasons that are more profound than those of terminology.

The first reason is a somewhat philosophical one, and one which Böhm-Bawerk apparently had inherited from his predecessors in the field, viz., that labor and nature are the only "original" factors, and that capital goods must, in the final analysis, be products of only these two basic factors. Since capital is itself produced it might be unreasonable or confusing to call it a third, independent, factor of production.

2. F. Hayek, *The Pure Theory of Capital* (Chicago: University of Chicago Press, 1950), pp. 4–5.

3. *Op. cit.*, chap. ii.   4. *Op. cit.*, p. 95.

The second reason is, however, the really fundamental one, or at least it seemed so to Böhm-Bawerk, Wicksell, and others who have been concerned with the mysteries of the productivity of capital. It is this: Suppose that it is true—and it is difficult to deny this—that capital is a product of labor and natural resources. To say that capital is productive—in the sense of being able to "more than pay" for itself—is not that the same thing as saying that labor and land yield more in some uses or processes than in others? And, if so, why does not the law of indifference in the market raise wages and rent to a level where the product of the most efficient roundabout method of production is just sufficient to pay for the basic factors?

If we consider capital as a factor of production without paying attention to its origin, we would leave out the fundamental problem of capital theory as Böhm-Bawerk and Wicksell saw it, viz., the problem of how current and "stored" labor could have different values in a given market. Böhm-Bawerk, of course, had the answer, which was that the *time element* had to be brought into the picture. His main problem became that of demonstrating how a certain rate of interest was in a sense both necessary and sufficient to prevent the diversion of all current output to the formation of capital.

This problem of why capital should be in a sense worth more than the labor put into it has apparently so completely spellbound Böhm-Bawerk and other great thinkers in this field that it seems unthinkable to them to get rid of the problem simply by introducing capital as a separate factor of production.

What Böhm-Bawerk and many others apparently have not been able to see is that including a variable called "capital" as a separate factor in a production function is not necessarily in conflict with the idea that this factor is itself a product of the other factors. There are two aspects of a factor of production that must be kept clear of each other. One aspect is the relation, if any, that the factor may have to other factors. Another aspect is the way in which the factor enters the production function.

Let us try to clarify this important point a little more. Suppose that by using an amount N_1, of the current labor and by *using up* an amount of capital, K, a product, x, can be produced according to the production function,

$$x = \Phi(N_1, K) .$$

Now suppose that K is the result of labor input only, and that this "stored-up" labor is, on the average, one year old. Let the amount of labor that has gone into K be N_2, and let us even measure K in such a way that $K = N_2$. It would obviously be nonsense to conclude from this that we

are dealing with only one factor. We can still speak of the marginal productivity of labor, $\partial \Phi / \partial N_1$, and the marginal productivity of capital
$\partial \Phi / \partial K$. And we must be very careful in distinguishing between what
$\partial \Phi / \partial N_1$ and $\partial \Phi / \partial K$ might be at a certain level of adaptation for N_1 and K
and what these marginal productivities might be in general. What would
it mean to say that "stored-up" labor N_2 is generally more productive
than immediate labor N_1? It would mean that $(\partial \Phi / \partial K) > (\partial \Phi / \partial N_1)$ for
all possible values of N_1 and N_2. This would certainly in most cases be a
very bad theory of production.

Suppose, for example, that the wage rate is w units of x per unit of
labor. It is quite possible that for a certain combination of N_1 and K we
could have $\partial \Phi / \partial N_1 = \partial \Phi / \partial K = w$, so that there would be no net marginal return on capital over and above its replacement cost. (This corre-
sponds to the case where the rate of interest is zero.) Does this mean that
no capital (or roundaboutness) would be applied? Obviously not. Because,
for a smaller amount of capital, the net marginal productivity of capital
may well be positive. For example, if the rate of interest be ρ, we may have
the following market equilibrium conditions:

$$\frac{\partial \Phi}{\partial N_1} = w , \quad \frac{\partial \Phi}{\partial K} \left(= \frac{\partial \Phi}{\partial N_2} \right) = (1 + \rho)\, w .$$

There is no technological mystery about the possibility of positive values both for N_1 and for K such that the conditions above are fulfilled, if Φ
is a production function of the general ultrapassum nature.

We do not—as Böhm-Bawerk seems to have thought—dodge the main
issue of why capital yields a surplus by considering it a factor of production. When he talks about the empirical fact that capital is something that
increases production, his ideas are perfectly well covered by a production
function of the type mentioned above. But later he gets so absorbed by the
idea of roundaboutness that he feels one should consider the roundabout
procedure, and not the *amount* of capital, as the real cause of productivity.[5]
This led him to the idea that an increase in capital is the same thing as
increase in roundaboutness. This idea, while itself not hopeless, has caused
an enormous amount of confusion in the theory of capital. One of our
many objectives in the following chapters will be to clarify this point.
Here it is sufficient to observe that it makes a great deal of difference
whether the connection between capital and roundaboutness is regarded
as a result of a certain kind of *economic equilibrium*, or whether we assume
the connection to be a technological phenomenon. These things must be
kept strictly separated.

5. Op. cit., p. 92.

II. The Wicksellian Model of the Roundabout Process

Böhm-Bawerk's ideas on the internal composition of capital and the notion of roundaboutness have become much more easily accessible through the razor-sharp logic and brilliant exposition in Knut Wicksell's writings.

Wicksell adopted wholeheartedly Böhm-Bawerk's idea that capital is stored-up labor (and stored-up land services). He made a sharp distinction between the problems of the dynamic process of capital accumulation and the problems of the internal composition of a given total amount of capital under hypothetical, stationary conditions. What we are interested in here is, however, not so much the final economic adaptation of the capital structure to the rate of interest as the technology of production which Wicksell assumes in order to explain the Böhm-Bawerkian ideas.

Let us first consider the celebrated model of wine production, as used by Wicksell.[6] We shall, however, use our own notations instead of Wicksell's since he used symbols which we need for other purposes. We shall also employ a formulation slightly different from his, but more useful for this study.

Suppose that the annual vintage (the output of grape juice) is constant over time and equal to v gallons (v being constant over time does not, of course, prevent us from considering alternative levels of v). Suppose that each year v is put into storage. The annual output of wine, although assumed to be the same number of gallons as the input v, is economically a different quantity. Let us call it x_τ for τ years old wine. Wicksell assumes that we measure x_τ *in value terms*, e.g., by multiplying v stored τ years by a given price for τ years old wine. Let p_τ be the price of τ years old wine. The prices p_τ are assumed "given from outside." Then we have

$$x_\tau = p_\tau v . \tag{5.1}$$

Suppose it is given that all wine is to be stored to a fixed age, θ. Then, in a stationary process, the total number of gallons in storage is $v\theta$. Defining this as the amount of "physical capital," K, we then have

$$K = \theta v . \tag{5.2}$$

Here we disregard problems of discontinuity at the beginning of each year. The definition (5.2) was not used by Wicksell. But we are interested in the role of K if introduced into the Wicksellian model. We can then write the "production function" for θ years old wine as

$$x_\theta = p_\theta \frac{K}{\theta} . \tag{5.3}$$

6. *Lectures*, I, 172–82.

This can be rewritten in various ways. Suppose, e.g., that the *price of grape juice is fixed*. Let it be p^*. Then we could write

$$x_\theta = \frac{p_\theta - p^*}{\theta} K + p^* v . \tag{5.4}$$

"Net output" from the storage operation could be defined as

$$(x_\theta - p^* v) = \frac{p_\theta - p^*}{\theta} K . \tag{5.5}$$

In a certain sense equation (5.4) can be regarded as a production function, the factors of production being v and K. It is a production function for alternative, stationary levels of v, K, and x_θ. However, for a given θ it is not possible within the conditions of validity of this function to change K without changing v. This is in line with Wicksell and Böhm-Bawerk's general idea that capital is not a separate factor of production. From their point of view, it is the land and labor services, as measured by v, that are the sole factors of production.

In considering the "production function" above we meet a fundamental problem in production theory, that of distinguishing between *physical output* and *physical input*. If we would measure output simply in gallons, we should have a very simple production function, viz., output = input of grape juice. But then we would lose the essence of the production process considered, viz., that wine is something different from grape juice. We could, of course, consider x_θ for every θ as a different product instead of different quantities of one product. However, we should then find it very difficult to apply such technological concepts as variable marginal productivities.

Wicksell now considers the market value of K. This value could be defined in at least two ways. The first, which Wicksell does not consider, except perhaps implicitly, is the value of the stock of stored wine if it were to be sold out *as wine*. This value, let us call it A_1, is evidently equal to

$$A_1 = \sum_{\tau=0}^{\theta-1} x_\tau . \tag{5.6}$$

The second meaning of the value of K is the usual one, which requires the introduction of a certain given market rate of interest. Let this market rate be ρ. Consider the present value (beginning of year) of the stock of wine, on the assumption that all wine is stored until the age θ and then sold. The present value, A_2, of the stored wine under this assumption is the discounted value of future sales, the first sale taking place after one year, the last after θ years, i.e.,

$$A_2 = \frac{x_\theta}{1+\rho} + \frac{x_\theta}{(1+\rho)^2} + \ldots + \frac{x_\theta}{(1+\rho)^\theta} = \frac{(1+\rho)^\theta - 1}{\rho(1+\rho)^\theta} x_\theta . \tag{5.7}$$

Suppose now that competition in the "factor market" would cause the cost of grape juice to be $p^* = [1/(1 + \rho)^\theta]p_\theta$ per gallon. Then the annual net returns from storing wine to the age θ would be

$$x_\theta - \frac{x_\theta}{(1 + \rho)^\theta}. \tag{5.8}$$

This net revenue is evidently *exactly equal to one year's interest* at the rate ρ on the value of capital as defined by equation (5.7).

We can here consider the product x_θ as a function of the value of capital A_2 and the value of "labor input," $x_\theta[1/(1 + \rho)^\theta]$. We have, from equation (5.7), the "production function,"

$$x_\theta = \rho A_2 + p^* v. \tag{5.9}$$

It must be emphasized, however, that equation (5.9) cannot be regarded as a production function in a technological sense. It depends on a certain adjustment to the market rate of interest, and it depends on market prices. We can already here begin to grasp the problems involved in considering such a thing as the *value* (or deflated *value*) of capital as a factor of production. The point, in connection with this kind of production process, is that the amount, or *stock*, of capital goods actually plays no direct technological role in creating the output. Time works (presumably) as well on one bottle of wine as on a large stock. The amount of capital is not technologically "instrumental." The collection of a physical stock is rather *incidental* to the process of bringing the time element to work. The situation would of course be quite different if we were to include such things as storage efficiency, or the productive activity of taking care of the storage operation.

In a more general model Wicksell considers[7] a Böhm-Bawerkian scheme where different types of capital are used simultaneously in producing a certain commodity. The meaning of different *types* of capital is, however, a very special one. First of all, capital is defined as a quantity of saved-up labor (and land services). Second, each kind of capital can be identified by one single parameter, its age, or storage period. Third, when a dose of capital is *used* in production, it is also *used up*. In fact, the more general model could be regarded as an extension of the wine example by considering a process where each year several kinds of grape juice are put into storage, each kind requiring one particular storage period. Each year's output would then consist of the sum-total of several types of mature

7. *Lectures*, I, 203–5. For an illuminating exposition of this model see R. Frisch's article on Wicksell in *The Development of Economic Thought: Great Economists in Perspective*, ed. Henry William Spiegel (New York: John Wiley & Sons, 1952), pp. 652–99.

wine. However, the model that Wicksell considers is somewhat more general than this, as he now also considers the possibility of each kind of capital having a different effect on the output, according to the volume of input (the volume of capital of a given age). This means that we now consider marginal productivities of capital in a more general way than was the case in the simple example of wine production. His model, as far as its technological aspects are concerned, can be described as follows.

We consider again alternative hypothetical stationary states of a production process. Let x denote annual output of finished products, measured in physical units. Using a discrete formulation, we assume that the output appears as a finite quantity at the end of each year. Let v denote the (stationary) volume of annual labor available at the beginning of each year. (For simplicity we may here disregard land services, although Wicksell, for reasons of completeness, put very strong emphasis on the inclusion of both land and labor.) Each year the total available amount of production resources v is divided into several parts according to their future age of maturity. A certain portion, v_0 is used directly in current production of x. Another part, v_1, is used next year. Still another part, v_2, is used the year after next. And so on, until the last part, v_n. (In Wicksell's formulation v_n is not defined.) Thus, we have

$$v = v_0 + v_1 + \ldots + v_n . \qquad (5.10)$$

Since we consider a stationary process, we also have that each year not only v_0, but previously stored quantities, $v_1, v_2, \ldots, v_n$, are *used up* in producing the output x. The production function considered by Wicksell can then be written as follows:

$$x = \Phi(v_0, v_1, \ldots, v_n) , \qquad (5.11a)$$

where now the subscripts of the v's denote their *age*. Wicksell considers the function Φ as a general production function, defining ordinary marginal productivity functions for each input v_i, $i = 0, 1, 2, \ldots, n$. (However, he assumes that Φ is homogeneous of degree 1.) If the v's can be added up in their original unit of measurement (e.g., labor-years), the total amount of stored-up labor or *physical capital*, K, at the beginning of each year is

$$K = v_1 + 2v_2 + \ldots + nv_n = K_1 + K_2 + \ldots + K_n , \qquad (5.12)$$

where K_i means the amount of capital which will be i years old when it is used in the production of x. We could, therefore, also write equation (5.11a) as

$$x = \Phi\left(v_0, K_1, \tfrac{1}{2}K_2, \tfrac{1}{3}K_3, \ldots, \tfrac{1}{n} K_n \right). \qquad (5.11b)$$

But one must carefully observe that while equation (5.11*a*) may be regarded as a given technical relation, equation (5.11*b*) is valid only when certain stationary conditions are in force.

We see that also this more general model is true to the idea that capital is itself not a factor of production. Capital is rather incidental to the use of the original productive powers in a certain roundabout way. Wicksell wants to use this model to show how the distribution of v over $v_0, v_1, \ldots, v_n$ is determined when there is a certain given price of the product x, and a certain given market rate of interest. He relies for this purpose on a principle of profit maximization. Because these problems of economic equilibrium are his main concern, he does not elaborate as much on the technology of the production structure involved as would have been desirable to discuss the technological role of capital in production.

We must also be very careful in interpreting the notion of investment in connection with such models as those above. What is called *net* investment in modern terminology is always *zero* in these models. The amount of capital is, for each stationary level, a constant, but revolving, stock. Each element of it is "invested" for a definite period of time. The amount of capital can vary from one stationary state to another for two reasons. One reason is simply the scale of operations, v; another reason may be a change in the internal composition of capital (the relative size of the v_i's).

Various notions of a "period of production" can be introduced in the Wicksellian model just discussed. But one must carefully observe that we are dealing with definitions that use conditions of a *stationary state*.

One concept of the period of production is the average storage time, T_v, of the physical inputs $v_0, v_1, \ldots, v_n$. This average is simply

$$T_v = \frac{1}{v} \sum_{i=0}^{n} i \, v_i. \tag{5.13}$$

T_v is then the average degree of roundaboutness measured in physical units.

But we could also take account of the fact that input consists not only of the v's which are annually used up but also of the "waiting" for the v's to mature. This is the concept of a period of production considered by Wicksell.[8] Obviously the psychological input element of waiting cannot be measured without introducing some economic evaluation parameters, such as the rate of interest. The period of production regarded as a period of waiting or a period of "investment" is, therefore, certainly not a purely technological concept.

8. See Frisch, *op. cit.*, pp. 664–65.

III. The Case of Durable Means of Production

The Böhm-Bawerkian theory of "circulating" capital as described above is a clear piece of theory as far as it goes. But admittedly it does not go very far. First of all, it treats only of alternative stationary states. Under these conditions it becomes possible to relate output to the volume of capital in a formal way. But this breaks down as soon as we consider a dynamic problem with net investment different from zero. Second, it deals at best with only a small part of the produced means of production, viz., those which deliver all their incorporated productive power after a definite period of processing or storage. The process of a growing productive power as a result of storage is somewhat mysterious, except in simple cases of natural growth or ripening processes where time itself is the active agent.

The central, but much more formidable, chapter of capital theory must be concerned with durable or fixed capital. Wicksell tackled this problem in a brilliant essay analyzing G. Åkerman's work on this subject.[9] Wicksell had, no doubt, a solid basis for the following statement with which he introduced his analysis of the problem:

This problem is clearly of great practical significance—no doubt much more so than the problems dealt with by Jevons and Böhm-Bawerk. They concentrated on the capitalistic process of production, in which labour resources (and probably land resources) ripened into immediate consumption goods, or what the author calls "variable capital." But his problem is so complex that the vast majority of economists, including the reviewer, have almost entirely passed it by as being much too difficult to be susceptible to analysis.[10]

The simplifying assumptions that Wicksell made were rather drastic (but even so the analysis itself is intricate indeed). First of all, the model includes only one kind of durable capital, all units lasting equally long and rendering full service while they last. Their built-in durability, or lifetime, is, however, a variable subject to economic adjustment by spending more or less labor in producing each unit. A second—and a really restrictive—assumption is that the production function is homogeneous of degree one in the two inputs, labor and physical capital. A third assumption which, however, concerns us less in the present context, is that capital is produced by labor only, and also that the time required for production of each capital unit is negligible as compared to its durability. Finally, all the variations within the model refer to hypothetical changes from one stationary state to another. There are no dynamics involved.

Under the assumptions made, Wicksell finds no difficulty in writing

9. *Lectures*, I, Appendix 2, pp. 258–99.
10. *Ibid.*, p. 258.

down a production function relating output (defined in a certain fixed unit of measurement) to the amount of current labor and the stock of capital. Measurement of the latter is no problem in this case, as there is only one kind of capital. We can simply count up the physical units, defined in some technological way. It is, however, necessary that the problem of defining a unit of physical capital has actually been solved. If K denotes the total amount of capital (number of physical units) present at any given time, and N is the number of workers using the capital to produce an output x, per unit of time, of some commodity, we may write the production function as

$$x = \Phi(N, K) , \qquad (5.14)$$

where the "productive effect" of N is labor services per unit of time and the "productive effect" of K is capital services per unit of time.

Suppose that each capital unit has a lifetime $= n$. On the assumptions under which equation (5.14) is supposed to be valid, n does not enter the production function! It comes into the picture only when we start calculating net revenue and other *economic* concepts. But n enters in an essential technological way into *another* production function which Wicksell considers, the production function for the *output of capital*. The necessary input of labor in order to produce one unit of capital varies with the durability, n, of the capital unit produced. (In Wicksell's specific numerical illustrations labor in this production function is assumed to be proportional to n^ν, where ν is a positive constant < 1.) One might think that by measuring the amount of capital as the amount of incorporated labor one could obtain an adequate measure of capital that would reflect both its physical volume and its durability. That is no doubt possible as far as its value in labor units is concerned. However, such a measure of capital is not the relevant measure of capital as a factor of production in equation (5.14). If two capital items differ only with respect to durability, the substitution of one for the other in equation (5.14) can have no effect upon x.

The situation is different if a change in durability is combined with a change in the quality, or efficiency, of each capital unit. If we measure capital as "number of machines," a change in their quality (apart from durability) would have to be reflected in equation (5.14), either as a change in the functional form Φ, or by "weighting" the variable K by some quality index, using this weighted amount of capital as a factor of production. This problem was mentioned by Wicksell,[11] but he did not elaborate on it.

11. *Lectures,* I, 299.

6

Controversial Aspects of the Idea of "Roundaboutness"

In the Böhm-Bawerk–Wicksell approach the notion of roundaboutness is clear enough in the case of a revolving stock of variable capital. Even in the case of fixed or durable capital equipment one could, by a somewhat artificial construction, consider a capital item as a sum of incorporated labor coming to maturity at various points of time until the instrument is worn out. Certainly there can be no disagreement concerning the general idea that the use of capital in production is related in an essential way to the idea of "lags" between inputs and outputs.

The really controversial issues seem to be the following:

1. The Böhm-Bawerkian idea would seem to suggest that, if the use of capital means a roundabout, or *indirect*, method of producing finished consumer goods, it should in each case be possible to visualize a *direct* method for comparison. Is this really a meaningful and realistic two-way classification?

2. Why should there be any economic gain connected with the presence of a lag between input and output, except in the case of natural growth processes when time itself is the active factor? Is not the lag in itself actually an economic loss rather than a gain?

3. Is there a meaningful constant technological relation between the degree of roundaboutness (in the sense of a time lag) and the quantity of capital, measured in some physical units? Is it realistic to consider such things as the period of production, or durability, as technological data?

4. Is there necessarily any relation between the amounts of "original factors," land and labor, incorporated in capital and its role as a tool of production? Why not simply regard an increase in output resulting from employing more capital per worker as a technological fact, and consider any "return to capital" as an economic question, a question of distribution?

We shall comment briefly upon these questions.

I. Roundabout vs. "Direct" Production

Böhm-Bawerk was, of course, aware of the fact that many consumer goods could not be produced at all except by the use of capital.[1] But in those cases it is obviously very simple to make a distinction between the

1. *Positive Theory of Capital*, trans. W. Smart (New York, 1923), p. 19.

direct and the indirect or roundabout method. The product of labor without the use of capital would be zero. However, it could be argued that if this is the case for the overwhelming part of consumer goods in a modern society, the reference to a direct method is rather useless. We should consider marginal effects of increasing the amount of capital. But then again, it becomes somewhat problematic how to measure the degree of roundaboutness.

Here one must at any rate make a very sharp distinction between production processes where the output is a continuous stream (e.g., the production of coal or electricity) and cases where the final product consists of large units produced discontinuously (such as houses). In the first case, if some labor is diverted to the making of more capital equipment, there is a temporary delay in output of finished goods, and the subsequent, increased, output could be said to be a result of this delay. In the second case, however, it could easily happen that the diversion of labor to the construction of tools and equipment would actually result in, e.g., a house getting finished earlier than if no "roundabout" method were applied.

However, the Böhm-Bawerkian idea of roundaboutness could perhaps be formally saved also in the latter case, by reasoning as follows: If more workers were diverted from their direct activity on a house under construction to the making of some tools, the remaining workers would take even longer to finish the house using the old equipment. Therefore, during the time when more workers make tools *a smaller part* of the house would get completed than if all the workers were active using the old equipment. Thus, the question of what a roundabout method means may depend on whether we consider finished houses or the "amount of house construction" as the final output. The matter becomes even more involved if we were to consider unfinished houses as part of "capital," and housing its tenants as the final output.

II. The Idea of "Productivity of Waiting"

In the case of the wine example discussed in the previous chapter, it is clear enough that there may be some positive gain in output simply by waiting for the wine to get better. The same applies to processes of feeding cattle, although here time is obviously only one of the factors involved. It also pays for the farmer to wait for the crops to ripen, but there is not much else he can do. The problem is why there should be a similar gain from waiting connected with lines of production where no physiological or biological ripening process is involved. Is not the situation here rather the other way around, i.e., that it is advantageous to use capital equipment in production; it is just too bad that it takes time to construct it!

Certainly it is not the delay in output which itself is "productive," but the fact that the more time we spend, the more capital we can construct.

Take the case of durable producer goods. Here it is certainly an advantage to produce such goods as quickly as possible if the productivity of labor making the capital goods is constant. Furthermore, it is no advantage that some of the services of such equipment belong to a distant future. The fact that the equipment is durable is an advantage mainly because the time rate at which we can extract the productive services of the equipment is limited (at least from an economic point of view). One should otherwise, in most cases, like to get the services out of the equipment as quickly as possible.

Thus, it may be more reasonable to say that "productivity" is a technological property of the capital equipment itself, whereas the need for waiting is the economic constraint on the amount of capital that we can afford to make.

We do not want to let the comments above develop into a fight over words. What we are aiming at is the next question of whether it is meaningful to consider such parameters as the period of production, or durability, as technical data needed for a fruitful definition of the factor "capital."

III. The Problem of Measuring Capital as a "Degree of Roundaboutness"

Very strong objections against the notion of capital as the "degree of roundaboutness" have been raised by J. B. Clark and, subsequently, by Frank Knight.[2] These writers and others have pointed out that to consider capital as a revolving stock, each unit being invested for a given span of time, is unrealistic, even meaningless, in most cases. In general, the idea of roundaboutness is held to be irrelevant to the notion of capital as a source of productive power. The whole idea of a lag between inputs and outputs is considered unrealistic, if taken to mean a transfer of productive services from one period of time to another. Labor and capital services are used simultaneously to produce output. An increase in the amount of capital means an instantaneous increase of the rate at which productive services of capital become available. The idea that it takes a technologically given period of time to produce a means of production, which at the end of the period is then *used up*, is held to be absurdly unrealistic. Likewise, it is

2. J. B. Clark, *The Distribution of Wealth* (Macmillan Co., 1920), pp. 117–40; F. Knight, "The Quantity of Capital and the Rate of Interest," *Journal of Political Economy* (1936), Nos. 4, 5. See also N. Kaldor's review article, "Annual Survey of Economic Theory: The Recent Controversy on the Theory of Capital," *Econometrica*, V (1937), 201–33, for extensive references on this controversy.

said that the durability of an item of fixed capital is certainly not a technological constant, and even if it were, this fact is not very interesting in the theory of capital. It may take a lot of time to produce a lot of capital, but that does not mean that it takes a certain given period to produce a capital item. Nor is it so that the more capital we have, the more durable it is. Capital lasts forever, when maintained.

The seriousness of these objections cannot really be evaluated except through a thorough study of the dynamics of production. We shall, therefore, not try to analyze these problems any further at this stage (cf. chaps. xv, xvii).

IV. Capital as Stored-up Labor and Land

It could be argued, as has been done by Frank Knight,[3] that the idea of a lag between input of productive services and the output of finished goods is meaningless. For each input there is always a simultaneous output, either of consumer goods or of investment goods (including half-finished products). The notion of roundaboutness is based on the idea that when capital is used (used up), this means a process of taking out of capital certain "original" resources that were put into it some time ago. This idea may not be particularly fruitful, or relevant, from a purely technological point of view. The amount of labor that has gone into a capital item may not tell us much about what this capital item actually does as a productive agent. So, even if we could find a measure of all the labor- and land-services incorporated in a capital item, this measure might not be a very interesting one.

However, one cannot deny that the Böhm-Bawerk–Wicksellian approach offers some kind of a rational explanation of the existence of capital and the economic reasons for its use in production. The objection that some capital is also used in producing capital itself is not really a serious one. There is no *formal* difficulty in constructing a recurrent chain from a given capital item back to the original factors labor and land (even if such a calculation may be impossible in practice). There is no denying that this way of looking upon the subject of capital can give us insight into the fundamental relation between capital and the time element, even if the procedure is somewhat artificial.

The Austrian model also poses sharply one of the fundamental problems of capital theory, the problem of choice between consumption and capital accumulation. It seems next to impossible to explain the phenomenon of capital accumulation except on the basis of some general notion of storage possibility as against a possibility of current consumption.

3. *Op. cit.*, pp. 453–57.

It is really not essential that we go back to a point in history where there was no capital. Even if we start at an arbitrary point of time with a given amount of capital, measured in some way, there is the problem of allocation of current productive resources. We cannot escape the conclusion that it is necessary for people to look toward the future in order to solve this allocation problem. And, unless the allocation be wholly arbitrary, it must have a basis in some *technological* connection between future results and the disposal of current resources.

I think that perhaps too much fuss has been made over the hard-boiled idea that we must go all the way back to pure labor and land services to find the true content of capital. The discussion on what is and what is not a "real" factor of production is not the essence of the matter. The hard-boiled scheme of the Austrians should rather be considered as an illustration. But it throws light on a really fundamental point, namely, that we need two kinds of data in order to solve the problem of allocation of current resources. We need (1) certain technological relations between allocation of current resources and future effects of this allocation, and we need (2) certain preference schedules to evaluate the relative merits of the various technological possibilities. Whether we should talk about a "direct" and a "roundabout" way of doing "the same thing" (producing consumer goods) or say that we choose between producing for the present and producing for the future, is largely a terminological question. Quite a different matter is the question whether the time lags involved in a theory of roundaboutness are stable and characteristic constants from an econometric point of view. These problems we shall study more closely in the chapters dealing with the dynamics of production.

7

Restatement of Problems in the Pure Theory of Capital

ONE could say that the field of capital theory as it now stands offers two kinds of problems upon which further work needs to be done: There are the issues where various authors have offered competing solutions and where they agree that they disagree! And there are questions which are recognized as important, but which have not as yet been seriously tackled. Both categories contain an abundance of possible research objectives. In the following chapters we shall concern ourselves with some of the problems that we cannot escape if we want to understand the economics of investment.

Let us here try to summarize the major issues as they emerge from the preceding review and analysis.

I. The Definition of Capital

It would seem rational and obvious that one should start a theory of capital by agreeing on what one is talking about, that is, by a definition of capital. However, strange as it seems, this question of definition has itself been one of the most controversial issues in the whole theory of capital. The reason is, of course, that it is very difficult to define capital as a physical object without referring to its economic functions. If we choose some a priori, statistical criterion to identify capital goods, we should very likely find that we end up with a rather heterogenous collection of objects, at least from the point of view of their economic function. On the other hand, if we define capital by referring to economic functions that all capital items have in common, we get into endless discussions as to how to measure the *amount* of capital, even if we allow ourselves to introduce variables representing various kinds of capital.

Nevertheless, there seems to be at least one aspect of capital which is not very controversial: That capital must have the dimensions of a *stock concept*, something *at a point of time, t*, and not something per unit of time. There is, perhaps, some degree of relativity attached to such a distinction between stocks and flows. Any function of time could be said to have the dimension of a stock as compared to its first derivative, while at the same time the function considered could be regarded as a flow concept in relation to its integral. However, if we choose consumption and the accumulation of capital as flow concepts, something per unit of time, there seems to be general agreement to the effect that capital should have the dimension of a stock.

But here the agreement on definition ends. A host of special problems arise, such as the question of whether only tangible objects should be included and not "good will" or the like, whether inactive goods stored in warehouses are capital, whether a half-finished house is capital, and so on. But this is just the beginning of the trouble. Far more formidable is the problem of how to *measure* the amount of various kinds of capital, once we have reached agreement on what kind of objects to include. The idea that capital should only be defined as a sum of values in money terms may be adequate for certain purposes, whereas for others it is nearly hopeless.

I think that the way out of this intricate maze must be to start out with no more of an a priori fixed idea as to what capital is and is not than to agree that it has the form of a stock of some kind of economic objects, and then to study more explicitly the role played by such stocks in various kinds of productive processes. Then we shall be able to find out to what extent it is possible to define capital by criteria that apply to larger groups of production processes, or perhaps to production processes in general.

II. Capital and the Time Element

Nearly all writers in the field of capital theory stress the importance of the time element. Actually, the time element shows up in three rather different ways. First, there is the question of the internal age distribution of capital. This way of introducing the time element should not be confused with the problem of making the theory dynamic. Obviously we can refer to the age of something without saying anything about changes over time or what historic point in time we are considering. The theories of Böhm-Bawerk and Wicksell concerning stationary states are in a sense timeless, even if the internal age composition and the time distances between input and output are absolutely central elements in these theories.

The second way that time comes into the theory of capital is through the formal relation that must exist between stock terms and corresponding flow terms. If capital is created by a process that has a continuous and limited output per unit of time, it will necessarily take some time to create a given quantity of capital. Similarly, if capital can only be used up or worn out at a finite rate per unit of time, it will necessarily take some time to exhaust a given volume of capital. In this connection the time element is really of fundamental importance, as it signifies the impossibility of spontaneous changes in the amount of capital.

The third way that time enters the theory of capital is, of course, through any approach toward a full-fledged dynamic model of the process of capital accumulation.

But it would be wrong to say that we could not conceive of a theory of capital or of capitalistic production without bringing in the time element. In certain production processes it is possible, and even quite adequate, to consider output as a function of alternative inputs of capital (or capital services) without regard to the time it takes to produce the capital or to wear it out. It would be quite unfounded to state, generally, that a theory of capital has to be dynamic. However, it is true that, if we have a model where it is necessary to consider both capital and its rate of growth, the model is automatically a dynamic model.

In the following we shall try to bring out more explicitly the role of the time element in various production processes.

III. THE PRODUCTIVITY OF CAPITAL

There is considerable disagreement on the question of *what function* capital actually performs in a production process, from a purely technological point of view. In the Böhm-Bawerkian model of circulating capital, the stock of capital as such actually does nothing, technologically speaking. It is just present as a consequence of a certain method of applying the original factors, labor and land. In the Wicksellian theory of fixed capital, however, the stock of capital is a service-yielding instrument in a technological sense. F. Knight and others seem to think that all capital should be regarded as a collection of service-rendering instruments.

One reason why discussions on this point are confused is related to the old mystery of why capital should do more than reproduce itself. But the main reason is, I think, that economists have so far not taken the study of the dynamics of production very seriously. What we have in this field is a hopeless mixture of vague technological notions and results of economic equilibrium mechanisms in a competitive market. It is one of our main objectives in the following to dig deeper into the purely technological aspects of the use of capital in production. We must try to distinguish clearly between the distributive "share" of capital and its technological role.

IV. PROBLEMS OF MEASUREMENT AND AGGREGATION

In what sense is it so much more difficult to find a physical measure for the volume of capital than it is to define an index of "total food consumption" or an index of the "volume" of foreign trade? The answer is certainly not merely that capital is composed of so many more different things. We can divide total capital into more homogeneous subgroups just the same way we construct subindices for the various kinds of food, or for commodities imported. In such cases we do in fact solve the insolvable problem of adding together very different things. In order to construct an index we have to specify what we are going to use it for or what general property the aggregate is supposed to measure. We can adjust an index to suit particular purposes by the choice of weights. This applies to the problem of constructing indices of the volume of capital as well as to any other kind of economic aggregate. In each case we have to evaluate what kind of approximation the index gives us and take this into account in drawing conclusions.

The fundamental problem of measuring capital, and one which makes this case somewhat different from an ordinary index number problem, is the following: We are actually confronted with the problem of constructing *four* different aggregates in such a way that they satisfy reasonable requirements of inner consistence and are interrelated in a meaningful and, preferably, simple way. The first aggregate is a measure of *real net investment* defined in such a way that is meaningful to say that net investment is the non-consumed part of real income. The second aggregate is the *amount of capital* defined as the *integral* over time of real net investment. The third aggregate is some measure of the volume of capital as a *technological factor* in relation to current physical output. And the fourth aggregate is *the rate of change* over time of the third aggregate (i.e., the accumulation of "productive power"). The relation between the first and the second pair of aggregates is sometimes fairly simple, as in the case where net real investment consists of a proportional increase in all kinds of physical capital items. But the relation may also be extremely complicated, e.g., when real net investment means making a certain kind of capital goods more durable without affecting its technological influence upon current output in the line of production where it is applied.

Considerable confusion exists in the literature about the four kinds of aggregates mentioned above. The main reason for this is, I think, the practice of using certain *market equilibrium conditions* to establish more or less simple relations between the real value of capital and the quantity of capital in the sense of a productive agent. If this is done and if, at the same time, we want to consider effects of certain variations which are bound to break the market equilibrium conditions, confusion is almost certain to occur.

8

The Time Element in Production

In economic textbooks on the theory of production we often find introductory remarks along the following line: "All production processes naturally take some time, but for the sake of simplicity we shall assume that the process is instantaneous." In certain cases, and for certain purposes, such a simplification may be quite legitimate and fruitful. But one must certainly be very careful about the kind of conclusions that can be drawn under this restrictive assumption. Thus, for example, if the inputs and outputs are finite quantities, and if we want to regard the instantaneous process as capable of repetition, we need some assumption of a finite time interval between the repetitions, otherwise we should have the nonsensical result that output per unit of time could be increased ad infinitum.

Another, perhaps rather trivial, observation is that a given production process may actually be regarded either as instantaneous or as time-consuming, depending on the way we interpret the process. Consider a process where the inputs are flows per unit of time and such that for all practical purposes the result is a simultaneous flow of output. If the process is continuous, the inputs and the output over an infinitesimal time interval will be of infinitesimal order. The process will, therefore, be a time-consuming one in the sense that it will take some time to produce a finite amount of output. We must be careful in distinguishing between processes that are time-consuming in this perfectly obvious sense, and processes where the time element has a more profound role. On closer inspection we shall find that the time element can play this more profound role in a number of rather different ways.

I. Productive Effects of "Time Itself"

The most obvious examples of time-consuming processes are those where a substance grows or ripens into a finished product. In some of these processes it is possible to accelerate or retard the process by other inputs during the growth or ripening period, as well as to change the quality or quantity of the final product. But most of these processes are, nevertheless, restricted by the need for time in a direct, technological sense.

It is perhaps a somewhat philosophical question whether we should regard time itself as an active productive agent in these processes or whether we should regard time only as a medium that permits the flows of services from other specified productive agents to cumulate into the product. The Böhm-Bawerk–Wicksellian approach corresponds, I think, to the latter interpretation. The distinction may be quite important in cases where the work intensity of the active, productive, agents can be regulated by human decision. In such cases the growth or ripening period may be very far from being a technological constant or a factor that uniquely determines output.

Even in these cases of obviously time-requiring processes, production could, in a certain sense, be regarded as instantaneous, if we regard output as the rate of growth of "goods in process," measured in units of the finished product. But an essential feature of such processes still remains, namely, that they require an accumulated stock of goods, or capital, in order to be kept going.

II. Processes That Require Successive Inputs

The processes previously mentioned are, of course, essentially of this type. However, there is a large number of other processes for which the operation of successive inputs is necessary even if time itself is not technologically important. In fact, the most common types of industrial production processes are of this nature. The completion of a finished product is carried out in steps which may or may not be interchangeable. Here the time element comes in, not necessarily because the product has to age, but because the various steps can be carried out only by a finite intensity of input per unit of time. Thus, for example, it may be technologically next to impossible to reduce the time of necessary transportation within a factory below a certain level. Or it may be impossible to increase the speed of input at a certain step in the process by increasing the number of workers concentrated at this step. The *economic* constraints upon a reduction of the time element in such processes may of course be much stronger than the purely technological ones.

An important feature of such production processes is that they necessarily have a stock- or capital-concept attached to them, namely the stock of goods in process (apart from other types of capital that may be involved).

III. The Idea of a "Construction Period"

The fact that it takes time to build a house or a ship is, of course, undeniable. However, the question of *constancy* of the building period is quite a different matter. During World War II ships were built in fewer hours than the number of days it usually took before the war. What counts here is, first of all, the number of man-hours that go into the finished product. The work may be concentrated or spread out in time. Technologically, the range is very wide, but economic considerations may narrow down the practical range of building periods.

Here again the process could, in a sense, be regarded as instantaneous, if we count the "rate of completion," measured in some unit, as output per unit of time.

IV. Time Elements in the Factors of Production

Even if a certain process is almost instantaneous as far as the time relation between direct inputs and outputs is concerned, the time element may be involved in an indirect way, via the age, or the processing period, of the factors themselves. This is particularly characteristic of machinery and other durable producer goods.

We may then find that the period of production of a certain commodity depends on the number of steps that are covered by the production function considered, i.e., the amount of vertical integration in the process for which the production function is assumed to be valid.

There may be a time element connected with the factors of production even if their production does not take much time and even if they are not durable. This may be the case if the inputs for some reason are stored before actually being used. Storage operations are production processes that have their own peculiarities which deserve some attention.

V. Storage Operations

In the case of the Wicksellian wine example, the storage operation is incidental to the production process considered, the production of mature wine. However, the idea of capital being productive due to roundaboutness does not seem particularly fruitful in connection with ordinary storage operations. There are many cases where the first-in-first-out rule does not apply. Also, there are many cases when the productivity of "aging" is plainly negative. It seems obvious that the "output" produced in a storage process must be something different from the net amount of goods taken out of storage. The output must be due either to a difference in the economic value of identical goods at different points in time or to some technological gain in making certain other processes more efficient, by producing a "smoothing" effect. If we want to include stock of goods in storage as capital, their technological role in production needs some clarification.

VI. The Time Element in Non-Stationary Processes

In the cases mentioned above, time enters in the form of the *length* of a time interval. In addition there is, of course, the question of historic time, or the amount of time that has elapsed since a certain process was started. It is time in this sense which is essential in economic dynamics. In a dynamic theory of production we must consider factors of production and outputs as functions of historic time, or time elapsed. A theory of production dealing with capitalistic processes must be dynamic if we want to use the relation between present capital and past investment to explain current output.

VII. The Measurement of Time

Can this really be a problem in the theory of production, unless we want to be philosophical? It can—and in a very practical and down-to-earth way. For example, if we say that it takes two days to produce some unit of output, it is not at all clear what this means. Does it mean forty-eight hours or does it mean two calendar days? If we were to compare two producers, one operating his factory continuously by using three work shifts, the other using an eight-hour day, we should definitely have to specify what we mean by "two days." If shiftwork is a matter of economic choice, it becomes exceedingly important to specify precisely what is meant, e.g., by a machine lasting five years. It could be five calendar years, but it could also be five years of continuous use on a twenty-four-hour basis.

In most of what follows we shall argue as if calendar time is the relevant measure. But this means, implicitly, that we have regarded the active part of the day as a constant fraction of twenty-four hours. Such an assumption is used implicitly in most of the theoretical literature on capital. Surprisingly little has been done on the economic theory of shift work. The problem is certainly an important one, and should be taken seriously in any would-be complete treatise on production. However, in what follows we shall have to neglect this problem, simply because we have enough of a theoretical task without it. (Some additional comments on this subject are given in chapter xiv.)

9

The Capital Element in Pure Aging Processes

WE have already analyzed the Wicksellian model of the process of aging wine. We want to consider such processes somewhat more generally, in order to clarify the technological role of capital in them.

I. The Simple One-Commodity Process

Let $v(t)$ denote the rate of input per unit of time of goods to be "aged." This variable is assumed to be measurable in some fixed physical unit (like the input of grape juice in the Wicksellian model). We shall here consider the simple case where, for some reason, the aging period θ must be *the same* for all units in the process. Let $x_\theta(t)$ denote the rate of output of finished goods aged θ units of time. The question immediately arises how to measure this variable. There are at least the following two possibilities: We could say that the physical measure of $x_\theta(t)$ is equal to the quantity $v(t - \theta)$ but that $x_\theta(t)$ in addition has a quality attribute. Or we could try to measure $x_\theta(t)$ in some unit that incorporates the quality attribute. Let us here consider the second approach. We may express this by writing

$$x_\theta(t) = \Psi^*[v(t - \theta), \theta] . \tag{9.1a}$$

We shall assume that this function is homogenous of degree one with respect to $v(t - \theta)$, so that we can write

$$x_\theta(t) = v(t - \theta) \, \Psi(\theta) \, . \tag{9.1b}$$

The second problem of measurement is the choice of a measure for the intermediary products. Here again we could measure goods which at time t already have been aged $\tau < \theta$ years simply as $v(t - \tau)$. We could, on the other hand, relate the measure of intermediary products to the measure of the final product $x_\theta(t)$ in some way. Or again, we could actually regard all intermediary products as final products of different kinds. It is, however, hard to visualize how one could make a sensible choice of such units of measurement without some reference to "economic value." We meet already in this simple case a fundamental problem in the theory of production, the problem of separating the purely technological aspects from the economic aspects of a production process.

One solution, which permits of several different interpretations, is to postulate that the rate $y_\tau(t)$ at which goods in process pass the age τ per unit of time is given by

$$y_\tau(t) = v(t - \tau) \, \Psi(\tau) \, , \qquad 0 \leqq \tau \leqq \theta \, , \tag{9.2}$$

where the function Ψ is the same as in equation (9.1b). Thus $x_\theta(t) = y_\theta(t)$.

Using this definition, consider the volume of goods in process defined as

$$K^*(t) = \int_0^\theta v(t - \tau) \, \Psi(\tau) \, d\tau \equiv \int_{t-\theta}^t v(\tau) \, \Psi(t - \tau) \, d\tau \, . \tag{9.3}$$

We have

$$\frac{dK^*}{dt} = v(t) \, \Psi(0) - x_\theta(t) + \int_{t-\theta}^t v(\tau) \, \Psi'(t - \tau) \, d\tau \, , \tag{9.4}$$

where Ψ' denotes the derivative of Ψ. The integral in equation (9.4) is the *internal increase* in K^* per unit of time. The term $v(t) \, \Psi(0)$ is the addition to K^* "from outside" while $x_\theta(t)$ is the "take-out."

We are interested in the interpretation of capital as a factor of production in this process. Let us define a simple, alternative measure of capital by

$$K(t) = \int_{t-\theta}^t v(\tau) \, d\tau \, . \tag{9.5}$$

Then, by a well-known rule of the calculus it may be possible to write

$$\int_{t-\theta}^t v(\tau) \, \Psi'(t - \tau) \, d\tau \equiv \kappa(t, \theta) \int_{t-\theta}^t v(\tau) \, d\tau \equiv \kappa(t, \theta) \, K(t) \, , \tag{9.6}$$

where $\kappa(t, \theta)$ is some mean value of Ψ'.

The identical expressions in (9.6) can be regarded as the output per unit of time at time t from the process of *holding the capital stock* $K(t)$. The coefficient κ will, in general, depend on t and θ, and it will also depend on the *functional form of the time function* $v(t)$. If we want to define the "marginal productivity" of $K(t)$, we obviously have to be very careful about the meaning of varying $K(t)$ at time t. We could think of $K(t)$ taking on different values at point of time t for the following reasons: (1) A change in θ to a different constant level (this change having taken place sufficiently far back in the past to make all units subject to the new θ); (2) a change in the form of the function $v(t)$. For these reasons $\kappa(t, \theta)$ will, in general, *not* be the marginal productivity of capital $K(t)$ at time t. Consider, however, the simple case where θ is constant while $K(t)$ takes on alternative different values by shifting a given series $v(t)$ up or down by a proportionality factor. In this case $\kappa(t, \theta)$ will be the marginal productivity of $K(t)$ and it will be independent of the value of $K(t)$. In this sense the process implies "constant return to scale."

Instead of (9.6) we could also write

$$\int_{t-\theta}^{t} v(\tau)\, \Psi'(t-\tau)\, d\tau \equiv \int_{t-\theta}^{t} v(\tau)\, \Psi(t-\tau) \frac{\Psi'(t-\tau)}{\Psi(t-\tau)}\, d\tau \tag{9.7}$$
$$= \kappa^*(t, \theta)\, K^*(t).$$

The problems of the interpretation of $\kappa^*(t, \theta)$ are similar to those discussed for the coefficient κ above.

Consider the case where $v(t)$ is a fixed time function and consider variations in $K(t)$ by ascribing alternative constant values to θ. In this case it is possible to define the marginal productivity of $K(t)$, or $K^*(t)$, as a function only of $K(t)$ or $K^*(t)$. These marginal productivities will, however, obviously not coincide with κ or κ^* as defined above, since the latter parameters depend on θ, and hence on $K(t)$ or $K^*(t)$.

Thus, we have found that in this sort of production process, there is, in general, no simple relation between the total *amount* of capital and the marginal productivity of capital, even when no other input elements are involved. Consider, however, the special case where $\Psi'(\tau)$ is a constant, $\bar{\kappa}$, independent of τ (in which case the "aging" means a linear growth). In this case we have, from identity (9.6)

$$\int_{t-\theta}^{t} v(\tau)\, \bar{\kappa}\, d\tau = \bar{\kappa} K(t), \tag{9.8}$$

where $\bar{\kappa}$ is independent of t, θ, and $K(t)$. Here $\bar{\kappa}$ is the marginal productivity of $K(t)$ in a very simple sense.

Consider, on the other hand, the special case where $\Psi(\tau) = ae^{\bar{\kappa}^*\tau}$, where a and $\bar{\kappa}^*$ are constants independent of τ. Then we have

$$\int_{t-\theta}^{t} v(\tau)\Psi(t-\tau)\frac{\Psi'(t-\tau)}{\Psi(t-\tau)}d\tau = \bar{\kappa}^*K^*(t), \qquad (9.9)$$

where $\bar{\kappa}^*$ is then the constant marginal productivity of $K^*(t)$.

In the simple cases above, the conclusions would hold even if we permit the stocks $K(t)$ and $K^*(t)$ to be currently modified by the purchase or sale of "goods in process," because the internal growth is independent of the composition of capital. But these are rather special cases. In general, the technological effect of capital on output in the model above cannot be expressed as a unique function of the volume of capital.

There are some important practical possibilities of simplifying the relations between capital and output, particularly if the stock of capital retains an approximately constant age distribution. This could be true under certain restrictions upon the series $v(t)$, or even if the holding of capital of various ages is modified by purchases and sales of goods in process. But even if such approximation were fairly good from a numerical point of view, this would not alter the fact that there is actually no unique technological relation between the amount of capital and the rate of output. One could say that, technologically, the aging process is not dependent upon the presence of many units being aged simultaneously.

II. A MULTI-COMMODITY PROCESS

Suppose that it is possible to regard goods in process also as finished goods (wine of different ages). Then, apart from economic limitations, we could regard the process as producing infinitely many different commodities. There is no difficulty in extending the scheme above to such a process.

Suppose that a certain generation of goods in process is sold out between age 0 and age θ, according to a certain fixed distribution $a(\tau)$, independent of t, such that

$$\int_{0}^{\theta} a(\tau)d\tau = 1. \qquad (9.10)$$

Then the rate of sales, $x(t)$, measured in the original units of the v's would be equal to

$$\int_{0}^{\theta} v(t-\tau)a(\tau)d\tau. \qquad (9.11)$$

And the rate of sales $x^*(t)$, measured in "finished commodity units," would be

$$x^*(t) = \int_{0}^{\theta} v(t-\tau)\Psi(\tau)a(\tau)d\tau. \qquad (9.12)$$

The portion of $v(t - \tau)$ that has been sold up to point of time t would be

$$v(t - \tau) \int_0^\tau a(z)\, dz.$$

Hence, we should find that the stock of capital at time t, measured in the unit of the v's, would be

$$K(t) = \int_0^\theta v(t - \tau) \left[1 - \int_0^\tau a(z)\, dz \right] d\tau. \qquad (9.13)$$

The volume of capital, regarded as finished goods in stock, $K^*(t)$, would be

$$K^*(t) = \int_0^\theta v(t - \tau) \Psi(\tau) \left[1 - \int_0^\tau a(z)\, dz \right] d\tau. \qquad (9.14)$$

The rate of internal growth of capital would be (cf. equation (9.4))

$$\int_{t-\theta}^t v(\tau) \Psi'(t - \tau) \left[1 - \int_0^{t-\tau} a(z)\, dz \right] d\tau. \qquad (9.15)$$

This formula could be discussed in a manner similar to the discussion of equation (9.7) above

III. POSSIBLE SIDE EFFECTS OF THE VOLUME OF CAPITAL

It is conceivable that the volume of capital could have some separate influence on the effectivity of the aging process, for example, if the possibilities of proper storage depend on the scale of operation in the whole process. This would, in general, mean that the quality, or value, of the finished goods would depend on the volume of capital present at each and every moment during the aging period. That is, output would in part bear a *functional* relation to the volume of capital. It might, under certain assumptions, be possible to approximate this relation by introducing a notion of average amount of capital during the aging period. Then the amount of capital could be regarded as a genuine factor of production in the technological sense, in addition to its being incidental to the process of aging.

The practical importance of the kind of processes discussed above is probably not very great as compared to other types of production processes. The aging processes were important in the Böhm-Bawerk-Wicksellian approach because these schemes served as good illustrations of a way of thinking which allegedly could be extended to nearly all kinds of capitalistic processes. The choice of the wine example and similar illustrations was, in a way, somewhat unfortunate. It is true that these examples carry a great deal of conviction as far as they go, but they fall very much short of telling the whole story of capital as a productive agent.

10

The Technology of Natural Growth Processes

IT may seem artificial to distinguish between aging processes and natural growth processes. In point of principle, they ought to be very similar. The distinction we have in mind is, however, that the practical difficulties of units of measurement may be rather different. In growth processes, like feeding of livestock, the raising of agricultural crops, production of timber, etc., it seems that we can get by with somewhat less trouble of defining output in technological units than is the case for the pure aging processes. The difference in this respect is, however, not an absolute one. Thus, for example, when a forest grows in terms of cubic feet content, the quality of each cubic foot usually depends in an important way on its age. Likewise, it is certainly not wholly adequate to measure beef merely in pounds. But the relevance of a purely physical measure of quantity seems, nevertheless, greater in such processes because of the fact that the physical volume usually changes enormously during the growth process and because the physical rate of growth often is a function of inputs which can be regulated by the producer. These processes are, therefore, somewhat more general, and certainly of more practical importance, than the pure aging processes.

I. Pure Natural Growth Processes

Consider, as an illustration, a forest which grows naturally, without any special caretaking. From one point of view the forest may be regarded as a certain *number of trees*. We may describe the content of the forest simply as an age distribution of trees. From another point of view the forest may at any time be regarded as a certain volume of wood or timber, e.g., a certain number of cubic feet. The age distribution of the cubic content will, of course, usually be very different from the age distribution of the number of trees.

If the forest is left undisturbed for a sufficiently long period, the total cubic content and its age distribution may settle down to a stationary state, or perhaps to some oscillations around a stationary level. If, on the other hand, the forest is being cut each year to some extent, it is usually possible to have a continuous net output which leaves the cubic content of the forest approximately constant. The cubic content at a given point in time can be regarded as a physical volume of capital which grows upon itself, or produces a net output.

55

However, it is only under very special conditions that the growth can be expressed as a function of the volume of forest capital measured in cubic content. The rate of growth will depend on the age composition of the cubic content. This means again that the rate of growth or "net output" at time t will depend on how the forest has been taxed in the past, what size of trees have been cut, how they have been picked among the trees standing, and so on. This leads to the conclusion that, unless we include in the technology certain *economic data*, such as the cutting policy of the forest operator, we should need at least two variables to characterize the production function of the forest, namely the cubic content, or volume of physical capital, and, in addition, a parameter describing the age composition of the physical capital. In this respect the process is similar to the aging processes discussed in the previous chapter.

Consider, as another illustration, the process of growing apples. And let us also in this case, for the sake of simplicity, disregard inputs of such things as labor and fertilizers. Suppose we regard the number of trees of fruit-bearing age as capital. For a given type and location of the orchard, the average annual crop of apples may be approximately equal to a function of capital measured as the number of trees. However, the yield of a tree will usually depend on its age, even if we disregard very old and very young trees. What is more important in this case is that there may be a relatively large number of young or newly planted trees that do not yield any output at all. If these trees are counted as capital, their effect on current output would be zero (or even negative in the case where the young trees compete with the older trees for water and nutrition).

The whole process could in fact be regarded as composed of two types of capitalistic processes, the first one an aging process of bringing trees to a fruit-bearing age, the second a process using durable capital as a means of production. Only under special conditions or by introducing elements of economic choice in the process could we express the output of apples as a function of the number of trees. Even if we include an additional parameter representing the age distribution of the trees, we should at best get only a rough approximation to a technological production function.

In processes like those above, the "inner growth" of capital may not be proportional to the volume of capital, even if the age distribution of the capital is fixed. There may be a scale factor which is not constant, due mainly to the fact that land is a fixed factor. The "density" of capital upon a given area may have an important effect upon the productivity of capital.

II. Feeding Processes

The most direct examples of this kind of processes would be the feeding of hogs or beef cattle, or other animal feeding processes. But there are also many industrial processes that have similar characteristics. In fact, there is some similarity between such feeding processes in the more direct sense and the construction of large capital units, such as houses, or power plants. But for the present we shall think of feeding processes in a more narrow sense. A feeding process can be regarded as a process of transforming and accumulating the effects of certain continuous inputs through a certain feeding period. In feeding processes that are based on some form of biological growth, there may be a complicated relation between the rate of inputs and the rate of accumulation or growth, due to limitations of "digestive capacity."

Consider as an illustration the feeding of hogs. Here the rate of growth of the individual animal will depend on such factors as the age and weight of the animal, as well as on the rate of input of feedstuff. For example, for a given age, weight, etc., there may be a rate of input of feedstuff that maximizes the rate of growth of the animal. There may be another rate of using feedstuff that maximizes the rate of growth *per unit of feedstuff*.

Now suppose we want to construct some index of physical capital involved in a feeding process. Such an index could be the number of hogs being fed times their average age, or perhaps the total live weight of the hogs. Could we then consider output in the sense of growth in pounds per unit of time as a function of the rate of input of feedstuff and the stock of "hog capital"? Apart from the obvious fact that there are many other influencing factors involved, there is the problem that two 100-pound hogs do not together grow in the same way as one 200-pound hog. On the other hand, if, within the range of practical variations, such problems could be neglected with a not too poor approximation, we could think of a feeding process as described by a production function

$$y(t) = \Psi[K(t), v(t)], \qquad (10.1)$$

where $y(t)$ is the total physical rate of growth per unit of time of all animals, $K(t)$ the amount of "hog capital" at t, and $v(t)$ the physical rate of total input of feedstuff per unit of time. The time element is here, in a sense, hidden in $K(t)$. However, it shows up more explicitly when we try to derive the production function for the finished product, slaughter hogs.

Suppose that a slaughter hog is defined as a hog of a given *weight*. And let us consider the production function for a typical animal. Let $\bar{y}(\tau)$ denote the rate of growth of an animal at age τ, let $\bar{K}(\tau)$ denote its weight at age τ, and $\bar{v}(\tau)$ the rate of feeding at age τ. Then we may have

$$\bar{y}\,(\tau) = g\,[\,\bar{K}\,(\tau)\,,\,\bar{v}\,(\tau)\,]$$

$$= g\,\left\{\left[\int_0^\tau \bar{y}\,(z)\,d\,z + \bar{K}\,(0)\,\right],\,\bar{v}\,(\tau)\,\right\}. \qquad (10.2)$$

Hence, if h denotes the prescribed weight of a slaughter hog, we have the condition

$$\int_0^\theta g d\,\tau = h\,. \qquad (10.3)$$

In this relation there are two variable elements, the feeding curve $\bar{v}(\tau)$ and the feeding period θ. These two variable elements must satisfy the condition of equation (10.3).

Suppose, in particular, that the curve $\bar{v}(\tau)$ is fixed for some reason. Then θ is determined by equation (10.3). Let $x(t)$ denote the output of slaughter hogs per unit of time. We might, under certain assumptions of continuity, be able to use

$$x(t) = \Phi[K(t - \omega_1), \bar{v}(t - \omega_2)] \qquad (10.4)$$

as a first approximation by appropriate choice of constant lags ω_1, and ω_2 (perhaps $\theta/2$ for both).

Suppose, on the other hand, that θ is fixed. Then the question of approximation is more complicated, since there will probably be many different curves $\bar{v}(\tau)$ satisfying equation (10.3). However, if we have some additional limitations on the curve $v(\tau)$, it may also in this case be permissible to use a production function of the form of equation (10.4) as an approximation.

However, in all these cases we see that, while the productivity of capital in the sense of the rate of internal growth may be an approximate function of the amount of capital currently present, the rate of output of finished products at a given point in time will not, in general, be a function of the volume of capital present at that time. There will at least be an approximately constant lag. The complications concerning capital as a factor of production depend to a great extent on whether it is the variable $x(t)$ or the variable $y(t)$ which we define as output. In the function Φ the amount of physical capital may well behave as an ordinary factor of production in the simple sense in which such factors are interpreted in the static theory of production.

The role of capital as a factor of production in these processes is somewhat peculiar. The presence of a capital stock is necessary as an instrument of accumulation. We could look upon the stock of capital as something which permits economizing with the input factor v. In one respect, the productivity of the capital stocks could be described, technologically, as the effect of changing the form of the input curve $\bar{v}(\tau)$ when the total input,

$$\int_0^\theta \bar{v}(\tau)\, d\tau,$$

is given.

III. INPUT OF CARE AND MANAGEMENT

The process described above can be regarded as a technical transformation process where the input of feedstuff is accumulated into a stock of goods in process. However, this transformation process may be greatly affected by the input of care and management. From a technical point of view the effect of care and management could, at least in part, be thought of as affecting the growth resulting from a unit input of feedstuff. The effect could take the form of avoiding direct waste and improving the digestive process in various ways. Thus, the input of care and management could be regarded as a method of saving feedstuff. But the effect could also be an increase in output for a given input of feedstuff.

Both the direct input of feedstuff and the input of care and management could, therefore, be regarded as something which gradually gets incorporated into the stock of goods in process. If we regard the rate of growth, $y(t)$, as the current output, and if $v_1(t)$ denotes the input of feedstuff and $v_2(t)$ the input of care and management (measured in workhours), we could have

$$y(t) = \Psi^*[K(t), v_1(t), v_2(t)], \qquad (10.5)$$

as an approximate production function of the firm, instead of equation (10.1).

Similarly, it may be possible, under certain conditions, to approximate the production function for the output of finished goods by

$$x(t) = \Phi^*[K(t - \omega), v_1(t - \omega_1), v_2(t - \omega_2)]. \qquad (10.6)$$

The lags ω, ω_1, ω_2 in this function would, however, generally depend on the economic organization of the feeding process. That is, the lags would depend on the form of the feeding curve, the labor input curve, changes in the number of units being fed, and so on.

One will notice that it may be possible to describe the processes discussed in this chapter as an Austrian scheme of roundaboutness. We could regard the capital involved at any time as an amount of stored-up labor- and land-services, the feedstuff being itself a product of land and labor.

However, it seems that such a scheme would take us unnecessarily far away from a straight technological point of view.

Obviously, the stock of goods in process may not be the only capital element in the process discussed above. There may, and there usually will be, fixed capital involved. In this respect feeding processes are not different from other kinds of production processes, and there is no particular need for discussing the effect of fixed capital at this particular point.

11

The Continuous Assembly Line

WE shall now discuss production processes that have the following general characteristics: (1) The output of finished products is in the nature of a continuous, or approximately continuous, *flow*. (2) The production of this flow of output consists in adding to each particle of the goods in process a certain sequence of successive inputs. (3) The inputs are intensities, something per unit of time.

There is a variety of well-known industrial processes that are of this nature, both among those that actually are assembly line processes, and others that do not literally involve an assembly line. The study of such processes may be useful in order to gain more insight concerning the time element in production. In particular, it is of importance to study to what extent the requirement of time is a technological question and to what extent it is a question of economic choice.

In the analysis to follow we shall continue to build on the usual simplification of assuming that the daily work-hours represent a fixed percentage of a calendar day of twenty-four hours.

I. A PROCESS OF STATIONARY FLOWS

In order to have something concrete, though extremely simple, to think about, let us associate the mathematical apparatus we are about to develop with the following process: Consider a continuous endless homogeneous strip of metal that runs through a factory building where it is being worked on while moving. The raw strip enters at one end of the building and comes out as a finished product at the other end. We assume that successive steps of work (or, more generally, some measurable inputs) are applied to each element of the strip as it moves along. Suppose that the building is L feet long, and let λ denote the distance from the entrance to a particular point along the assembly line. Let $v(\lambda)$, $0 \leqq \lambda \leqq L$, denote the *intensity of input* per foot per unit of time, applied to the strip at the point λ. In what follows we shall assume that the function $v(\lambda)$ is independent of time. The process can be visualized schematically as in Figure 1.

Let us first assume, tentatively, that the metal strip is being moved by discrete "jerks" at equal time intervals Δt. For each jerk, the strip is assumed to advance a distance $\Delta\lambda$ at infinite speed and then come to rest

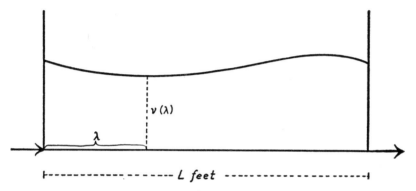

FIG. 1.—Assembly line

for a period Δt. Let us choose $\Delta\lambda$ such that $n\Delta\lambda = L$, with n an integer, and let us number the elements $\Delta\lambda$ Nos. 1, 2, . . . , n, starting from the entrance. For each of these segments, say i, the strip will receive a certain amount of productive input, or "value added." Suppose that this value added is measurable. Let $y(i)$ denote the average rate of value added per foot per unit of time over segment i of the line. The total value added over the segment i for each segment of the strip of length $1/n\ L$ would then be $y(i)\Delta\lambda\Delta t$. Let us analyze a little more in detail the determinants of this value-added element.

Consider the "effect variable" $y(i)$. It must, first of all, depend on the value of the factor input intensity $v(\lambda)$ over the ith segment of the line. There is obviously a direct value-added effect of the length of the time interval Δt, but this is already taken account of in the product $y(i)\Delta\lambda\Delta t$. However, it is reasonable to assume that the length of Δt will also affect $y(i)$ to some extent, for the reason that eventually *too much work* of a certain kind might be done on the strip if it stays too long in the same spot.

In general, we must, therefore, assume that, for a given work intensity

$v(\lambda)$ over a given segment of the line, the effect variable $y(i)$ will be a more or less complicated function of the average speed with which the strip moves or, what comes to the same, a function of its resting periods Δt.

Let $v(\lambda_i)$ denote the average intensity of factor input upon the segment i. For certain processes it might be a sufficiently good approximation to assume that the amount of value added per foot during Δt, i.e., $\Delta t y(i)$, depends only on the amount of factor input during Δt, i.e., $v(\lambda_i)\Delta t$. In such cases we could write $\Delta t y(i) = f[\Delta t v(\lambda_i)]$. This would mean that the work of two workers during twenty minutes would have a value-added effect equivalent to the work of four workers during ten minutes. However, in most cases this would be unrealistic, as it may not be feasible to crowd more than a very limited amount of labor input into a certain spot along the line. In general, we must assume that $y(i)$ will be a function of $v(\lambda_i)$ and Δt separately. And this function will probably also depend on which of the line segments we consider. Hence we should presumably write

$$y(i) = g[v(\lambda_i), \Delta t, i] . \tag{11.1}$$

This is, in a sense, a production function expressing the "internal rate of growth" of the product at the stage i. Since Δt is a constant, the total time, T, that a certain point of the metal strip remains in the factory building would be equal to $n\Delta t$. As long as n stays constant, we could, therefore, also write

$$y (i) = g\left[v (\lambda_i) , \frac{T}{n}, i\right] = g^* [v (\lambda_i) , T, i]. \tag{11.2}$$

The form of the functions g and g^* will, in general, depend on the number of segments, n.

Now consider the case where the metal strip moves continuously, with constant speed. We cannot safely "derive" the result in this case simply by a mathematical limit operation ($n \to \infty$) because we do not know how in reality the functions g, or g^*, would behave under such an operation. But the simple result that would be completely analogous to equation (11.1) or (11.2) in the continuous case is obviously

$$y(\lambda) = \Phi[v(\lambda), T, \lambda] , \tag{11.3}$$

where Φ is a certain function and where $y(\lambda)$ denotes the rate of "value added" per foot per unit of time at the point λ of the assembly line.

The somewhat complicated *dimension* of $v(\lambda)$ and $y(\lambda)$, "value added" per foot per unit of time, must be carefully observed. The reason for the "per unit of time" dimension is obvious. But the "per foot" dimension may need a word of explanation. It derives from the fact that we have to measure the intensity of work input per foot along λ. The total input of work per unit of time must by definition be equal to

$$\int_0^L v(\lambda)\, d\lambda.$$

Since this is to be a finite rate of total work input per unit of time and since $d\lambda$ has the dimension "feet," $v(\lambda)$ must have the dimension work per foot per unit of time. An exactly similar reasoning applies to $y(\lambda)$.

As long as the strip moves with constant speed, the total output or value added, x, per unit of time for all the steps along the line can easily be calculated. We obtain

$$x = \sum_{i=1}^{n} g^* [v(\lambda_i), T, i] \, \Delta\lambda \tag{11.4}$$

and

$$x = \int_0^L \Phi [v(\lambda), T, \lambda] \, d\lambda, \tag{11.5a}$$

for the discontinuous and the continuous case, respectively.

The speed of a point on the metal strip in the continuous case is obviously L/T. The time, τ, that it takes for a point on the strip to move the distance λ is, therefore, $\tau = (T/L)\lambda$. Thus, we could also write equation (11.5a) as

$$x = \frac{L}{T} \int_0^T \Phi \left[v \left(\frac{L}{T} \tau \right), T, \frac{L}{T} \tau \right] d\tau. \tag{11.5b}$$

The number of feet of finished product per unit of time is obviously equal to L/T. The value added to such a section of the strip is the sum of values added to each part of it while it is in the factory building. This sum is obviously *equal to* x, because x is the total value added per unit of time and because the process is stationary in the sense that the accumulated value added inside the factory building must remain constant.

Let us now look at the amount of capital, in the form of goods in process, inside the factory building. We shall here neglect the possible value of the raw metal strip. Consider an infinitesimal cross-section $\Delta\lambda$ of the strip at the distance λ from the entrance. This section has been under work for $\tau = T(\lambda/L)$ units of time. Its value added can, therefore, be regarded as proportional to the average of the rate y, from zero to λ, times $T(\lambda/L)$, the proportionality factor being $\Delta\lambda$. The total value of goods in process must be the sum of all such infinitesimal cross-sections within the factory building. The result can be written as

$$K = \frac{L}{T} \int_0^T \left[\int_0^\tau y \left(\frac{L}{T} z \right) dz \right] d\tau. \tag{11.6}$$

If, in particular, $y(\lambda)$ would be a constant $= \bar{y}$, independent of λ, we should have, from equation (11.6), that K would be equal to $\frac{1}{2}\bar{y}LT$. From this result we see certain obvious relations that must hold between the input intensities, the speed of the metal strip, the amount of goods in process, and the "quality" of the finished product. Suppose, for example, that the speed of the strip would be doubled. Then K would be cut by 50 per cent while the rate of output, x, would stay the same. However, each foot of the finished strip would have only one-half as much value added as before, which of course would be nonsensical if the finished strip has to be of a certain prescribed quality. If, however, $\bar{y}$ is doubled at the same time as T is reduced by one-half, capital in the form of goods in process would be unchanged while the rate of output, x, would be doubled. But it may not be technically possible to change the input intensity $v(\lambda)$ along the assembly line in this simple way.

Still, from the considerations above we see that the amount of capital, in the form of goods in process, behaves in some respects like a factor of production. There are some sort of substitution possibilities as between the stock of capital and the intensity of work input. For a given $v(\lambda)$ function there may be a certain amount of capital that maximizes output.

One could ask whether there are any obvious technological reasons why the process above should lead to a significant average lag between inputs and output. Could not the process be speeded up to an almost instantaneous process by increasing the input intensity along the assembly line? We have already mentioned the simple capacity problem in this connection, the question of space for the workers along the assembly line. But there may be other reasons. In some cases there may be a ripening—or aging—process involved at a certain step along the line. The rate of supply of raw metal strip may be limited, the technological possibilities of handling the finished product may be limited, and so on. The technological as well as the economic role of capital in the form of goods in process is that it permits a spreading out of the current input elements, thereby increasing their effect on the finished product.

In the process above we have not counted the value of the raw metal strip as part of capital or goods in process. If we did, the addition would obviously be a constant independent of the speed at which the strip moves along the assembly line. This is a cost element which may make it profitable to speed up the process to some extent.

II. A Process of Variable "Production Starting"

In the preceding model we assumed that the amount of raw materials that enters the process per unit of time was a constant, independent of time. If the speed of the process varied, we should not get a homogeneous final product unless we made adjustments of the $v(\lambda)$-function over time. The same thing would happen if, in the previous model, we imagine that we could vary the width of the metal strip while keeping its speed through the factory building constant. Presumably, the rate of value added at a given point along the assembly line would then be spread out across the metal strip, the thinner the wider the strip. Therefore, the wider parts of the strip would come out with less value added per square foot than the more narrow parts. However, if the $v(\lambda)$-curve could be varied over time, e.g., in such a way that $v(\lambda)$ would be proportional to the width of the metal strip passing at any time, the final product might still be fairly homogeneous.

Suppose that, as an example, the metal strip originally was assumed to be one foot wide, and that the $v(\lambda)$ function, for a given processing time T, was such as to give a finished product of a specified quality. And suppose now that we consider a work input intensity function $\bar{v}(\lambda, t)$ which is equal to $v(\lambda)$ times the width of the metal strip passing the point λ at time t. The cross-section of the strip that enters the process at time t_e passes the point λ at time $\tau = t_e + T(\lambda/L)$. Let the width of the strip entering at t_e be $\nu(t_e)$ feet. We then have

$$\bar{v}\,(\lambda, t) = v\,(\lambda)\,\nu\left(t - T\,\frac{\lambda}{L}\right), \tag{11.7}$$

and, perhaps, as an approximation to the intensity of value added at t per foot per unit of time at the point λ,

$$y(\lambda, t) = \Phi[\bar{v}(\lambda, t), T, \lambda], \tag{11.8}$$

with the same Φ as in equation (11.3).

If we denote by $x(t)$ the rate of value added in the whole process per unit of time at t, we should then have

$$x\,(t) = \int_0^L y\,(\lambda, t)\,d\lambda = \int_0^L \Phi\left[v\,(\lambda)\,\nu\left(t - T\,\frac{\lambda}{L}\right), T, \lambda\right]d\lambda. \tag{11.9}$$

But now this rate of total value added per unit of time would *not* in general be equal to the rate of output of finished products. This latter rate might be larger or smaller than that given by equation (11.9), depending on how the series $\nu(t_e)$ varies with time. The rate of output of finished products would be

$$x^*\,(t) = \int_0^L y\left[\lambda, \left(t - T + \frac{T}{L}\lambda\right)\right]d\lambda$$
$$= \int_0^L \Phi\left[v\,(\lambda)\,\nu\,(t - T), T, \lambda\right]d\lambda. \tag{11.10}$$

Thus, for example, if $\nu(t_e)$ is increasing with time we should expect to find $x^*(t) < x(t)$.

Also the volume of goods in process will now be a function of time. At time t the amount of capital, $K(t)$, will be

$$K(t) = \frac{L}{T} \int_0^T \left\{ \int_0^\theta y \left[\frac{L}{T} \tau, t - (\theta - \tau) \right] d\tau \right\} d\theta \quad (11.11)$$

(cf. equation (11.6)). The stock of capital will depend on how much work has been started in the past.

There is, in general, no simple relation between $K(t)$ and either $x(t)$ or $x^*(t)$. However, each element of $K(t)$ plays the role of being present as a recipient of further work input.

III. REMARKS ON THE PRODUCTIVITY OF GOODS IN PROCESS

We have seen that capital in the form of goods in process can be regarded as a necessary receptacle for the inputs of other factors and that the effect of these other factors may depend on the amount of goods in process. To bring out this essential point more clearly, let us consider the simple case where the value-added intensity, $y(\lambda)$, is a constant $= \bar{y}$ along the whole assembly line of length L. Let us also assume that the "breadth" of the process as well as its speed are constants. There we have the simple relation (cf. equation (11.6) or (11.11))

$$\bar{K} = \tfrac{1}{2} \bar{y} L T , \quad (11.12)$$

where $\bar{K}$ is the constant amount of goods in process. The corresponding constant rate of output, $\bar{x}$, would be equal to

$$\bar{x} = \bar{y} L . \quad (11.13)$$

The process can be described, somewhat freely perhaps, as follows: L denotes the "size of plant," while L/T describes the speed of output, $\bar{x}/(L/T) = \bar{y}T$ is "value" per physical unit of output, or "quality." The rate of total output is $\bar{y}L$, while $\bar{K}$ is the amount of "variable capital" used.

Let us first look at the possible effects of trying to reduce $\bar{K}$ while keeping the same output, both quantitatively and qualitatively. These latter requirements can be described as follows:

$$\bar{y}L = \text{constant, e.g., } = \alpha ,$$

$$\bar{y}T = \text{constant, e.g., } = \beta .$$

We see at once that, in order to meet these requirements, the speed of the process, L/T, must be kept constant. From equation (11.12) we then get

$$\bar{K} = \frac{1}{2} \frac{\alpha\beta}{\bar{y}} .$$

This means that in order to reduce $\bar{K}$, the intensity $\bar{y}$ must be increased. Now this may be difficult or costly. The choice of the combination $(\bar{K}, \bar{y})$ may, therefore, be very important and of the same nature as the substitution problems we know from the ordinary, static, theory of production.

Let us look at the process from a different angle. Suppose we should wish to increase the rate of output $\bar{x}$, without loss of quality and without expansion of capital. Since $\bar{y}T$ must be constant, we see at once from equation (11.12) that L must remain constant in order to have $\bar{K}$ unchanged. Hence the possibility that remains is to increase $\bar{y}$ and decrease T such that their product remains constant. That means to speed up the process by using a greater work intensity along the assembly line. This may meet with the difficulties of space and efficiency that we have mentioned before.

The illustrations above suggest that capital in the form of goods in process behaves much like a factor of production in the more usual meaning. We shall find that this is true also for other types of time-consuming processes.

12

The Production of Large Units

THE term "large" units may be somewhat ambiguous. What we have in mind are products that have the dimension of a *stock*, such that if a certain finite number of these products were produced during each consecutive time interval Δt the output per unit of time would become "infinite" if $\Delta t \to 0$. The point is simply that, even if we have a continuously operating production process, the output from this process may not become a "product" until a certain bulk of accumulated inputs has been reached. Such products are not necessarily durable goods. For example, it may take some time to produce a guided missile but not much time to "consume" it. Also, the product may sometimes be regarded as continuous output in a technical sense but not in an economic sense, as, for example, the building of a road from one town to another (when nobody has any business going to a point between the two towns).

The reason why the production of such units is time-consuming may simply be that it takes a lot of labor input to accumulate one unit, and that the rate of possible labor input per unit of time is limited for technological or economic reasons.

I. Construction Work as a Process of Simple Accumulation

Suppose that the current output, $y(\tau)$, of a certain continuous process is so defined that if

$$\int_{t}^{t+T} y(\tau)\, d\tau = 1 ,\qquad(12.1)$$

it means the completion of *one unit* of a certain bulk product (a machine, a ship, etc.). We could then say that the total "period of construction" of this unit is T, and that a certain part of one unit or a certain number of units of finished products have been produced *per unit of time*.

Let us for simplicity assume that the continuous input which produces the flow $y(t)$ can be measured by a single index, $v(\tau)$, such that

$$y(\tau) = \Phi[v(\tau)] ,\qquad(12.2)$$

where $v(\tau)$ has the dimension of input per unit of time, and where Φ is independent of the stage of the accumulation process as well as of historic time. The average age, θ, of the inputs incorporated in a unit of finished product will then be

$$\theta = \frac{\int_{0}^{T} (T-\tau)\, v\,(t-T+\tau)\, d\tau}{\int_{0}^{T} v\,(t-T+\tau)\, d\tau} .\qquad(12.3)$$

Suppose we have the special case where $v(\tau)$ is constant $= \bar{v}$ and, therefore, $y(\tau)$ constant $= \bar{y}$. Then we obtain from equation (12.1) that $T\bar{y} = 1$. And from equation (12.3) we get $\theta = \frac{1}{2}T$. The time interval T can thus be shortened by an increase of $\bar{y}$. However, it is by no means certain that Φ would be such that $\bar{v}$ and $\bar{y}$ would be proportional. We may have a general economic problem of substitution as between T and $\bar{v}$.

During the period T the average capital in the form of goods in process is, of course, simply a fraction of 1, if the finished products are produced one at a time, as assumed above. If y is constant $= \bar{y}$, this capital is equal to $\frac{1}{2}$. The average output of finished products per unit of time is $1/T$. Hence the average ratio of capital to output is equal to $\frac{1}{2}T$. This ratio can, therefore, be reduced by increasing $\bar{y}$. In this sense we can here talk about a possibility of substitution between capital and current input $\bar{v}$.

In the case of constant $v(\tau) = \bar{v}$, the total number of man-hours or "input-hours" in a unit of finished product would be $\bar{v}T$. However, even if $T\bar{y} = 1$ for alternative values of T and $\bar{y}$, this does *not* mean that $\bar{v}T$ would stay constant if T is changed. If we want to use $T\bar{v}$ as a variable in the production function we obtain

$$T\bar{y} = 1 = T\Phi\left(\frac{\bar{v}T}{T}\right).$$

Only if Φ were homogeneous of degree 1 could the output of the finished product unit be regarded as a function only of *total input* $T\bar{v}$. In general, if $T\bar{v}$ is given, T will be *determinate*, not arbitrary.

II. Staggered Lines of Production

We want to consider the technology of an enterprise which produces some kind of large units, e.g., a standard type of house, under the following conditions: (1) Only one input factor (labor or a fixed proportion of labor and equipment) is applied. Of course, building materials are needed but we shall regard these inputs as fixed auxiliaries in the process. (2) A certain constant rate of input per unit of time is prescribed for each house. For the sake of simplicity let us call this rate of input "labor" and denote it by $\bar{n}$. (3) For a given $\bar{n}$ we assume that the total building time of a house is a constant $= T$. We shall assume that T is an integer in the time unit chosen. (4) At equal discrete intervals of time $t = t_0, t_0 + 1, \ldots$ work is started on a new batch of houses m_t in number.

Under these conditions we shall have that the level of total employment, N_t, at the beginning of each time interval will be

$$N_t = (m_t + m_{t-1} + \ldots + m_{t-T+1})\bar{n}, \quad t = t_0 + T,$$

$$t_0 + T + 1, \ldots. \tag{12.4}$$

(N_t is a stock concept, but, by convention, it is numerically equal to the total amount of work done per unit of time.)

In the special case where m is constant $= \bar{m}$, total employment will be equal to $\bar{m}\bar{n}T$. The annual output of finished houses will then, of course, be equal to $\bar{m}$. However, it would *not* in general be true that this rate could be maintained by, e.g., doubling $\bar{n}$ and reducing T by one half; T must be regarded as a function of $\bar{n}$. It may, e.g., be that $\bar{n}T$ would be at a minimum for a certain value of $\bar{n}$.

The amount of accumulated input (labor) Y_t incorporated in all the houses under construction, including houses just finished, will be

$$Y_t = [m_{t-T}\,T + m_{t-T+1}\,(T-1) + \ldots + m_{t-1}]\bar{n},$$

$$t = t_0 + T, \quad t_0 + T + 1, \ldots. \tag{12.5}$$

If, in particular, m_t is constant $= \bar{m}$, we get $Y_t = \bar{Y} = $ constant, viz.,

$$\bar{Y} = \frac{1+T}{2}\, \bar{m} \bar{n} T. \tag{12.6}$$

Suppose that $\bar{n}$ is increased sufficiently to make T a smaller integer than before. This may mean that the product $\bar{n} T$ will have to increase, for reasons already explained. Even if $\bar{m}$ is constant, the increase in $\bar{n}$ does not necessarily mean that $\bar{Y}$ is decreased, although the factor $(1 + T)/2$ contributes to this effect. It all depends on the behavior of the product $\bar{n} T$ for different values of $\bar{n}$.

The stock-concept Y_t is a part of the total capital of goods in process. But there are also the building materials to be considered. If we could assume that the rate of input of building materials could be measured in the same units as $\bar{n}$ and that the two rates were proportional, the total working capital would be proportional to Y_t. Because of the assumed variability of the product $\bar{n} T$, the amount of working capital could, in a sense, be regarded as a factor of production.

Above we have assumed that the work on each batch of finished products was started at the beginning of each year, or whatever the unit of time may be. It may be of some interest to see what happens if the starting takes place more frequently or, alternatively, less frequently. For simplicity, let the starting points remain equidistant. Suppose that the equidistance is a units of time, where a is either an integer or a rational proper fraction, while T remains an integer. And let us consider only the case where m_t is equal to $\bar{m}a$, where $\bar{m}$ is a constant, (i.e., the average starting of new units per unit of time is a constant). We then have

$$\bar{Y}(a) = (a + 2a + \ldots + T)\, a\bar{m}\bar{n} = (a+T)\frac{T}{2}\,\bar{m}\bar{n}, \tag{12.7}$$

$$\left(\frac{T}{a}\ \text{terms}\right)$$

where $\bar{Y}(a)$ is defined for points of time that are equidistant with interval equal to a.

From equation (12.7) we see that if a becomes a small fraction of T, then $\bar{Y}(a)$ will be approximately equal to $(T^2/2)\bar{m}\bar{n}$. Of course, if this consideration is to make sense, $\bar{m}a$ must remain an integer.

What the above considerations show is that the frequency of starting points for new units may not be really essential for the stock of goods in process. It is likewise obvious that the average rate of output of finished products per unit of time is not affected in any fundamental way.

III. A Continuous Approximation

An essential characteristic of the processes just discussed is that it takes time to produce each unit of finished product because each unit is a *stock* of some size. Only a certain finite number of such finished units can be produced during each unit of time or, what comes to the same, only a finite number of units can be started in each unit of time. No matter how many units are started during each unit of time, the starting can never actually become a continuous flow.

Nevertheless, if the starting points are spread out in time so that there are several units starting during each unit of time, it may be possible to *approximate* the process by a continuous analogue without losing the central features of the dynamics involved. This may be particularly true if T is large in relation to the unit of time and if there are frequent startings within each unit of time. Then the inaccuracy in the exact timing of startings and final outputs that one gets by considering these time points as, e.g., centered averages over one unit of time may be immaterial.

Let $z(t)$ denote the number of units started per unit of time at t, disregarding the fact that $z(t)$ actually would have to be an integer. The result analogous to equation (12.5) would then be

$$Y(t+T) = \bar{n} \int_0^T z(t+\tau)\,(T-\tau)\,d\tau. \qquad (12.8)$$

If $z(t)$ were a constant $= \bar{z}$, we should have $\bar{Y} = (1/2)T^2\bar{n}\bar{z}$, a result which could be anticipated from our considerations earlier in this chapter.

Here $\bar{n}T$ represents the amount of work required to produce one unit of finished product. If $\bar{n}T$ is a constant, independent of $\bar{n}$, i.e., if T is inversely proportional to $\bar{n}$, we should have that the amount of incorporated work in the goods in process would be proportional to T. If this were the case, the entrepreneur might have every reason to make Y as small as possible by operating with a very large $\bar{n}$. The level of total employment would be

$$N(t) = \bar{n} \int_0^T z(t-\tau)\,d\tau, \qquad (12.9)$$

or $\bar{N} = \bar{n}\bar{z}T$, when $z(t)$ is constant $= \bar{z}$. Thus, if $\bar{n}T$ were constant for changes in $\bar{n}$, total employment would stay constant, while $\bar{Y}$ could be reduced. However, as we have already pointed out, there are many reasons why $\bar{n}T$ would not be independent of $\bar{n}$.

IV. An Illustration of the Effect of Limited Capacity

Suppose that we have a process of the type described in the previous section, but that the level of total employment N (or, more generally, "factor input") is limited. There may be several reasons for such a limitation. One reason may be that the size of the plant or the number of necessary tools per worker is limited. Another reason may be that the enterprise is set up to manage a given size of total employment. We shall, at any rate, assume that N is a constant, independent of time. We shall be interested in the possible effects of variations in the rate of starting of new units of construction.

If the number of units started is variable over time, there are many possibilities concerning the use of total employment, N. For example, if the influx of new construction units were particularly large, it could be that, at first, only a token amount of work would be done on the new units. We should then, in fact, have a backlog of orders instead of units actually under construction. Alternatively, we might find that total employment would be spread out over more units, thus slowing down the speed of construction, perhaps in a somewhat planless manner. In other cases it might be irrational to use full employment.

For the sake of illustration we shall here consider only one simple alternative, viz., that the same amount of employment is always applied to all units under construction and that this amount simply is $= N$ divided by the total number of units under construction at any time. The amount of employment per unit under construction will therefore, in general, be a function of time. Consequently, if a certain given amount of work is required to finish a unit, the construction period T will be a function of time. We shall set up an explicit model for this case.

The following variables have to be considered in this connection:

$N(t)$ = total employment (numerically equal to total work input per unit of time)

$z(t)$ = number of construction units started per unit of time

$Z(t)$ = number of units under construction at t

$y(t)$ = total rate of "value added" to all units per unit of time

$\bar{y}(t)$ = average rate of "value added" per construction unit per unit of time

$T(t)$ = construction period for a unit started at t

$x(t)$ = number of units of finished product per unit of time

Formalizing our assumptions above concerning the process to be considered, we have

$$N(t) = N = \text{constant, independent of time ;} \qquad (12.10)$$

$$z(t) = \text{a given, exogeneous, function of time .} \qquad (12.11)$$

There is a simple bookkeeping relation involved, viz.,

$$\dot{Z}(t) = z(t) - x(t) . \qquad (12.12)$$

This must hold as long as no unit is lost in the process.

Our assumption concerning the use of the total productive force, N, can be expressed by the definition

$$\bar{y}(t) = \frac{y(t)}{Z(t)} . \qquad (12.13)$$

Now we have to make an assumption concerning the value-added *effect*, $y(t)$. It is obvious that this effect will depend on how the labor force is distributed over the various units in process, and it will certainly depend on the total number of such units. If there are too few units in $Z(t)$, the work places may be crowded, resulting in a loss of efficiency. If $Z(t)$ is too large, there may be difficulties of getting efficient teamwork (too small teams). To simplify our model we shall ignore the question of distribution of the productive resources over the various stages of production, but take account of the effect of $Z(t)$. We express this by the "production function"

$$y(t) = \Phi[N, Z(t)] , \qquad (12.14)$$

where we assume the form Φ to be independent of time. Here $\partial\Phi/\partial Z$ may depend on Z in a somewhat complicated manner. The function Φ must be such that $y = 0$ when $Z = 0$. For the following analysis it is also necessary to assume that $\bar{y}(t)$ remains finite for every $Z > 0$.

One unit of output (e.g., one house) is defined by the relation

$$\int_t^{t+T(t)} \bar{y}(\tau) \, d\tau = 1 , \qquad (12.15a)$$

where now T must be regarded as variable over time. We assume, tentatively, that T can be expressed as a continuous function of the *starting point*, t, for the particular product unit considered.

The equation (12.15a) is assumed to be an identity in t. That is, it must be true for every value of t. This means that the relation is a restriction upon the two *functions* $\bar{y}(t)$ and $T(t)$.

We now consider the rate of output, $x(t)$. Let us look at the product units on which work was started between t_0 and $t_0 + dt$. There are approximately $z(t_0)dt$ such units. Suppose, for example, that the function $\bar{y}(t)$ is steadily decreasing. Then the units started early in the interval dt

will obviously be finished within a relatively shorter period T than the units which were started toward the end of the interval. The result can be pictured graphically as in Figure 2. The problem of finding $x[t + T(t)]$ is solved if, for every t, we can find the differential dT that corresponds to dt.

One thing is obvious, namely, that the units of finished product will be completed in the *same succession* as the one in which they were started.

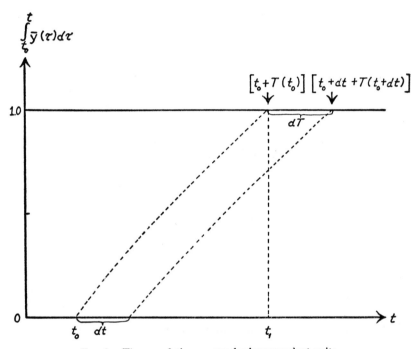

Fig. 2.—The completion process for large product units

There will always be more work incorporated in an older unit than in a newer. And while both are under processing they grow at the same rate. That is, we must have $t + T(t) > t_1 + T(t_1)$, when $t > t_1$. It is therefore obvious that the relation between the starting and the finishing of units must be

$$\int_{t_1}^{t} z(\tau) \, d\tau = \int_{t_1 + T(t_1)}^{t + T(t)} x(\tau) \, d\tau, \qquad t > t_1. \qquad (12.16a)$$

Under proper assumptions we can derive the following relation by taking the derivative with respect to t in equation (12.16a)

$$z(t) = x(t+T)\left(1 + \frac{dT}{dt}\right), \quad \text{or} \quad x(t+T) = \frac{z(t)}{1 + \frac{dT}{dt}}. \quad (12.16\,b)$$

Our dynamic system is now complete, apart from certain necessary information on initial conditions.

Consider the definition (12.15*a*). By differentiating this relation with respect to t we get

$$\frac{dT}{dt} = \frac{\bar{y}(t)}{\bar{y}(t+T)} - 1, \quad (12.15\,b)$$

which of course shows that if $\bar{y}$ is constant over time, T will be a constant. However, even if $z(t)$ is a constant, $\bar{y}(t)$ is not necessarily a constant, because $Z(t)$ may be growing or decreasing, depending on the function Φ and the constant value of z.

The system above may be formally solved in the following way.

Suppose that the whole process started at $t = t_0$. And suppose that $t = t_1$ is the first point of time that any finished goods at all come out of the process. We do not know t_1, but this point of time can be found by the two relations

$$\int_{t_0}^{\tau} z(s)\, ds = Z(\tau), \quad (t_0 \leqq \tau \leqq t_1), \quad \text{and} \quad \int_{t_0}^{t_1} \frac{\Phi[N, Z(\tau)]}{Z(\tau)}\, d\tau = 1.$$

Since the series $z(t)$ is assumed to be known, we can plot the curve $Z(t)$ and the integrand in the last equation. And by exact or approximate integration we can find t_1. Then $Z(t_1)$, $y(t_1)$, $\bar{y}(t_1)$, $T(t_0) = t_1 - t_0$, and $x(t_1)$ are known.

After $t = t_1$, we can find the time functions involved by solving the system of difference-differential equations (12.12), (12.16*b*), (12.15*b*), using equations (12.13) and (12.14).

Many interesting questions could be posed in connection with this model. We could, for example, try to find the series $z(t)$ which in the long run would maximize output $x(t)$. Or we could ask what series $z(t)$ would minimize the amount of working capital, $Z(t)$, for a given long-run stable level of $x(t)$. Looking at the model as a global model for the economy as a whole, we could study the effects of starting too much or too little construction work when the "capacity," N, is given. For example, after World War II many countries experienced inefficiencies in the construction industries, because people were too eager to get new projects started (a too high level of $z[t]$ above).

13

The Productivity of Warehouse Stocks

In many of the cases we have studied so far we have seen that it may be possible, with the use of some imagination, to squeeze the theory of capital into the Böhm-Bawerkian framework. When it comes to the process of holding stocks of finished goods, however, the Austrian approach of the roundabout method becomes rather hopeless. Certainly, the ripening of goods in warehouses is usually not productive in any economic sense. It is true that it takes time to produce a certain stock of goods and that the process of *using* stocks for some purpose is dependent on something that has been done earlier. But the age of the individual particle of goods in a warehouse stock is usually not in itself advantageous.

In order to see in what sense a warehouse stock is capital in production, it is necessary to study the purpose of storage operations. The output of the process of holding stocks is certainly not the net amount of goods taken out of storage per unit of time. "Output" must be something else, some sort of advantage obtained by the stock *being present*.

I. Buffer Stocks

The function of such stocks can be described in a formal and fairly general way as follows.[1] Let $Y(t)$ denote the stock of a certain commodity (raw materials, semimanufactures, or finished goods). Suppose that the outflow, $x(t)$, and the inflow, $y(t)$ can be regarded as continuous flows. Then we have

$$\dot{Y}(t) = y(t) - x(t) . \tag{13.1}$$

Here $x(t)$ may include some outflow in the form of waste, etc. More generally, one could consider $x(t)$ as made up of several flows, and similarly for $y(t)$. But, for simplicity, we shall ! ere adopt the definition (13.1).

The variables in (13.1) are subject to certain obvious constraints,

$$a)\ \ Y(t) \geqq 0 ,$$

$$b)\ \ y(t) \geqq 0 ,$$

$$c)\ \ x(t) \geqq 0 , \tag{13.2}$$

1. See Edwin S. Mills, "The Theory of Inventory Decisions," *Econometrica*, XXV, No. 2 (1957), 222–38.

d) Additional "practical" constraints of the type

$$Y(t) \leq A, \quad y(t) \leq a, \quad x(t) \leq b, \quad \text{or} \quad y(t) = \text{a}$$

given time function.

Usually, the operation of holding a positive stock, $Y(t)$, will involve expenses. In order for the operation to be advantageous, there must be some kind of yield resulting from the storage. In some cases the stock manager can himself decide the inflow $y(t)$ and the outflow $x(t)$, subject to the constraints (13.2), but his decisions will have consequences for something which he wants to maximize, e.g., total discounted net revenue over a given horizon. In other cases one of the flows $x(t)$ or $y(t)$ may be given from outside, so that he has only one of the flows at his disposal for the purpose of obtaining a maximum result.

The "result" to be maximized could be several different things. A fairly general assumption would be that the result depends on the form of some function of the series $x(\tau), y(\tau)$ and $Y(\tau)$ over a given horizon θ, and on the level of the stock at the end of the period. For example, the result could be the discounted value of sales over purchases plus the discounted value of the net increase or decrease in stock at the end of the planning period. The data in this calculation could be certain given price- and cost-series and discount rates.

Let the current "result" of the operation be a function, Π, of $x(\tau), y(\tau)$, $Y(\tau)$, and present time, t; and let $V[Y(t + \theta), t]$ denote the result as far as status at the end of the planning period is concerned. Furthermore, let $\lambda(t, \tau)$ denote the "weight" of future results as seen from the point of time t. Then the objective of the process could be described as that of maximizing

$$\int_t^{t+\theta} \lambda\,(t,\ \tau)\,\Pi\,[x\,(\tau)\,,\ y\,(\tau)\,,\ Y\,(\tau)\,,\ \tau]\,d\tau \tag{13.3}$$
$$+ \lambda\,(t,\ t + \theta)\ V\,[\,Y\,(t + \theta)\,,\ t]$$

with respect to the functional forms $x(\tau), y(\tau), Y(\tau)$, subject to the constraints (13.1) and (13.2), and under the assumption that the initial stock $Y(t)$ is a datum.

The results to be maximized would depend on the stock of capital in various ways. First, alternative levels of the initial amount of stock, $Y(t)$, could play a role, similar to a factor of production. Second, this would be true for the stock of goods at each and every moment between t and $t + \theta$. Finally, the stock, $Y(t + \theta)$, could be regarded as producing the result $V[Y(t + \theta), t]$.

What is difficult, however, is to define and measure the product of the process above in any technological sense. Nevertheless it seems fairly rea-sonable to suppose that even if we should choose some rather obscure measure of result or product, we would still choose this measure in such a way that it would be related to the physical quantity of capital. Therefore we could still maintain the idea of the volume of stocks as a factor of pro-duction.

II. SPECULATORS' STOCKS

The holding of goods in storage is often regarded as an operation dis-tinct from that of maintaining stocks for purely technological purposes. The reasons for speculators' storage operations are usually some known, or expected, differences in economic value of a given commodity at different points of time. Such storage operations are, however, covered by the model above, in particular if we assume that anticipated as well as known developments of prices and costs can be used in evaluating the functions II and V.

One might ask what the productivity of stocks is in this case. It is some-times thought that gains and losses will automatically cancel out for a market as a whole. However, this is certainly false. There may be a real gain for society as a whole by storing, e.g., part of a good year's crop and consuming the stock in a bad year, even if the stock actually depreciates in a quantitative sense during storage. Here again the amount of capital operates as a factor of production, but in a process where the product is somewhat obscure, from a technological point of view.

14

Instruments of Production

ALL the capital concepts that we have considered so far have been in the nature of working capital, that is, a stock of goods which are themselves a *product* of the production process in question. We have not yet considered capital in the form of stocks that work *upon* the goods in process. This most important type of capital comprises all kinds of tools, machinery, factory buildings, transportation equipment, etc. Sometimes these objects are identified as durable producer goods. However, this relation is dubi-ous, not very profound, and sometimes really misleading. In fact, even the distinction between working capital and instruments of production is not as profound as one might think. In chapter xvii we shall come back to these questions. For the time being, let us try to understand the characteristic functions of the instrument of production in such production processes as we have already discussed.

I. What Is the "Input" from Instruments of Production?

The Austrian theory of capital tried to squeeze even the instruments of production into the framework of "final goods en route." This idea was illustrated by such examples as the following: Instead of collecting kindling wood with his bare hands, a man takes time off, perhaps temporarily shivering a little from lack of heating, and produces an ax. Thereafter, the ax can gradually be turned into firewood, so to speak. However, Wicksell showed clearly how difficult it would be to determine how much of the ax should be regarded as incorporated in a unit of wood.[1]

The idea, often advanced, that the "input" from a capital instrument is simply equal to its rate of depreciation is in fact very dangerous and misleading. This idea may lead to ridiculous technological conclusions, or it may require a very abstract notion of depreciation. However, it is easy to understand how the idea has come about. It stems from the efforts to explain the "paradox of the rate of interest." A positive productivity-rate of interest must mean that the use of capital yields something more than full depreciation. From here the idea that "depreciation goes in and something more comes out" is not far away. To see how hopeless this idea is from the point of view of production theory, consider the case where a capital instrument requires little or no depreciation. Then the input of such capital in production would be very small or zero, while the interest from using it could be a large revenue item.

This confusion is, I think, the result of attempts to consider the input of capital as actual physical inputs of aged or stored-up land and labor services. Capital is supposed to give these services back with interest sufficient to pay for "waiting." If capital yielded more than this, we should have a something-for-nothing possibility which is incompatible with a fundamental axiom of economics. Now, this reasoning is perfectly all right as far as it goes. The trouble with it is that it tends to confuse two very different things, the actual return to capital in a *market equilibrium situation* and the *technological effect* of employing various amounts of capital in production.

The way out of this confusion seems rather simple. We have to remove the mystery of stored-up land and labor from the definition of instruments

---

1. Wicksell, *Lectures*, I, Appendix 2.

of production and regard them as being productive, rendering a productive service by *being present* in a production process. We can draw a perfect analogy between labor being present and in action for a certain number of hours and instrumental capital being present and in use for a certain number of hours.

What we mean when we write a production function with the number of workers and the amount of capital as factors is that we assume labor input per unit of time to be a known function of the number of workers present and, similarly, that the input of capital services per unit of time is a known function of the quantity of capital present. This is what we mean when we write a production function as

$$x = \Phi(N, K) , \qquad (14.1)$$

where x is the rate of output, N is the number of workers and K the amount of instrumental capital, measured in some defined physical unit.

In equation (14.1) it is obvious that $\partial\Phi/\partial K$ need have nothing whatsoever to do with a market rate of interest, unless we impose some particular market equilibrium conditions. Furthermore, it is obvious that if K is measured in units relevant from the point of view of production technology (number of machines), then, for arbitrarily fixed values of K and N, there need be no direct relation between the productive effect of K and the amount of work that has gone into its making, or the age of this work. We must try to keep the technological concepts in the production function separated from the market equilibrium notions of the cost of a factor in terms of its own making. The idea, in itself sound enough, that capital is the result of some other more basic productive agents can be perfectly well accounted for by requirements of equivalence between certain *market values*, instead of trying to squeeze such things into the technological production functions.

There are, however, some very serious problems involved in using a production function of the type (14.1), and some of these problems have to do with the use of the physical stock of capital as the only variable to describe how capital affects production. This may be all right as long as we can assume that there is a unique relation between the amount of capital and the productive service it yields. However, we have to consider the fact that capital can be used more or less *intensively*, and try to see how this element can be accounted for in the production function.

Some people have seen this as a reason for using the rate of depreciation of K in the production function, instead of K. It is, however, easy to see that neither the use of depreciation alone as a factor of production, nor the use of only K itself as such a factor would solve this problem. The case of capital items that are technologically identical except for durability shows the difficulty of the first procedure, while the case of variable intensity of the use of a capital item shows the difficulty of the second procedure. We obviously need the amount of capital K in the production function, as a scale factor of the volume of capital services. In order to decide what to do about variations in the intensity of the use of capital we have to consider, more concretely, how the intensity of the use of capital could be described or defined.

The idea that a producer could decide to put more or less intensity of "capital use" into the process does not seem very relevant. The machines, etc., are there, and intensity is not a question of cutting smaller or bigger parts out of the machines to be put into the product, even if we should think of these "parts" as something very abstract. It seems that, in most cases, the decision to change the intensity of the use of capital must be *indirect*, in terms of a change in some *other parameters* that affect the strain on the capital equipment. Now, one such parameter is already in the production function (14.1), namely, the amount of labor. This factor could work both ways. In some cases more labor could spare the machines from wear. In other cases, perhaps the more common ones, more labor would mean more wear upon the existing capital equipment. Another parameter, which might be the actual decision parameter, is the rate of input of raw materials. This could conceivably influence output even if K and N stayed constant, in which case both capital and labor would be used more intensively. (Then we should have the input of raw materials as a variable in Φ besides N and K.) Then there is the possibility of letting the machines run faster in order to do more work on a given flow of raw materials with a given amount of labor. But here the technologically relevant parameter would be such things as input of electric power or, more directly, the speed of the machines.

The conclusion that we reach from these considerations is, I think, simply this: We have to use the variable K as a factor in the production function. If this is not sufficient, the solution is not to replace K by some other variable such as depreciation, but to include some other parameters *in addition to K*. Many of the seemingly insurmountable difficulties connected with the use of K as a variable in the production function disappear if we rid ourselves of the idea that the only other factors are land and labor.

The problems discussed above are, in fact, only part of a general problem related to production functions of the type (14.1), viz., the problem of justifying the assumption that output can be regarded as uniquely determined by the values of certain factors of production. This general problem has two angles. The first, and most obvious, is the question of specifying the factors that it is necessary to take account of, or to assume constant, in order to have a unique relation. The other is the need for some basic assumption concerning *efficient use* of input elements. It is obvious that behind a production function of the type (14.1) there must be a lot of economic organization and management. The effects of these things are hidden in the functional form of Φ. It is, therefore, more than doubtful whether we can talk about production functions of the type (14.1) as being purely technological data. The term "technological" becomes highly relative, depending on where we draw the line of demarcation between the domain of production engineering and the domain of economic decision-making.[2]

II. A Fundamental Problem of Measurement

Part of the difficulties mentioned above goes back to the puzzling problem of how to measure the *quantity of capital*, in particular, the volume of instruments of production. The main problem can be described briefly as follows. Consider two production processes which are identical in every respect, except that one of them employs capital equipment that is more *durable* than the other. Then it is only the physical quantity of machines, etc., that counts in the production function for the two processes. If we tried, instead, to measure the amount of capital in some real cost units, we could not use this variable as a factor of production. The durability of the capital employed would affect *depreciation* and, hence, *income* in the two processes, but not the rate of physical output.

This matter is obvious, but it is not so obvious what we are going to do about the practical problem of actually measuring physical capital so as to make it a relevant variable in a production function. We shall deal more extensively with this problem in chapter xviii. Here we shall mention only briefly two econometric aspects of this problem.

Suppose, first, that we want to compare the production processes of two simultaneously operating firms producing the same kind of product. We may be interested in whether one of the firms uses more capital than the other. Their capital equipment may be rather different, so that it is difficult to find a relevant, technical, unit of measurement. In such cases we usually have to settle for some measure in terms of value or cost. But here we meet the problem of durability right away. If we neglect this, we

2. On this subject the reader is referred to T. Koopmans (ed.), *Activity Analysis of Production and Allocation*, Cowles Commission Monograph No. 13 (New York: John Wiley & Sons, 1951), and to the extensive literature now available on Linear Programming. See also T. Koopmans, *Three Essays on the State of Economic Science* (New York: McGraw-Hill, 1957).

may find that one firm produces the same amount of output using the same amount of labor as the other firm, but uses much more capital. The difference will show up in the net revenue of the two firms. But to derive the production functions of the firms we have to devise some way of "deflating" the value of capital to eliminate the durability component.

Suppose, next, that we have a problem of comparing the production activities of a firm at different points in time. And suppose that we know the form of the production function and the value of annual net investment over the period considered. What relation is there between the value of investment and the net increase in the amount of capital equipment measured in a way that is relevant to the production function?

In chapter xviii we shall offer some positive suggestions on how to overcome these difficulties by the use of certain approximations.

III. Comments on the Use of Shiftwork

Suppose that, in connection with the production function (14.1), time is measured as *calendar* time, but that the form Φ is fixed under the implicit assumption that the *active* part of calendar time is a constant (e.g., an eight-hour day). Let the part of calendar time during which equation (14.1) is active be denoted by h. We may think of h as a fraction of a week. Then we could write equation (14.1) more explicitly as

$$x = \Phi^*(N, K, h) . \qquad (14.1a)$$

Here x still means output per unit of *calendar* time. N means labor force present during h units of time per unit of calendar time. And likewise for K. But while the same machines K may be present during full calendar time, this is, of course, not the case for the workers. Suppose that there is a fixed workweek, h_0, for each worker. And let N^* be the total labor force (number of standard workweek persons) employed in the process. Then we could write,

$$x = \Phi^*\left(\frac{h_0}{h} N^*, K, h\right). \qquad (14.1b)$$

Could we assume that the function Φ^* would be homogeneous of degree 1 in N^* and h, for fixed K, when $0 < h < 1$? There are many reasons why this assumption could be very wrong. First of all, there are the well-known starting and stopping problems. For small h's there may be any product x at all. Furthermore, the capital K may need rest, for repair, cooling, etc. There is also the influence of varying efficiency over the day, due to changing amounts of light, temperature, etc. (On the other hand, one should not confuse the issue by mentioning overtime pay for nightwork. This is a *cost* element, not a technological factor in the production function.)

In connection with the production function (14.1*b*), one must be very careful about the interpretation of *marginal* productivities. Thus, the marginal productivity of the labor intensity, N, for fixed K and h, is equal to $\partial\Phi^*/\partial N$. But the marginal productivity of the total labor force, N^*, is $(\partial\Phi^*/\partial N)\,(h_0/h)$ for fixed K and h. The marginal productivity of h, if N^* and K are constant, is

$$-\frac{\partial\Phi^*}{\partial N}\frac{h_0\,N^*}{h^2}+\frac{\partial\Phi^*}{\partial h}.$$

But the marginal productivity of h when (N^*/h) and K are constants is $\partial\Phi^*/\partial h$. The marginal productivity of N^* when N^*/h and K remain constant is

$$\frac{h}{N^*}\frac{\partial\Phi^*}{\partial h}=\frac{h_0}{N}\frac{\partial\Phi^*}{\partial h}.$$

(If we are at a level of N^*, K, and h where

$$\frac{h_0}{N}\frac{\partial\Phi^*}{\partial h}>\frac{\partial\Phi^*}{\partial N^*},$$

it would indicate an underoptimal use of shiftwork.)

However, there is the question of *depreciation* of K, and also the question of interest charges. These are *economic*, not technological questions. If depreciation depends only on the time during which capital is actively at work, the advantage of continuous shiftwork is generally weakened. In most cases depreciation will depend both on the degree of active use and on calendar time. Interest charges would certainly be related to calendar time.

In judging the efficiency of shiftwork we must carefully distinguish between the case of a single entrepreneur facing an unlimited supply of labor at given wages, and the case of a closed, full-employment economy. In the first case output can be influenced by changing, independently, both N and h. In the second case N and h have to be adjusted under the constraint that N^* is approximately constant. Then the use of shiftwork is a means of increasing the capital-labor ratio. Whether or not this is an economic gain depends, e.g., on people's attitudes toward nightwork. It also depends on the kind of capital used and the way it depreciates.

In what follows we shall have to neglect the important problem of shiftwork. We shall assume that the parameter h is a constant not subject to managerial choice. No particularly good reason can be given to justify this, except a desperate need for simplification.

15

The Period of Production

ONE of the most controversial ideas in the pure theory of capital has been that of a period of production. Of course, nobody can deny that there may be a considerable time lag between the input of certain productive agents and the output of a final product. Our analysis of various types of production processes has illustrated this lag phenomenon. The controversy is, mostly, concerned with such questions as how to *define* the period of production, how constant it may be, and what *relation* the period of production has to *the volume of capital.*

The usefulness of the concept of a period of production may be questioned. Nevertheless, the problems of its definition are in themselves rather interesting, and a study of them may help toward a better understanding of the intimate relation between the concept of capital and the element of time.

I. LAGS IN THE PRODUCTION FUNCTION

Consider a production function which, as a first approximation, can be written as

$$x(t) = \Phi[N(t - \omega_1), K(t - \omega_2)], \qquad (15.1)$$

where $x(t)$ denotes a continuous rate of output per unit of time, and N and K represent number of workers and stock of capital, respectively. For our purpose here we may think of K as durable instruments of production.

Let us explain the meaning of equation (15.1) a little more in detail. It is, of course, not N and K that themselves go into the product x, it is the productive services of N and K. The assumption is that these services can be regarded as fixed functions of N and K respectively, e.g., in the form of simple proportionalities. The lags ω_1 and ω_2 could have various interpretations. One possibility is that, actually, the services of N and K work at $t - \omega_1$ and $t - \omega_2$, respectively, and that there is a necessary aging—or growth period—between the time of these inputs and the time, t, of final output. Another possibility is that the services of N and K are spread out, as in our model of the assembly line process, and that the lags ω_1 and ω_2 are averages. Then equation (15.1) is in general only an approximation to the actual production function.

Suppose now that we should ask the question: What is the *average* time interval between total inputs and output? There are two problems that must be solved before this question can have any meaning. The first problem is that of defining the rates of services from N and K per unit of time. The second problem is to devise a common unit of measurement for both these services. One possible answer to the first problem is simply to use man-hours and capital-hours. Then the natural answer to the second question would be to represent these services by their money cost or to use some other coefficients of value of the two inputs, so that they could be added up. Another idea could be to use the rate of depreciation for K as a proxy for capital input and to calculate its value in terms of labor. More generally, if we assume that $f(N)$ measures the rate of input of labor services, and $g(K)$ the rate of input of capital services, such that the sum $f(N) + g(K)$ exists as a meaningful quantity, we could define the average processing time for $x(t)$ as

$$T(t) = \frac{\omega_1 f[N(t-\omega_1)] + \omega_2 g[K(t-\omega_2)]}{f[N(t-\omega_1)] + g[K(t-\omega_2)]}. \tag{15.2}$$

The interval $T(t)$ would, in general, depend on t. The effect upon T of a partial change in K would depend on whether $\omega_1 \gtreqless \omega_2$, among other things.

II. The Age of Factor Inputs

The formula does not take account of the fact that K already has a certain age and that, therefore, the services of K are themselves produced at an earlier date. (The same is, of course, true of N, but usually we take less interest in the "investment" in N, although it may be a highly relevant thing in, e.g., a theory of economic growth.) Suppose that the services $g[K(t-\omega_2)]$ were already ω years old. Then we should have, instead of equation (15.2),

$$T^*(t) = \frac{\omega_1 f[N(t-\omega_1)] + (\omega+\omega_2) g[K(t-\omega_2)]}{f[N(t-\omega_1)] + g[K(t-\omega_2)]}. \tag{15.3}$$

One of the central issues in discussions on the period of production has been the interpretation of ω_2, the age of capital services. The problem is in what sense the quantity of capital services, $g[K(t)]$, can be identified with a definite rate of earlier productive inputs, e.g., of labor. If this operation is not possible, the concept of a period of production will not make sense.

The Austrian theory of capital suggests that the solution to this problem is to consider the input of capital as equal to its rate of depreciation and to identify the rate of depreciation with a rate of labor input ω years earlier. Suppose, however, that the relevant variable K in equation (15.1) is an index of the number of machines, etc., *regardless of age*. And suppose that all machines last equally long, e.g., θ years, and are equally efficient while they last. Then we should find that the technological depreciation which would be relevant for K *as a factor of production* would be the rate of production of machines θ years earlier. But the rate of depreciation, from an *economic* point of view, would obviously be related to the fact that each of the machines loses something like $1/\theta$ of its value each year. These two depreciation concepts need not coincide except under stationary conditions.

It is obviously a somewhat philosophical question whether one should say that "incorporated labor" in a machine is taken out gradually, as the machine is in use, or whether one should say that this all happens at the time of "death" of the machine. We see, for example, that if the machines are of constant utility until the age θ, production could, technologically speaking, be carried on according to equation (15.1) by, e.g., buying $(\theta - 1)$-year-old machines every year. A particular firm following this procedure would then have much less capital in terms of its value than another firm which uses younger machines. This shows that, unless K is measured as "number of machines," a function $g(K)$ may not have a sensible meaning as capital input.

Suppose that we disregard all these difficulties and assume that the formula (15.3) makes sense. Then this formula is interesting in connection with another question, namely, the question of whether or not a larger K means more "roundaboutness" in the sense of a larger T^*. This is not obvious, unless $(\omega + \omega_2) > \omega_1$. This assumption may, however, perhaps be regarded as obviously true in practice. What is more important is that the lags ω_1 and ω_2 may be affected by the amount of capital used. For example, the use of more capital may make it possible to speed up the process of producing x. This shows another dubious aspect of the period of production if one has the idea that it can be used to measure "capital intensity" of a firm, or of a whole economy.

III. The Period of Production as the Inverse of a Rate of Turnover of Capital

If, in equation (15.1), both K and x are measured in units of *value* and if we compute the ratio $T_x = K/x$, this ratio has the dimension of time.[1] This is also true of $T_N = (K/N)$, if N is interpreted as number of man-years per year. These ratios could be interpreted as periods of production, perhaps in a somewhat peculiar sense. Thus, T_x could be interpreted as the number of years it would take to convert the stock K into final output at

---

1. Cf. Hawtrey, *Capital and Employment* (London: Longmans, Green & Co., 1952), pp. 11–28.

the annual rate x. And, similarly, T_N could be interpreted as the number of years it would take to liberate K into current labor services. Thus, these ratios could be said to describe by how much past efforts have been ahead of schedule in producing a flow of final output.

The situation in regard to these and other similar measures of the period of production as well as those previously discussed is that if we have stationary conditions they are all more or less equivalent. But then, again, under stationary conditions we can do without these time concepts and instead consider only the volume of capital, either in physical units or in value terms. It is under non-stationary conditions that the notion of a period of production really becomes interesting, but unfortunately it is precisely then that the concept becomes really controversial. Under stationary conditions, the period of production may retain some explanatory value in connection with the phenomenon of the rate of interest. But as a description of production technology it may be of little use.

16

Remarks on the Concept of Capacity

THE notion of productive capacity is used somewhat loosely both in everyday language and in the economic literature. Sometimes it seems to mean a definite boundary for output in a physical sense, sometimes it may mean a quantitative limitation on one or more factors of production, and often it simply means that an output larger than a certain level would be uneconomical. It is not at all certain whether a notion of capacity in any one of these senses really is useful as a separate concept in the theory of production. But since its redundance is not obvious, the matter may be worth a few comments.

I. THE NOTION OF CAPACITY AND THE PRODUCTION FUNCTION

Let us again consider a production function of the type

$$x = \Phi(N, K) , \qquad (16.1)$$

where x is rate of output per unit of time, N is employed manpower, and K the amount of capital equipment present. We may think of this process as one where inputs and output are simultaneous, in which case we can drop the direct reference to the point of time.

One way of interpreting equation (16.1) is as follows: For a given x, and a given K, there is a smallest amount of labor N which permits the production of the output x. Suppose that K is fixed and equal to $\bar{K}$. And suppose that Φ is such that, for the admissible values of N, x (1) is non-negative, (2) has a lowest upper bound $\bar{x}$, and such that (3) there exists at least one value of N for which $x > \bar{x}$ if $K = \bar{K} + \Delta K$, where ΔK is positive and finite. Then one could describe $\bar{K}$ as "capacity," or as a capacity-limiting factor. However, suppose that the admissible values of N are limited to $0 \leqq N \leqq \bar{N}$, say. Then it is quite possible that x could be increased beyond $\bar{x}$ by increasing $\bar{N}$ with $\bar{K}$ constant. In that case $\bar{N}$ could be said to represent the capacity limitation. But we should then simply be back to the simple statement that the values of N and K determine maximum output. That is just another way of describing the production function (16.1).

Suppose that there should exist a boundary across the admissible set of values of N and K, say $g(\bar{N}, \bar{K}) = 0$, such that on this boundary the maximum value of x is constant and equal to $\bar{x}$, and such that $x \leqq \bar{x}$ for any admissible pair N, K on one side of this boundary while $x < \bar{x}$ for any pair N, K on the other side of this boundary. Then neither capital nor labor can be regarded as *the* capacity-limiting factor.

However, all these considerations say no more than what is said by specifying the function Φ and the domain of admissible values of N and K.

The case where the maximum output x is not uniquely determined by N and K but can be influenced by a parameter, say α, of variable work intensity and a parameter, say β, of variable intensity of the use of K is somewhat more interesting. Suppose that the function

$$x = \Phi^*(N, K, \alpha, \beta) \qquad (16.2)$$

expresses the maximum output, x, that can be produced with given values of N, K, α, β. Now it is quite obvious that even if there were an upper limit to x for given K, under admissible values of N, α, β, this would not be a very interesting capacity limit. For variations in α and β would presumably mean a variable cost element, in addition to standard wages, let us say. Suppose, for example, that x and K could be measured in the same physical units. Then x minus depreciation might cease to increase long before the effect on x of increasing N, α, and β would be zero. Here again there would seem to be no particular gain in introducing a concept of capacity, in addition to what is already contained in the specification of equation (16.2).

II. The Case of Limitational Factors of Production

Suppose that instead of the "classical" production functions discussed above we have a technology which is defined as follows:

$$x = F(N), \text{ when } K > g(N)$$

$$x = G(K), \text{ when } K < g(N)$$

$$G[g(N)] \equiv F(N) \qquad (16.3)$$

$$0 \leq N \leq \bar{N}$$

$$0 \leq K \leq \bar{K}.$$

Suppose that each of the functional forms F, G, and g is variable over a certain given functional field, but subject to the restrictions (16.3), and that all possible values of x that could be generated in this manner would represent actual production possibilities. Each triple of admissible functions F, G, and g could be described as a given technology. Then we could have $\bar{N}$ as a capacity limit, or $\bar{K}$, or both, or neither $\bar{N}$ nor $\bar{K}$. However, for every N and x there will, under reasonable assumptions, be a smallest K such that x cannot be increased by increasing N while holding K constant.

If neither $\bar{N}$ nor $\bar{K}$ determines maximum output in the production structure above, it is usually attributed to the constancy of some third factor, implicit in every admissible triple of functions F, G, and g.

Also in this model it is evidently possible to define certain precise concepts of capacity. But what we achieve is nothing but a renaming of certain things that are implicit in the definition of the production function.

Some commonly used phrases regarding the notion of full capacity may be misleading, such as the statement that we must use both labor and capital to full capacity. If this means the employment of an arbitrarily given $\bar{N}$ and an arbitrarily given $\bar{K}$, the problem may be insoluble unless we admit waste.

In connection with the question of shiftwork, the interpretation of capital as capacity has a more straightforward meaning. If, e.g., capital and labor are limitational factors, capacity could mean output on a 24-hour basis. But it is by no means certain that this is "capacity" in an economic sense. It may be out of the question to assume that an absolutely continuous production process could be economically feasible. Even from a purely technological point of view it may be next to impossible to operate a fully continuous process.

17

Conclusions regarding Capital as a
Factor of Production

In the preceding chapters we have tried to clarify some of the technological features of capitalistic production processes. Even if our analysis is far from exhaustive, it points toward some very simple, but important, conclusions, which may serve to remove part of the apparent mysticism about the notion of capital as a factor of production. It may be useful to restate briefly these simple conclusions.

I. Capital Is a "Stock" Concept

This conclusion seems obvious and perhaps even too trivial to mention. Whatever one thinks of capital as a productive agent or of the difficulties of regarding capital as an input element, it should not be difficult to agree on the simple definition that capital as such is something which has the dimension "quantity *at time t*" and not something "per unit of time." This applies to goods in process as well as to "instruments." Difficulties of measurement may have led to doubts about the possibility of a meaningful quantitative definition of capital. But that such a definition, whatever its nature, must have the dimension of a stock is, I think, not a matter for controversy.

Trivial as this observation may seem, it leads to some rather fundamental conclusions. The first of these is that, if capital as such has any influence on the output of a continuous production process, this influence must be due to *capital being present* in the process and not to the fact that certain parts of it are used up in the process. For example, if warehouse stocks are to be regarded as productive agents, they function in this role by being *maintained*, and not as something of which we continue to take out more than we put in. This does not mean that all stocks have to be productive agents. It means that *if* capital has anything to do with productivity, this is due to whatever services it yields as a result of its existence.

Another conclusion also follows, viz., that the distinction between durable and non-durable capital is actually meaningless when applied to capital as a factor of production. It is true, of course, that some goods, when used in a production process, are *used up* or go out of existence while others, like tools, are used over and over again. It is also true that we could

91

have a stock of both kinds of economic objects. But there is no necessary connection whatsoever between the size of such stocks and the physical durability of the items of which the stocks are composed.

It can be stated as a simple tautology that *all capital is durable,* in the sense that if the rate of exhaustion per unit of time is finite, it will always take some time to exhaust a finite stock.

Confusion on this point probably goes back to confused ideas concerning the meaning of the input of capital in production. We shall now try to summarize our conclusions on that subject.

II. The Productivity of Capital

The Austrian approach on this subject was, as we have seen, to regard capital as something which was in a sense incidental to a *method* of production, a characteristic symptom of a roundabout process. In this scheme there is no room for capital as a separate factor of production.

This may be a perfectly tenable point of view. Much of the confusion around it has been rather unnecessary and could have been avoided by the following formulation: Suppose we take a particular, stationary, production process as an initial condition. The output of this process is a stationary flow of consumer goods. Suppose now that there exists a set of alternative, known, stationary processes leading to alternative stationary levels of output of consumer goods. We can conceive of these alternatives as a set of possible production technologies, or "activities." With each of them there may be associated certain necessary, or unavoidable, accumulated stocks of goods of various kinds. The idea of a larger or smaller degree of roundaboutness in connection with each alternative technology then has to do with the process of transition from the initial state to one of the alternatives. Presumably, it would take more time to reach an alternative requiring more capital than one requiring less. The capital requirements in each case could be looked upon as a necessary evil attached to the particular method of production. The usual argument about the efficiency of a more roundabout method or—which would be the same— the use of more capital, could then be turned upside down in the following way: A larger degree of roundaboutness is not necessarily more efficient, but because more capital is a necessary evil, a larger degree of roundaboutness *will have to be more efficient in order to be chosen.*

This would be a perfectly logical scheme. There would be no need to worry about whether or not capital as such is "productive" in any philosophical sense. The trouble comes in when we want to combine the idea of roundaboutness with the modern ideas of a production function where output is determined by variable amounts of a certain set of physical inputs. It is then that we get into the problems of defining in what sense capital "goes into" a product. The immediate, but superficial, idea here would seem to be that it is the depreciation or depletion of capital stock that goes into the product. From this point of view it is, so to speak, only an unfortunate circumstance that we have to have machines standing around in a factory when, actually, what we want is only a flow of input corresponding to the rate of depreciation! Likewise, the input from a producer's stock of raw materials would naturally seem to be the amount of raw materials that is used up per unit of time. But what is then the use of the stock as such? To make the confusion complete one needs only to add the idea, near at hand, that a production process would be the more "capitalistic" the larger the annual depreciation charges connected with the process!

The trouble with the idea of capital as something that "goes into" the product is perhaps not that the idea in itself is entirely hopeless, but that it is unnecessarily complicated from a technological point of view. It is the result of a difficulty that perhaps most of us have of understanding how something can be used and render a yield in a process without itself being destroyed or depleted. Of course, we have the same problem in connection with labor, but that apparently does not bother us as much as is the case in connection with the use of capital. However, in all the cases of capitalistic production that we have studied in the preceding chapters it is perfectly possible and natural to regard the role of capital as that of *being present in a production process and yielding a productive service per unit of time.*

In the case of aging processes, for example, it is true that we can describe the production technology without the use of a capital concept. That is, we do not need to introduce the amount of working capital in order to describe the process of output of the finished product. But if we ask about production per unit of time in the sense of "value added," it becomes necessary to introduce the notion of a capital stock which is productive by having an internal growth. It is a somewhat philosophical question in this connection whether we should say that the actual input in this process is time, or whether we should say that the stock of capital produces a growth per unit of time. Similar remarks could be made on what we have called natural growth processes.

When it comes to the various kinds of goods in process in industry, it is likewise perfectly natural to regard such capital as an active element co-operating with labor and other inputs in the production of "value added" per unit of time.

In the case of instruments of production we need only think of extreme cases where depreciation is nearly zero to see that it must be possible for this kind of capital to affect output by being present in the process as an active service-rendering agent.

In what follows we shall, therefore, use the notion of capital as a stock which renders productive services by its presence in a production process. That is, we shall use it as a separate factor of production which is perfectly analogous to an employed labor force. However, it would be very hasty to conclude that this choice means getting rid of the problems of defining capital as a factor of production. First of all, there are the problems of measurement. These problems we have already touched upon on several occasions, and we shall deal with them more extensively in the next chapter. But there is also the problem of how to define production functions where capital is involved, even if we assume the problems of defining and measuring capital to be solved.

III. Problems of Capital as a Variable in Production Functions

It will be remembered from the various dynamic production processes that we have discussed, that we encountered serious problems in trying to express output of finished goods as a function of the amount of capital (and other factors) even in the cases where the physical volume of capital consisted of perfectly homogeneous items. This was the case for all kinds of goods in process, because there need not be any unique connection between the volume of such goods in process and the current rate of output of finished goods. Even if we regard output as some sort of "value added," it is only under special conditions that the role of total capital (of goods in process) can be expressed by simply using the *amount* of capital as a variable. In connection with instrumental capital we may have the problem of intensity of use as a separate variable in addition to the amount of capital.

The question of whether or not the role of capital can be fully represented by using the amount of capital as a variable in a production function should not be confused with the general problem of whether or not capital as such is a factor of production. Exactly similar difficulties arise in connection with labor. Here it is only on rare occasions that the amount of labor (the number of labor-hours) fully describes the effect of labor input. For example, in the assembly line process discussed in chapter xi, the rate of output would, in general, depend not only on total input of work-hours, but also on the distribution of this input along the assembly line. In regarding total employment in a process as a simple factor of production we rely, implicitly or explicitly, on two basic assumptions, first, that the rate of labor services is uniquely determined by the number of workers present, and second, that the effect upon the product of the labor input can be represented by a single parameter. These are formidable assumptions, in view of the possibilities of differences in work intensity and in the organization of the sequence of work operations, etc. In connection with capital we have all these difficulties and perhaps some in addition, due to the fact that measurement of the amount of capital is itself very problematic.

It seems, however, that in much of the literature that is critical concerning capital as a factor of production, a degree of perfection concerning the treatment of this particular factor is required which is out of proportion to what general theory has asked for in connection with labor and "land." The Austrians discarded the idea of capital as a factor of production on somewhat philosophical grounds. Modern writers[1] have thought that capital is hopeless as a factor of production because there are "too many kinds of capital." Both views represent a tendency to forget that what we can hope for is at best some simple model that simulates the process of capitalistic production, not a model that accounts for everything.

18

Problems of Aggregation

Some of the problems of aggregation that we meet in dealing with capital as a factor of production are of a perfectly general nature. There is no reason for us to go into details on such problems, except perhaps for the purpose of separating them from the problems of aggregation that are particular to capital theory. The special problems of aggregation in the theory of capital are connected with the variable durability of instruments of production. These problems deserve special attention here. But let us first consider briefly the "ordinary" aggregation problems as we encounter them in dealing with capital as a factor of production.

1. Cf. Joan Robinson's article, "The Production Function and the Theory of Capital," *Review of Economic Studies*, XXI (1953–54), 81–106.

I. The Question of Several Kinds of Capital
in a Production Function

From a technological point of view it is obvious that things we call "capital" can be very different and serve very different functions. This is obviously true when we consider the capital of a whole industrial sector or of a large community. But even within a single firm an itemized list of the stock of capital would, in most cases, be quite long. Moreover, it is usually easy to establish, by simple inspection, that the various capital items play different roles in the production process, and that each item often may be adjusted separately, as far as its quantity is concerned. All this points in the direction of using not one, but several, variables to represent capital as a factor of production. Even for relatively simple production processes, one could often specify so many separate capital concepts that the production function would become absolutely unmanageable. Therefore, a problem of aggregation arises in the attempt to bring the number of factors down to a small number, or perhaps to just one factor.

There is really no difference between this problem and the problem of accounting for various kinds of consumer goods in a preference schedule, e.g., various kinds of food. In the case of factors of production, representing various kinds of capital, the problem can be formalized as follows. Let

$$x = \Phi(K_1, K_2, \ldots, K_n) \qquad (18.1)$$

denote a production function where x is output and where K_i represents quantity of some particular kind of capital. And suppose we want to try to reduce the number of specified factors of capital to one. Obviously this cannot be done except either under some particular, restrictive conditions or by introducing some idea of approximation to equation (18.1).

Let $K = g(K_1, K_2, \ldots, K_n)$ denote some chosen formula for an index of total capital. We could ask: Does there exist a single-valued function, F, such that $x = F(K)$, identically in $K_1, K_2, \ldots, K_n$? This will in general not be true. But there are cases where the relation would hold over a restricted set of values of $K_1, K_2, \ldots, K_n$. For example, if all the variables K_i vary as given function of one single parameter, a formula $x = F(K)$ could be found which would be valid over this particular set of K_i-values. If the production function is "well behaved," it may be possible to find a wider region in the factor space such that a formula $x = F(K)$ would hold to within a certain degree of approximation. As we have already pointed out, these problems are exactly similar to those we meet in dealing with other kinds of economic relations, e.g., demand functions.

II. The Aggregation of Different Production Functions

Suppose that we have several different production processes, each using various amounts of capital, which may be of n different kinds. More specifically, suppose that we have

$$x_i = \Phi_i(K_{i1}, K_{i2}, \ldots, K_{in}) , \quad i = 1, 2, \ldots, m , \quad (18.2)$$

where x_i denotes output for process No. i (all x's representing the same kind of product), and where K_{ij} represents the amount of capital of type j used in process No. i.

Let us now assume that we have defined the following aggregates, or indices:

$$x = f(x_1, x_2, \ldots, x_m) , \quad (18.3)$$

$$K_j = g_j(K_{1j}, K_{2j}, \ldots, K_{mj}) , \quad j = 1, 2, \ldots, n . \quad (18.4)$$

We could pose the following question: Under what conditions does there exist a function F such that

$$x = F(K_1, K_2, \ldots, K_n) \quad (18.5)$$

identically in the nm variables K_{ij}? Obviously it will not in general be possible to find any such function F, if we require it to be single-valued. But a formula (18.5) may hold for a particular restricted set of values of the variables K_{ij}. Or, again, a formula (18.5) may be found that possesses a certain, more or less satisfactory, degree of approximation.

In point of principle, there is obviously no principal difference between the problem of aggregation as described above and the problem of aggregating demand functions for different individuals. However, this may be of meager comfort to those toiling with the problem.

III. Aggregation of Capital of Different Durabilities

In connection with the "ordinary" problems of aggregation discussed above, it is assumed that we are able to measure the various kinds of capital in well-defined physical units, relevant to the production functions (18.1) or (18.2). It is further assumed that the capital indices g are such as to preserve the idea of capital as a physical quantity, relevant to a meaningful, aggregated production function. Both these assumptions cover some really intricate problems of quantitative research on capital as a factor of production. It is impossible to conceive of a common unit of measurement for various kinds of capital except through the introduction of some kind of weights, based on the *value* of the various kinds of capital.

Now, this does not in itself represent an insurmountable obstacle. If the value of each type of capital could change for only *two* reasons, that is, as a result of a change in physical volume or in price, or both, we should have a problem similar to that of measuring total real consumption. But the value of capital of a certain kind has, as it were, *three* dimensions, viz., its quantity as a factor of production, its durability, and its price (i.e., the price as a variable under fixed durability). If we disregard variations in durability and measure the quantity of capital of a particular kind by its deflated value (to take account of nominal price changes) we may very easily get such absurd results as a decrease in output by adding more capital, even when it is obvious that the process is very far from saturated with this kind of capital.

In practice, there are various possible ways out of this difficulty. We shall indicate two of these.

The first possibility, which may work in some cases, is to group the various kinds of capital in a production process according to their durability and to represent each such group by a separate variable in the aggregated production function. If such a grouping were relevant and workable as an approximation, we could then consider a change in the average durability of capital as a relative change in volume of the various kinds of capital. We shall try to formalize this idea a little more.

Suppose that the various kinds of capital in a process can be completely characterized by their durability. We assume, in other words, that each kind has a fixed durability, but that there may be possibilities of substitution between them. Let $K_1, K_2, \ldots, K_n$, represent an exhaustive list of the types of capital used in the process, and such that K_1 represents capital of one year's duration, K_2 that of two year's duration, and so on. And suppose that the production function is

$$x = \Phi(K_1, K_2, \ldots, K_n),$$

where the various kinds of capital are measured in physical units. If, instead of the K_i's, we observe $K_i^* = \lambda_i K_i$, where the λ's are fixed weights (e.g., real prices), the production function becomes

$$x = \Phi\left(\frac{K_1^*}{\lambda_1}, \frac{K_2^*}{\lambda_2}, \ldots, \frac{K_n^*}{\lambda_n}\right) = \Phi^*(K_1^*, K_2^*, \ldots, K_n^*). \quad (18.6)$$

It may then, under certain conditions, be possible to condense the number of factors by an approximation formula, e.g., of the following kind

$$x = \Phi^{**}(\bar{K}_{\theta_1}^*, \bar{K}_{\theta_2}^*), \quad (18.7)$$

where

$$\bar{K}^*_{\theta_1} = g_1(K^*_1, K^*_2, \ldots, K^*_m), \qquad m < n$$

$$\bar{K}^*_{\theta_2} = g_2(K^*_{m+1}, K^*_{m+2}, \ldots, K^*_n). \tag{18.8}$$

Here m could be chosen so as to make the approximation (18.7) "as good as possible," in some sense or other.

However, if we have the situation that each kind of capital can have variable durability, the approximation (18.7) may lead to serious errors, even if it would be a very good approximation for the case of fixed durabilities. It seems necessary to try to introduce some general procedure of "deflating" the various kinds of capital for the effect of changes in durability. This certainly applies if our measure of the amount of capital, of various kinds, runs in terms of "real value," or "incorporated labor," or similar economic units. We want to consider the practical possibilities of finding such deflating procedures.

For the purpose of illustration, consider the case where production depends on only *one kind of capital*, regarded as a factor of production, but where this kind of capital may have variable durability. Let K denote a physical measure of the volume of this kind of capital (e.g., number of machines). And assume that we have the production function

$$x = \Phi(K). \tag{18.9a}$$

The problem we have before us arises out of the fact that K *may not be directly observable*. Let us assume that, instead of K, we observe K^* and that this measure is a *known function* of K and of the durability, θ,

$$K^* = G(K, \theta). \tag{18.10}$$

Then, if equation (18.10) defines K as a function of K^* and θ, i.e., $K = G^*(K^*, \theta)$, we have

$$x = \Phi[G^*(K^*, \theta)]. \tag{18.9b}$$

This means that if we regard K^* as a factor of production, θ will appear as a parameter in the production function.

This procedure can readily be extended to the case where the production function depends on several different kinds of capital. The result will obviously be that we get the durability of each kind of capital as a parameter in the transformed production function corresponding to (18.9b).

The procedure is formally simple but it raises several intricate practical problems. One problem is that K may be composed of items of different durability. Another problem is to obtain actual measurements of these durabilities. And a third problem is how to determine the form of the function G (or several such functions in the more general case). To illustrate a possible procedure which could yield a first approximation in a practical case, we shall consider the following problem.

Let us assume that the production function is of the form (18.9a), and that K is composed of two parts, K_1 with durability θ_1, and K_2 with durability θ_2, and such that $K = K_1 + K_2$ is a measure relevant for the technological relationship (18.9a). Suppose, further, that K_1 was acquired (new) at time t_1 and that K_2 was acquired (new) at t_2, and that both items are younger than their respective maximum durabilities. We assume that capital is equally efficient as a productive agent throughout its lifetime. The quantities K_1 and K_2 cannot be directly observed, but we assume that we can observe the following economic quantities:

    a) $K_1^* =$ the purchase value of K_1 at t_1

    b) $K_2^* =$ the purchase value of K_2 at t_2

    c) θ_1 $=$ the durability of K_1

    d) θ_2 $=$ the durability of K_2

    e) ρ $=$ the rate of interest at t_2

Here K_1^* and K_2^* denote "real" capital in the sense that they are measured in terms of *constant prices*, i.e., K_1^* and K_2^* are deflated by a price index for capital of *standard durability*. But even so it would not make sense to replace K in equation (18.9a) by $K^* = K_1^* + K_2^*$, because the quantities K_1^* and K_2^* are affected both by their physical volume and by their different durabilities. The problem is to derive an index for the variable K.

This can be done by utilizing certain assumptions concerning *market equilibrium*. These are (1) that the rate of interest ρ was expected by the buyer of K_2 to remain constant from t_2 to $t_2 + \theta_2$, (2) that the annual (deflated) income, r_2, from owning K_2 from t_2 to $t_2 + \theta_2$ was expected to remain constant from t_2 to $t_2 + \theta_2$, and (3) that the purchase value of K_2 was equal to the discounted income from t_2 to $t_2 + \theta_2$. Then we have, using a continuous formulation,

$$K_2^* = \int_0^{\theta_2} r_2 e^{-\rho\tau} d\tau . \qquad (18.11)$$

Now, if K_2 had been of the same durability as K_1, but otherwise equivalent, it would still have earned r_2 but for the period θ_1. Because of the law of indifference, the market value, K_2, of the hypothetical K_2 at t_2 would then have been

$$K_2^{**} = \int_0^{\theta_1} r_2 e^{-\rho\tau} d\tau . \qquad (18.12)$$

Hence, from equations (18.11) and (18.12), we have

$$K_2^{**} = K_2^* \frac{1 - e^{-\rho\theta_1}}{1 - e^{-\rho\theta_2}} . \qquad (18.13)$$

We then find that $K_1^* + K_2^{**}$ should be *proportional to* K. Choosing conventionally $K_1 = K_1^*$, we could write (remembering that we use deflated values)

$$K = K_1^* + K_2^{**} , \qquad (18.14)$$

where K_2^{**} is defined by equation (18.13).

From equation (18.13) we see that K_2^* would overestimate K_2 as a factor of production compared to K_1^* if $\theta_2 > \theta_1$ and that K_2^* would be an underestimate if $\theta_2 < \theta_1$.

If, for example, K_2 is regarded as "investment" in addition to K_1, $(t_2 > t_1)$, this investment could apparently have two purposes, first, to increase the amount of capital as a factor of production, and second, to change annual depreciation expenses. It is only the first part of this investment which is relevant as added capital in the production function.

The illustration above suggests a very simple principle for converting a time series of capital values into a series representing an index of the physical volume of capital as a factor of production. If we have data from a competitive market, the series should first be deflated to obtain "constant-dollar" figures. Then the deflated value figures should be converted to an "equal-durability" basis by formulas of the type (18.13). It is my guess that such a procedure, even if it is very rough and approximate, would be a definite improvement over the customary, but unfounded, method of measuring K simply as $K_1^* + K_2^*$.

This concludes our study of the technological aspects of capital as a factor of production. It is, as we have seen, a rather intricate subject, and if we were to carry all the difficulties over into the field of investment behavior we should be taking on much more than could possibly be managed by the use of reasonably simple models. However, we believe that some of the main results that we have described are really fundamental to the understanding of investment behavior. The development of an investment theory without a solid foundation in the theory of capital would be superficial and risky, to say the least. Even if we cannot take account of all the problems of defining and measuring capital as a factor of production, it is helpful to keep these difficulties in mind when we try to evaluate the use of the simplified investment theories which we may have to settle for in explicit analytical, or empirical, work.

PART III

*Savings and Investment in a
Centralized Economy*

It could be argued that the really fundamental problems of economic theory arise precisely out of a fact which we now are about to disregard, namely, that an economy is composed of a complex set of more or less independent decision-makers with different and partially conflicting preferences and aspirations. The use of Robinson Crusoe models has often been ridiculed for this reason. On the other hand, it is a common view in economics that even the most decentralized economy tends, in some sense, to operate as a whole, guided, as it were, by Adam Smith's invisible hand. Also, it is far from correct to say that the economic theory of a centralized economy is "no real problem." Practical experience from planned economies has emphasized this. Some of the most fundamental problems of economic theory retain their relevance in a centralized economy and are, in fact, made to stand out more sharply than may be the case in a decentralized system. Some people would even argue that it is only after we rid ourselves of the confusing details in a decentralized economy that we see the really profound problems of economic theory and of economic policy. This may be particularly true in the field of long-run capital development and economic growth.

Theoretical models based on the assumption of a centralized economy may be more general than they appear to be at first sight. In a direct way, they simulate, of course, economies that are in fact centralized. But they can also sometimes be used to analyze certain economic fundamentals that are more or less independent of whether or not the economy is actually centralized, in some political sense. The assumption of a centralized economy can also sometimes be used, with some caution, as an *approximation* in the analysis of certain phenomena in a complex, decentralized economy. The idea of clarifying basic issues of economic theory by using the "as-if-centralized" construction has been relied upon to no less extent by the most hard-boiled liberalists than by various kinds of planners. The trick of assuming a centralized economy is merely an application of the general scientific principle of moving by stages from the simple to the more complex.

There are some other, natural, simplifying assumptions that are in line with this general principle. One of these is the assumption that we are dealing with a closed economy. This assumption is sometimes harmless, sometimes very restrictive. If, e.g., we discuss the question of whether or not the growth of capital per unit of time has to be a finite flow, the assumptions of no export or import of capital is, of course, absolutely decisive. In chapters xx–xxiv we shall assume that we have a closed economy. In chapter xxv we shall try to study some effects of the economy being open to capital exports and imports.

Another assumption, which can only be justified as a stepping stone, is that technology is constant, except for such changes in technology as may be covered, implicitly, by the definition of the capital concept used. In chapters xx–xxv we shall largely ignore the problem of changing technology and—even more important—changing knowledge of technological possibilities. In chapter xxvi we shall, however, consider briefly some aspects of general technological change.

19

The Choice of a Descriptive Framework

THE process of capital accumulation is something very complex, even from a purely descriptive point of view. Already the seemingly modest problem of finding out what we want to talk about in this field is itself no mean task. Even if we imagine that the purely economic aspects of the process can be singled out as objectives of a separate body of theory, it is by no means obvious what the phenomena or the variables to be explained are. We have already seen that the stock of capital at a given moment can be composed of many very different things. We have also seen that the problems of measurement depend very much upon whether we are concerned with a stock of wealth or a stock of a "productive agent." Even more complex is the relation between capital accumulation and the gross output of capital goods. And when we come to the final question of the relation between capital accumulation and economic progress in the sense of utility or welfare, the problems of choosing the relevant descriptive variables could take us into quite philosophical lines of thought. The model picture that an economist can hope to handle will be a very dry and skinny one, as compared to the real spectacle of dynamics that we have before us.

However, even if the number of variables we can handle has to be rationed, we do not necessarily have to select them from yearbooks of current statistics. It may sometimes be more fruitful to develop theory in terms of variables which we *should like to* measure, or which could be measured *in point of principle*. We may derive deeper understanding even by using abstract and auxiliary variables that could not conceivably be observed. We want to comment briefly upon the adequacy of the standard framework of national accounts in the light of these philosophical remarks.

I. The Descriptive Framework of National Accounting

The simple *tableau économique* of modern macrotheories has been the following: The annual gross national product is divided into three parts. One part is consumed. One part is necessary to cover depreciation and obsolescence. The remaining third part is the rate of capital accumulation. This is a simple bookkeeping principle. It has been of fundamental importance in discussions of effective demand and employment. It has brought order into the discussions on such matters as "excess savings" and "disposable income." The use of national bookkeeping principles has become so widespread and so commonly accepted, that many people regard this framework as containing all the variables with which we need to concern ourselves in economic models on the macro level. If other variables are to be considered they must, it is held, be variables *in addition* to those defined in national accounting. The relations in national accounting are held to be "obvious" and unavoidable.

It is not the purpose here to try to reduce the fundamental importance of national accounting. We must, however, try to be clear about one thing: Any system of national accounting is a conventional, descriptive framework. The only reason why we sometimes regard a system of national accounts as "factual" and indispensable is that we have business—and private—accounting as realities of economic life. It is, however, quite conceivable that we could picture economic reality by an entirely different descriptive framework, which could give us a different, and perhaps better, kind of understanding of what economic life and its evolution is all about. We do not, of course, suggest that economic theory should be thrown into a state of anarchy which does not make use of the idea of certain bookkeeping principles. But we do want to emphasize that the reliance upon the national accounting principles to keep track of what happens in an economy may create some very dangerous pitfalls. This is particularly true in the field of capital accumulation and economic growth. We want to point out some of these pitfalls.

The first and most obvious pitfall would be to regard the rate of net investment as the rate of growth of productive capacity, that is, as the rate of growth of the amount of capital in the technological sense. The difference between these two concepts of growth has been repeatedly emphasized in preceding chapters.

Another, perhaps somewhat philosophical, question is whether we should use the idea that net growth of the value of capital equals gross investment minus depreciation. Unquestionably we can adopt this convention. But is it necessarily a fruitful one? The simplicity of the relation is gained at the expense of a somewhat "mystic" content or meaning of at least one of the three concepts involved. If, for example, depreciation is defined as all changes in the value of capital that are deviations from the rate of gross investment, we shall have a difficult task explaining what real economic actions this kind of depreciation corresponds to.

Another, really sophisticated, question is whether it is possible to subdivide the annual flow of goods and services into mutually exclusive subflows, such as consumption and gross investment. In the case of education, for example, it may be very problematic to say that it is *either* consumption *or* accumulation of productive power. It may be both, without any possibility of saying which part is "consumption" and which part is "investment." The problem we have in mind is not the ordinary ever-present problem of "correct classification." What we have in mind is the problem of whether the linear system of national bookkeeping is a good basis for defining fruitful economic concepts. The only thing that I am trying to emphasize here is that the answer may sometimes be yes, sometimes no.

In general, the situation with regard to the choice of a descriptive framework seems to be something like this: Suppose we start out by defining the variables and concepts to be considered in such a way that they fit a convenient and simple bookkeeping system of some kind. Then we may find that we have pushed the problem of complexity over into the field of technological and behavioristic relationships. That is, we pay for the simplicity of the variables in terms of very complex, perhaps impossible, problems of deriving meaningful relations of technology and behavior. If, on the other hand, we permit ourselves to use more abstract, and perhaps only loosely defined, economic variables that could give us better hope of relatively simple technological and behavioristic relations, these variables may be unwieldy and nasty from the point of view of an orderly and convenient classification of visible economic facts. This means that in our choice of descriptive framework we shall often be faced with an unpleasant problem of substitution between simplicity of description versus simplicity of explanation.

II. An Impressionistic Picture of the Process of Capital Accumulation

Let us start out with only vague ideas about the quantitative aspects of the variables we talk about. Imagine that we cut into the evolutionary process of an economy at a certain point in time, observing what it looks like at that time and what happens to it during a certain subsequent time interval.

At a given point in time we shall find a certain human population engaged in a variety of economic activities. We find certain stocks of economic objects of various kinds. Some of these will be stocks for no other purpose than to be exhausted at some later date. Others are there for the purpose of security against unforeseeable events. They render a service simply by their presence. Other stocks consist of goods in process. And there will be stocks of goods that are more actively at work in a variety of technological transformation processes. We also observe a *flow of total output* which, during a certain time interval, could accumulate into new stocks of various kinds. At the same time we observe certain flows of things that go out of the picture. One such flow is human consumption, the final objective of the whole process. Then we see that the various stocks are subject to deterioration, outflow, or leakage of various kinds. At the same time a certain part of the flow of total output goes into each kind of stocks. We also observe certain changes going on in the size of the population.

If this process goes on for a certain interval of time, what will the economy look like at the end of that interval? To give a precise answer to this question is a problem of finding precise and relevant descriptive variables to account for the phenomena that we have referred to only in vague terms. To answer the question of *why* the economy must look like it does at the end of the interval, given its state of affairs at the beginning, is the problem of an explanatory economic theory.

A general explanatory theory must try to answer two kinds of questions in order to be complete. The first is this: What effects do the various stocks of capital and the available manpower have upon the flow of total output and also upon the rate of change of the human population? These effects are influenced, in various ways, by human decisions and will not be purely technical. The second kind of question is: How does the use of the various stocks of capital and the disposal of total output affect the various stocks of capital and the size and qualities of the population present at the end of the time interval considered? This is, to a large extent, a question of the attitude that the population has concerning the future as compared to the present.

This is, broadly speaking, the kind of descriptive outline we have to start from, if we want to aim at a determinate, dynamic theory of capital accumulation. In Part II of this study, we have tried to gain some insight into the possible technological relations between the various kinds of capital and productive output. What we have to look for now is some rational theory of how such capital comes into existence and how it is managed, once it has been created.

20

The Meaning of Optimal Growth

IT is a simple matter to construct a *formal* theory of capital accumulation. Using a traditional approach, we could reason as follows: We assume that the economic community as a whole has a utility *functional* stretching into an indefinite future, and with the time shapes of the total rate of consumption and the total human labor input as its two arguments. We assume that the amount of total output that could be produced by employing certain amounts of labor and certain amounts of capital of various kinds is known for every point of time into the future. We assume that the rate of depreciation for the various kinds of capital is known. We assume that it is known what addition can be made to each kind of capital at any time by means of one unit of total output.

In this way certain definite constraints will be established concerning admissible time functions for consumption and for labor input. Maximizing the utility functional with respect to the time functions of consumption and labor input within the admissible field of such functions, we may find a unique pair of such functions as a solution. The optimal rate of gross capital accumulation would be the difference between the time function of total gross output and the optimal time path of consumption. We could also deduce the optimal net growth of the various categories of capital. There is just nothing to it. Except for the following which may cause some trouble:

We know very little about the utility functional involved, except that people seem to like both to have progress and to have a high current standard of living. We do not know to what extent people actually include population increase in their plans for the future. Judging from the rate at which population increases at present in most countries, while people are at the same time shouting for a higher current standard of living, one is led to believe that there is not much planning for the future in this matter. Our utility functional would imply that the present generation would determine, not only the size of future generations, but even the kind of economic preferences that these future generations should have, or can be expected to have.

Very little can be known at any given time about the kind of capital equipment that could be produced in the future. This is not just the same as saying that the path of the evolution of technology cannot be foreseen. We should have to know much more than a forecast of this kind. We need to know the set of all possible *alternative technologies*. This certainly is not known. Thus, if the production functions involved are assumed given, this assumption may hold precisely because of the *lack* of knowledge. This means that all the constraints upon the maximization procedure considered are, at best, only vague notions of the possibilities within which a choice can take place.

This does not mean that the general idea behind the model we have outlined is not meaningful and valuable. But it would, I think, be rather futile to fill pages with a formal mathematical apparatus, giving results with a look of precision which they could not possibly have. Instead, we want to investigate a much more simple version of the general model, one that could tell us something about the decisions to save and to invest, over relatively short periods of time.

I. A Framework of Short-Run Alternatives

Consider a planning period which is "short" in either one of the following senses: The period should be long enough so that, judging from past experience, a substantial amount of existing capital would be due for renewal within the period, but not longer than to make it reasonably well known what alternative *kinds* of capital there would be to choose from. The interval should be such that the adult population present at the beginning of the period would represent a substantial majority of the adults at the end of the period. The period should not be longer than to make most people "really concerned" about their economic conditions also for some time after the end of the period. Now this certainly does not give a very precise determination of the planning period involved. The length of the period could vary greatly from one economy to another, and might depend in an essential way on previous experience concerning the relation between plans and factual development. To try to be more specific let us assume that an interval of five to ten years would represent a period which would have roughly the properties described.

At the beginning of such a period a wide variety of paths of development are open to the economy. A substantial increase in the immediate rate of consumption could perhaps be reached by devoting a larger part of total output than before to consumer goods. Stocks could be depleted. Theoretically, there would be virtually no limit to the instantaneous rate of consumption at the beginning of the period. But a very high rate of consumption, say one larger than total gross output, would presumably begin to cause difficulties in maintaining production long before the end of the planning period. There would also be a theoretical possibility of going to the other extreme, reducing the rate of consumption drastically and keeping it down for the whole planning period. Then a very high rate of capital accumulation could be achieved, perhaps doubling the amount of capital of all kinds during the period.

Presumably, there would also be several alternatives with regard to the *kinds* of capital to be accumulated. There is, first, the accumulation of simple stocks of goods and goods in process. Such stocks may be rather "passive" elements in the decision to accumulate, stocks and goods in process being more or less a direct consequence of the scale of total output. But this kind of accumulation would, nevertheless, have to be counted as requiring a part of total output. Accumulation of the more active kinds of capital, the instruments of production, could take many forms. Thus, it could take either the form of "more of the same things," or it could take alternative technologically known forms, or both. In particular, the accumulation could take the form of *more durable*, or *less durable*, capital. The purpose of making capital more durable would be to reduce the rate of necessary depreciation for a given rate of gross output.

Another object of choice would be the development of the rate of labor input during the period. This choice would have the development of population as practically a datum. Likewise, it would presumably have as a rough datum the amount of total output that could be produced with given amounts of capital and labor.

II. Outline of a Scheme of Adjustment Preferences

What will be the actual choice of development for the planning period described above? A really basic theory should make it possible to deduce the development from some scheme of given preferences, precisely defined initial conditions, and technological constraints. However, we do not have much to build on in the way of actual knowledge regarding the possible invariants in such a scheme. Going to the other extreme, we could leave all theory aside and be satisfied with the simple factual observation that a modern society seems to have a strong propensity to maintain a positive rate of capital accumulation, and that it is a matter of bookkeeping to register more precisely how much net addition to the various kinds of capital is made each year. We could have some kind of theory in the form of a simple projection of the recent past into the immediate future.

However, it may not be necessary to choose any one of these two extreme views. Even if we cannot define any precise preference function for the theoretically possible alternatives open at the beginning of the planning period, we may try to use past observations to indicate, roughly, some aspects of people's preferences that seem to prevail. That is, we can probably use past observations, not merely as a means of mechanical extrapolation, but to some extent as observations of certain, more general, ways of thinking that seem to underlie actual economic planning. Another way of describing what we have in mind is that we can consider the choice to be made for any given planning period as a matter of *adjustment* in relation to what was done in the previous period. This means that we assume that observations from the past will show, approximately, the nature of the economic development that people want. In this way the set of relevant alternatives for a given planning period may be narrowed down considerably.

Let us try to register some of the apparent "facts" concerning economic preferences that seem to rule economic development in a modern society.

First, consider the propensity to *consume*. It is probably fair to say that people have extremely strong feelings *against* a consumption policy which would mean a *lower* rate of consumption during the planning period than what they have had in the immediate past. It usually takes such things as wars or some very spectacular possibilities of using resources for other purposes in order to alter the strong feeling against a setback in standard of living. In fact, we could probably even make the stronger statement that people will have a very strong preference against a slowdown in the *speed of improvement* of their standard of living. Recognizing these facts, we can then probably assume that the rate of consumption at the beginning of the period will represent some kind of floor under the various, alternative developments of consumption. A stronger statement would be that, in addition, the rate of increase in consumption should not be smaller than the current rate anywhere in the planning period and that it must be nondecreasing.

There are also strong *upper* limitations on the rate of consumption. A relatively weak assumption—which I think it is safe to make—is that the rate of net output at the end of the planning period must not be smaller than the rate of consumption reached at that time. To break this rule would be against very strong human feelings that it is "wrong," thoughtless, and almost immoral to live upon the future. In fact, many economists would think it safe to make the much stronger statement that there would be very strong feelings against leaving the economy in a less favorable position with regard to the possibilities of further *expansion* at the end of the planning period than was the case at the beginning.

All of these statements on preferences can probably be made still somewhat stronger by the fair assumption that the preferences expressed will tend to run in terms of per capita figures, at least if the planning period is not too long.

What would be the preferences in regard to labor efforts? The standard economic theory is that the input of labor will depend on remuneration. But this statement is, I think, one that is particularly related to alternatives at a given point in time, a response to hypothetical shifts in the possible remuneration. For our purpose here we may assume that such adjustments have already taken place insofar as they represent really big changes in the supply of labor. It may then be reasonable to assume that people will expect *not to work any harder in the future* than they have done in the immediate past, except under very extraordinary conditions, such as wars. This would put a ceiling over the amounts of labor input per worker that could be regarded as practical alternatives. The initial conditions of the economy and the requirements concerning consumption as outlined above would represent a floor under the possible alternative developments for the labor-input factor. Also, expected changes in population would play a role. However, the precise preferences concerning labor input are very hard to evaluate.

This outline of a scheme of preferences is, of course, very rough and perhaps somewhat subjective, or at least speculative. Nevertheless, it is my guess that the hypotheses suggested are almost as good as those we are able to make about the production technology and the relation between gross investment and the rate of increase in productive capacity. These things, usually assumed to be something that we really know in economic theory are, as we have seen in the previous part of this study, of such a complexity that we should talk very softly about precisely given technological conditions. We shall return to some of these problems in chapter xxii. But let us now first, as an illustration, try to study a somewhat more rigorously formulated planning model using the general framework outlined above.

21

A Model Illustrating the Dynamics of Planning

In the theory of capital accumulation one of the major questions has been why people save and accumulate in spite of the fact that they are assumed to prefer present goods to future goods. This has been the central issue in discussions about the "mystery" of a positive rate of interest. It has, of course, been realized that a preference for the present over the future is not sufficient to prove the need for a positive rate of interest. Account must be taken of the expected total supply of goods available at the future date as compared to what is available for the present. It was one of Böhm-Bawerk's fundamental assumptions that people in general tend to believe that there will somehow be more goods forthcoming in the future than at present. This, together with a supposedly lower degree of concern for the future than for the present, would indicate the need for a positive reward for "waiting."

A theory built on these ideas requires two sets of data which are both very difficult to obtain. The first of these is the human preferences concerning present and future goods. The second is the question of what consequences present economic decisions will lead to, as far as the supply of goods in the future is concerned. As we have already pointed out, the latter set of data may be very difficult to evaluate. It is much too simple to name these data the "technological constraints" and to assume that they are known to the planners. But even so, it would undoubtedly be bad theory to assume that the future supply of goods is completely unknown. It must be assumed that people know—or think that they know—a good deal about what the alternatives are for the future and that they feel that they can in part determine the future by present actions. If this be the case, we should be left with one major problem to be answered in order to determine the current rate of capital accumulation, viz., the nature of people's preferences regarding present and future rate of consumption. A formal solution of this problem would mean the setting up of a dynamic preference function to be maximized, subject to the technological constraints. However, we have already observed that this may lead to just a lot of empty algebra, unless we introduce more specific knowledge concerning the concrete nature of preferences. And we have suggested certain general ideas in this respect. We want to consider an explicit model that uses some of these ideas, while keeping in mind that to operate with the idea of "known technological constraints" is to dodge a major problem.

I. A Dynamic Preference Function Defined by Inequalities

In economic literature dealing with dynamic preference functions, it is often argued that such functions can formally be regarded as similar to a static preference function by considering goods at different points in time as different goods. However, one cannot help feeling that, somehow, a part of the true dynamics of the matter is lost in this way. The procedure tends to divert interest from the importance of the "flux" of time in the whole picture. It is the time sequence of development that matters. It may very well be that the idea of utility per se for a given point in time is meaningless and that a meaningful definition would require reference to a sequence of time points or a stretch of time. It may very well be that people are, mainly, concerned about what the future is going to be *as compared to the past* and that they have only vague ideas about what their future standard of living is going to be when reckoned in some kind of *absolute* terms. We want to consider a very simple model based on these ideas.

Let us assume that in the economy considered we have a well-defined measure of *total net output* of goods and services. We shall leave out all the admittedly formidable problems of depreciation of capital by assuming that it is a known function of the volume of capital and that we can deduct it from some observable measure of gross output. Let total net output per unit of time be $x(t)$. Let $c(t)$ denote the rate of total consumption and assume that the rate of capital accumulation, $\dot{K}(t)$, in the sense of additions to the amount of *physical capital*, $K(t)$, is a *known function* of $x(t) - c(t)$. For simplicity, we shall assume that this function is of the usual form

$$\dot{K}(t) = x(t) - c(t) . \qquad (21.1)$$

In order to keep the model as simple as possible, we shall assume that population and available manpower can be regarded as approximately constant for the planning period considered. We also assume that there is no cost of raw materials, etc., except what is accounted for by labor input.

We shall make a very simple assumption concerning the preferences of labor input, namely, that people will be very much *against an increase* in efforts per worker, while they do not have any significant desire to reduce input for the planning period considered. We shall interpret this to mean that we can take labor input as a constant. Using this assumption, we shall consider the simplest possible form of a production function valid for the planning period, namely,

$$x(t) = AK(t) + B , \qquad (21.2)$$

where A and B are constants.

Let the planning period be denoted by θ. It is assumed to have the general properties of a "moderately long" period as described in the preceding chapter. Consider $t = 0$ conventionally as the beginning of the planning period. At that time $K(0)$ and $x(0)$ are data to the planners; $c(0)$ is not a datum, but the rate of consumption at time immediately preceding $t = 0$ is a datum. Let this rate be $\bar{c}(0)$. The rate of consumption might take a discontinuous "jump" at $t = 0$, if the planners should so desire.

If the planners know these data and the relations of equations (21.1) and (21.2), how will they plan for the period $t = 0$ to $t = \theta$? As we have said, the following assumptions concerning the general properties of people's preferences may not be too unreasonable: First, there will be a strong feeling against the rate of consumption being lower than in the past, i.e., lower than $\bar{c}(0)$, for any part of the planning period. Second, there will be strong feelings against postponing the enjoyment of the result of progress during the period to the very end of the period. Third, there will be strong feelings against any setbacks at any point of time during the planning period. Fourth, there would, under these conditions, be a desire to reach as high a rate of consumption as possible by the end of the planning period. *But*, there would be strong preferences against the economy having less productive capacity by the end of the period than what would be necessary to produce output at least equal to the rate of consumption reached at that time. That would probably be considered "irresponsible."

Under these general assumptions there is still a great variety of possible time paths of production, consumption, and accumulation between $t = 0$ and $t = \theta$. We want to narrow down these possibilities by making a very special, but still perhaps not too restrictive, assumption that planning runs in terms of *linear alternatives* for the development of the rate of consumption. This means that we restrict the possible developments of consumption to a form

$$c(t) = at + c(0) , \quad 0 \leqq t \leqq \theta , \qquad (21.3)$$

where a and $c(0)$ are *constants to be chosen*. (An alternative could be $c(t) = c(0) \, e^{a*t}$. However this would not lead to anything essentially new as compared to equation (21.3), and it is even doubtful whether people actually think in terms of the higher derivatives involved in a non-linear expansion.)

The assumptions we have made above concerning the preferences place the following restrictions upon the choice of a and $c(0)$:

$$at + c(0) \geq \bar{c}(0) , \quad 0 \leq t \leq \theta ; \tag{21.4}$$

$$a\theta + c(0) \leq x(\theta) ; \tag{21.5}$$

$$a \geq 0. \tag{21.6}$$

This implies that $c(0) \geq \bar{c}(0)$. We further assume as a known fact that $x(0) > \bar{c}(0)$.

Under these assumptions the actual choice will depend on the planning objective. This could be maximum immediate consumption, maximum average consumption over the period, or maximum rate of consumption at the end of the planning period. As an illustration we shall consider the last of these alternatives.

II. Maximizing the Rate of Consumption at the End of the Planning Period

We consider first the development we should get as a result of a particular choice of a and $c(0)$, subject to the constraints (21.4)–(21.6). From equations (21.1), (21.2), and (21.3) we have

$$\dot{K}(t) = AK(t) - at + B - c(0) . \tag{21.7}$$

The solution of this differential equation can be written as

$$K(t) = \frac{1}{A}\left[AK(0) + B - c(0) - \frac{a}{A} \right] e^{At} + \frac{a}{A} t$$
$$+ \frac{1}{A}\left[c(0) - B + \frac{a}{A} \right], \quad 0 \leq t \leq \theta . \tag{21.8}$$

The corresponding development of output $x(t)$ would be

$$x(t) = \left[AK(0) + B - c(0) - \frac{a}{A} \right] e^{At} + at + c(0) \frac{a}{A} , \tag{21.9}$$
$$0 \leq t \leq \theta .$$

Let us now consider the implication of assumption (21.5). Setting $t = \theta$ in equation (21.9) and requiring that $x(\theta) \geq c(\theta)$, we obtain

$$\left[AK(0) + B - c(0) - \frac{a}{A} \right] e^{A\theta} + \frac{a}{A} \geq 0$$

or, more conveniently written,

$$\frac{1}{A}(e^{A\theta} - 1) a \leq [AK(0) + B - c(0)] e^{A\theta}. \tag{21.10}$$

From this we see that the larger a is, the smaller must the lowest upper bound of $c(0)$ be. If $a = 0$, the maximum value of $c(0)$ is $AK(0) + B$. For the minimum value of $c(0)$, which is $\bar{c}(0)$, the maximum value of a is

$$a^{(max)} = [AK(0) + B - \bar{c}(0)]\frac{A}{1 - e^{-A\theta}}. \qquad (21.11)$$

The "possibility region" for a and $c(0)$ can be pictured as the shaded area in Figure 3.

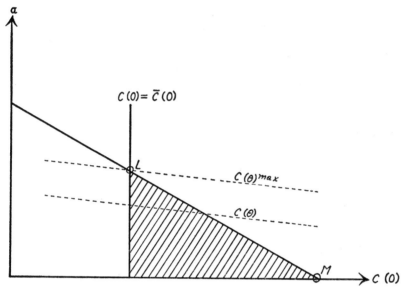

FIG. 3.—The possibility region for a and $c(0)$

What are the values of a and $c(0)$ which will maximize $c(\theta) = a\theta + c(0)$? The slope of the straight lines $a\theta + c(0) =$ constant, if drawn in the diagram (Fig. 3), will be equal to $-(1/\theta)$. The slope of the straight line LM in Figure 3 is $-A/(1 - e^{-A\theta})$. The slope of the line LM will be steeper than $-(1/\theta)$. Then the combination a, $c(0)$ which maximizes $c(\theta)$ must be the point L. This means that if the society has had a positive rate of accumulation immediately before the beginning of the planning period, accumulation will continue to be positive, and consumption would not make a jump at $t = 0$, but would rise gradually.

Would output at the end of the planning period be equal to the rate of consumption then reached? The answer is yes. The rate of accumulation would be reduced gradually until it reached zero at the end of the planning period, at which time there would be just enough capital accumulated to produce a net output equal to the level of consumption reached at that time.

Thus, in order to maintain the rate of accumulation beyond $t = \theta$, it seems that we would have to make some assumption of *stronger concern about continued growth beyond the planning period* than the one we have expressed by (21.5).

One possibility of a higher rate of accumulation than what we have found above could come as a result of *gradual revision* of the original plan. It might be reasonable to assume that, as consumption possibilities increase, the concern about future increases becomes greater, so that, actually, not the full amount available for consumption under the scheme above would be used. Thus, if we consider the planning point of time as mobile, while θ remains fixed, the model above could be regarded as determining only the α relevant for the consumption policy of the immediate future; α could then become variable over time.

A variety of other questions could be analyzed by means of the model considered or by modifications of it. We shall, however, not carry this study any further, as it was meant mainly as an illustration. We think that this illustration may have served to emphasize something which is important in the theory of capital accumulation, namely, that some fairly strong desire for continued *growth as such* may be necessary in order to produce a maintained or accelerated rate of accumulation.

22

Structural Changes in the Propensity To Accumulate

We have seen that the interest, or willingness, that a society shows in the direction of maintaining a previously positive rate of accumulation will depend on two general sets of circumstances. The first is the kind of concern that people have for the future. The second is the technological possibilities of doing something about the future by present actions. The concern for the future may be an "endogenous," economic, variable—to some extent. It may change as a result of repercussions from the economic development itself. But there may also be effects of factors regarded as external to the "strictly economic" forces, although the distinction is a dubious one. Thus, we sometimes regard population development as an external factor, either because we think that it does not depend much on economic conditions or because this dependence is not a result of economic decision-making. But these assumptions should certainly be regarded with suspicion. We also sometimes regard development of technology and know-how as external, an assumption which probably is a gross violation of the facts of economic evolution.

The ardent defender of a materialistic interpretation of history could maintain that the idea of external shifts affecting economic conditions is nonsensical, because everything actually grows out of the past. The apparent phenomena of shifts could be due simply to the fact that we have only incomplete models. This philosophical problem is not very likely to be settled in any near future. Even if assumptions of external shift could be shown to be unrealistic, it is quite possible that we can get an approximate solution to the questions we ask by the trick of an "as-if" hypothesis. The discussion below must be judged in the light of these remarks.

I. Population Changes

Population changes may have an effect on decisions to provide for the future in two different ways. First, it may be that the decision-makers include a planned or expected population change as part of their economic planning. Second, they may plan more or less on the basis of the current size of the population but change the plans as changes in population actually take place.

As far as the *ability* of society to provide for the future is concerned, population changes have two kinds of effects. One effect is that of a simple scale factor. If we disregard changes in the relation between productive manpower and total population, total output will, presumably, in most cases increase as a result of there being more people at work. But the scale factor also affects consumption. Therefore, as population increases, the possibilities of consumption, or of accumulation, in terms of per capita figures, may or may not improve.

Even if the current *ability* to accumulate is adversely affected by current increase in population, the *willingness* to accumulate may be stimulated by the concern for future consequences of a continued population increase. We may illustrate some of these ideas by means of the simple model of linear preferences described in the previous chapter.

Suppose, first, that the model applies to total figures for consumption, production and capital, and that population increases are simply disregarded. Then the production function (21.2) would probably be "wrong." Suppose, for example, that the effect of a gradual increase in population could be accounted for by adding a trend, say βt, to the production function. If the optimal rate of total consumption were strictly adhered to, the result would be a higher rate of accumulation and a higher production potential at the end of the planning period. This would be so, both because of a larger $K(\theta)$ and because of the term $\beta\theta$. However, we should most likely also have some "unexpected" expansion of consumption. For this reason the final position at $t = \theta$ might be either worse than planned or better than planned, as far as productive capacity per capita is concerned.

Consider, as an alternative, the case where the same model actually was set up in terms of per capita figures for consumption, production, and the amount of capital. In order to know the corresponding absolute variables, the planners would have had to know, or have estimated, population changes. Let $N(t)$ denote total population. Then $N(\theta) K(\theta)$, $N(\theta) x(\theta)$, and $N(\theta) c(\theta)$ would represent the status at the end of the planning period, in terms of the total variables. Now if the optimal plan derived on the basis of per capita figures should be strictly adhered to (this would require the knowledge of the series $N[t]$), we should have $\dot{K}(t) = 0$ at $t = \theta$. This would mean that the absolute rate of accumulation at that time would be equal to $K(\theta) \dot{N}(\theta)$. Thus, the fact that population may be increasing at the end point of the planning period could be the cause of a positive absolute rate of capital accumulation at that time.

II. Effects of Improved Production Technique

An Illustration

To emphasize the importance of technical progress is almost the same as saying that we do not know the actual production structure which should form the basis for a planned rate of capital accumulation. The knowledge we have of the determinants of technological advancements is certainly very scanty. We probably know a little more about their economic *effects*—*if* they happen. To illustrate this let us again consider the simple model of linear preferences described in the preceding chapter.

Let us assume that, at the beginning of the planning period, a new kind of capital has become known. We assume this capital to be such that if measured in the same units as the old capital it has an effect upon net output, which is larger than that of the old kind of capital. We shall further assume that the old capital is composed of approximately equally many units in each age group. For simplicity we shall assume that the depreciation of the old machines consists in an equal number of machines "dying" per unit of time. And, to make matters even simpler, we shall take the planning period θ to be exactly the time it takes before the last of the old machines are worn out. Let the stock of the new (and better) capital be denoted by $K^*(t)$. We shall assume that we record total output, $x(t)$, *net* in the sense that deductions are already made for depreciation of the *new* kind of capital (but not for the old). We write the production function as

$$x(t) = AK(t) + aK^*(t) + B, \qquad 0 \leq t \leq \theta, \quad (22.1)$$

where A, a, and B are constants. (Note that A here is different from A in chapter xxi.) Let the depreciation of $K(t)$ per unit of time be a constant equal to $(1/\theta) K(0)$. If $K^*(t)$ is a more efficient kind of capital than K when both are reckoned in x-units, it is obvious that the old capital will not be replaced. Thus we have

$$\dot{K}^*(t) = x(t) - c(t), \qquad (22.2)$$

which is net investment as far as K^* is concerned, but gross for K and K^* taken together.

Consider now a consumption plan of the form (21.3) and assume that the plan must satisfy the inequalities (21.4)–(21.6). How will a and $c(0)$ be chosen to maximize $c(\theta)$?

We first derive the possible developments of $K^*(t)$ and $x(t)$. From our assumptions concerning $K(t)$ we have $K(t) = K(0) (1 - t/\theta)$. Using this, we find

$$K^*(t) = \frac{1}{a}\left[AK(0) + B - c(0) - \frac{AK(0) + a\theta}{a\theta}\right]e^{at}$$

$$+ \frac{AK(0) + a\theta}{a\theta} t - \frac{1}{a}\left[AK(0) + B - c(0) \right. \qquad (22.3)$$

$$\left. - \frac{AK(0) + a\theta}{a\theta}\right], \qquad 0 \leq t \leq \theta.$$

And for $x(t)$ we have

$$x(t) = \left[AK(0) + B - c(0) - \frac{AK(0) + a\theta}{a\theta}\right]e^{at}$$

$$+ at + c(0) + \frac{AK(0) + a\theta}{a\theta} \qquad 0 \leq t \leq \theta. \qquad (22.4)$$

In order to satisfy condition (21.5) we must have

$$\left[AK(0) + B - c(0) - \frac{AK(0) + a\theta}{a\theta}\right]e^{a\theta}$$

$$+ \frac{AK(0) + a\theta}{a\theta} \geq 0. \qquad (22.5)$$

(Incidentally, it can readily be verified that this inequality holds for $t < \theta$ if it holds for $t = \theta$.) The largest $c(0)$ that satisfies this condition is the one for which the equality in (22.5) holds when $a = 0$. We find that, *if improved technology means $a > A(1 - e^{-a\theta})$*, we shall have

$$c(0) \leqq A K(0) + B - \frac{A K(0)}{a \theta}(1 - e^{-a\theta}). \qquad (22.6)$$

This means that it would not be optimal to consume only the whole net product, if consumption were to be kept constant. A part of the capital "liberated" by depreciating K may be consumed since the rest, when applied to K^*, is more effective. But an additional part can be consumed by *letting the gross product decrease gradually up to $t = \theta$*, since no depreciation is required after $t = \theta$. This shows that if consumption was at the level of net output at the beginning of the period, i.e., $\bar{c}(0) = A K(0) + B - K(0)/\theta$, the result of the technological improvement of capital would mean that the level of consumption could take a positive jump of a magnitude equal to

$$c(0) - \bar{c}(0) = \frac{K(0)}{\theta}\left[1 - \frac{A}{a}(1 - e^{-a\theta})\right] \qquad (22.7)$$

and stay at this level for the whole planning period.

However, if the purpose would be to maximize the rate of consumption at the end of the planning period, we shall have to consider the optimal value of a, under the constraints assumed. We find that we must have

$$a^{(\text{max})} = \frac{a}{1 - e^{-a\theta}}[A K(0) + B - \bar{c}(0)] - \frac{A K(0)}{\theta}. \qquad (22.8)$$

If a is large enough, and $A - 1/\theta$, equals the A of (21.2), we see from (22.6) and (22.8) that the point corresponding to L in Figure 3 will now be higher. Thus we find the result, which could be expected, that the technological improvement makes it possible to reach a higher level of consumption at the end of the planning period.

The rate of net accumulation at the beginning of the planning period will be the same as the old going rate at that time. (We have assumed that this rate was non-negative.) It is equal to $A K(0) + B - K(0)/\theta - \bar{c}(0)$. It will, however, fall gradually, reaching zero at $t = \theta$.

One might think that if a were large, one might get a more rapid growth, and that it might pay even to close the planning period with the amount of capital still growing. The reasons why this is not the case under the kinds of preferences considered here are quite clear. The conclusion would even hold for more general forms of consumption development. Intuitively, this can be seen as follows: Suppose that we are close to the end of the planning period with the rate of net investment still being strongly positive. That means that productive capacity is much larger than would be needed to maintain consumption at the current level. Consumption could be increased and there could still be enough capital accumulated at the end of the period to maintain the level of consumption then reached.

What we have found, however, is that technical progress is bound to increase output capacity at the end of the planning period. But it can be achieved with a lower rate of accumulation than before, reckoned in terms of the saved part of total net output.

23

Depreciation and the Concept of Net Investment

T HE scheme analyzed in the preceding two chapters illustrates two fundamentally different aspects of capital as a factor of production. On the one hand, we have the output that capital creates as an agent in the productive process. On the other hand, we have its cost of maintenance and replacement. Accumulation could aim at an increase in the former, positive, effect, as well as at a reduction in the latter, negative, effect. We have repeatedly mentioned this problem. Now we have to consider it somewhat more in detail, in order to see whether the problem of depreciation can be dealt with in a way that is reasonably manageable, from an analytic point of view.

For this purpose it may be of some interest to try to define depreciation in a fairly general way, even if subsequent simplifications will be absolutely necessary for practical purposes.

I. A GENERAL DEPRECIATION FORMULA

The kind of depreciation which we shall be concerned with here has to do with capital as a *factor of production*. We are *not* concerned with the depreciation of the *value* of capital, except insofar as statistical observations on depreciation in value terms may be used to evaluate depreciation of the quantity of capital as a variable in the production function.

It is clear that the various kinds of physical capital may wear out, or become obsolete, in different ways. The simplest case is when time wears upon the quantity of capital at a constant absolute or relative rate, regardless of the intensity of use, and when this wear simply means a corresponding reduction in the *volume* of physical capital. Stocks of goods in warehouses or goods in process may have this kind of physical depreciation and also some auxiliary materials used over and over again in industrial processes. Even in the case of tools and machinery, it may happen that the reduction in efficiency due to wear can be regarded as if we had a reduction in the *quantity* of such equipment, when measured by some kind of "constant-quality" index.

Another, relatively simple, case is when each unit of capital has a fixed lifetime, regardless of use. Strictly speaking, there is probably no such capital. But we may find that a model of this kind would be approximately correct within a certain practical range of intensities of use.

In more complicated cases—which probably are the rule—the rate of deterioration of capital will depend on its use. Moreover, the intensity of use will not be a technological datum but will be subject to *economic adaptation* to varying prices and costs. Both the efficiency of a capital item during its lifetime and its maximum life may be variables that could be subject to economic adjustments. The possibility of *shiftwork* would be very important in this connection. The use of calendar time to measure durability depends, as pointed out earlier, essentially on the length of the workday being fixed. In what follows, the problem of shiftwork is neglected, not because it is not important, but simply because we have to ration the amount of complications that we should try to handle.

Finally, two capital units which are equivalent as parts of capital in a production function may have different durabilities, that is, different built-in qualities as far as withstanding a given amount of strain and wear is concerned.

Consider a certain type of capital, the quantity of which is a relevant factor of production in a given production function. Let the amount of such capital at time t be $K(t)$. Assume that labor is the only other factor of production and that labor input is proportional to employment, $N(t)$. Let $z(t)$ denote the rate of gross addition to the stock of capital, i.e., gross investment in the sense of additions to the quantity of capital in the production function. Assume that the element $z(t)dt$ has a certain given durability which depends only on t. Let θ_t be an index of the degree of durability. We shall assume that this index measures, in a general way, the resistance to wear and tear of the capital units, as well as resistance to deterioration for reasons of age.

Consider one unit of such capital *new at t*. Its future fate as part of capital in the production function will depend on how hard it will be used and on its own durability. Suppose that at any time all the units in the stock of physical capital are being used equally intensively. Let $h_{t,\tau}$ denote what is still left, as a part of $K(\tau)$, of one unit of capital new at t; $h_{t,\tau}$ will be a non-increasing function of τ and such that $h_{t,t} = 1$. It is reasonable to assume that $h_{t,\tau}$ will depend on what combinations of K and N it has "lived with" from t to τ. We can express this in a simplified way by writing

$$\frac{\partial h_{t,\tau}}{\partial \tau} = \delta\,[K(\tau),\,N(\tau),\,\tau - t,\,\theta_t]\,, \qquad \tau \geqq t, \qquad (23.1)$$

where δ is a function such that $h_{t,\tau}$ will be positive and non-increasing and presumably approaches or becomes practically zero for a sufficiently large τ, depending on use and durability. Therefore, δ is never positive and generally negative. Presumably, the absolute value of δ will be the smaller, the larger is $K(\tau)$, and the smaller is $N(\tau)$, whereas it may be difficult to say how pure age, $\tau - t$, will affect δ.

The maximum age that any capital unit can reach may be formally set as "infinite," provided δ is defined for all $\tau \geqq t$. We shall then have

$$\dot{K}(t) = z(t) + \int_{-\infty}^{t} z(\tau)\,\delta\,[K(t),\,N(t),\,(t-\tau),\,\theta_\tau]\,d\tau \qquad (23.2)$$

as net investment in the sense of the rate of net additions to the volume of capital as a factor of production.

Even after the various simplifications made in order to write down equation (23.2), it is obvious that this formula may be extremely complicated. Moreover, if we want to use it for an aggregated capital variable, we should find that the function δ would be different for different kinds of capital. It is, therefore, important to look into the possibilities of approximations and the kinds of error that would be committed by using such approximations.

II. Approximate Depreciation Formulas

Conceptually, the depreciation scheme where each capital item has a fixed lifetime is probably the simplest, but from a mathematical point of view a constant percentage rate of depreciation is undoubtedly the easiest one to handle. This latter scheme corresponds to the function δ in equation (23.1), being an exponential function of $(\tau - t)$ only. If $-\gamma$ is the coefficient of this exponential, we have

$$\int_{-\infty}^{t} z(\tau)\,\gamma\,e^{-\gamma(t-\tau)}d\tau = \gamma K(t) \qquad (23.3)$$

as the current rate of depreciation of the physical amount of capital.

The depreciation formula (23.3) may be exactly or approximately correct for certain kinds of capital, such as warehouse stocks. For other kinds of capital it may represent a part of actual depreciation, and for still other types it may be an approximation formula when the rate of gross investment and the intensity of use are restricted to a certain narrow practical range.

Let us now take the case of capital with a fixed lifetime. This corresponds to the function δ being practically zero, except for a certain narrow range of the variable $(\tau - t)$ in equation (23.1). Suppose that the lifetime is exactly equal to a constant, θ. Then the rate of depreciation at point of time t will simply be:

$$\text{depreciation at } t = z(t - \theta) . \tag{23.4}$$

Even if θ is not entirely independent of time, this formula could sometimes be used as an approximation, with a constant *average* θ.

One could ask, under what circumstances formula (23.4) can be replaced by (23.3). This can obviously be done in the case where $K(t)$ is stationary. Then we should have $\gamma = (1/\theta)$. Otherwise γ would in general depend on t. If we regard γ as a function of time, $\gamma(t)$, we should have

$$\gamma(t) \, K(t) = \frac{z(t - \theta)}{\displaystyle\int_0^\theta z(t - \tau) \, d\tau} \, K(t) . \tag{23.5}$$

If it can be assumed that $z(t)$ moves "regularly" or "slowly," in some sense or other, various approximation formulas could be derived. If, for example, $z(t)$ changes approximately at a constant percentage rate over a time interval about equal to θ, we may have, as a workable approximation,

$$\gamma(t) = \frac{1}{\theta} - \beta \, \frac{\dot{K}(t)}{K(t)} . \tag{23.6}$$

It is intuitively obvious that if $z(t)$ is growing, then the current rate of depreciation, regarded as a fraction of capital, will be smaller than if $z(t)$ is constant or falling.

Suppose that we have the case where each capital unit depreciates by a constant absolute amount each year. This corresponds to the case of fixed lifetime, but with gradual wearing out. Suppose that each year a capital unit is reduced by $(1/\theta)$ of its original quantity. Then we should have

$$\text{depreciation at } t = \frac{1}{\theta} \int_0^\theta z(t - \tau) \, d\tau . \tag{23.7}$$

The amount of capital at t would be

$$K(t) = \int_0^\theta z(t-\tau)\left(1-\frac{\tau}{\theta}\right) d\tau. \qquad (23.8)$$

If $z(t)$ changes slowly in relation to the time interval θ, we see that the ratio of depreciation to capital, $\gamma(t)$, would be of the order of magnitude $(2/\theta)$. Actually we have

$$\gamma(t) = \frac{1}{\theta - \bar{\tau}_t}, \qquad (23.9)$$

where $\bar{\tau}_t$ is a weighted average of the age of the various capital units at time t. If the amount of gross investment, $z(t)$, is a growing series, $\bar{\tau}_t$ will be smaller than $(1/2)\theta$ and, hence, $\gamma(t) < (2/\theta)$.

In situations where the amount of capital is actually an aggregate of various types of capital, the various coefficients discussed above would have to be interpreted as some kind of averages. The degree of approximation that could be reached by using such averages has to be investigated in each case, if the question is one of practical, econometric work.

All the formulas above disregarded the possibility of varying intensity of use of the capital equipment. Going to the other extreme and assuming that there is no fixed durability but that it is only the intensity of use that matters we could have such approximations as

$$\gamma(t) = \gamma_1 \frac{N(t)}{K(t)} + \gamma_0, \qquad (23.10)$$

where γ_0 and γ_1 are certain constants. Here γ_0 could be interpreted as the wear and tear upon capital due to time itself. Such formulas would, however, largely neglect the fact that the various capital units may be subject to different wear according to their age. Changes in durability of new capital units over time could, however, be taken account of, to some extent, by making γ_0 and γ_1 functions of time.

The use of appropriate depreciation formulas may be of great importance in actual, quantitative, research. However, for the purpose of analyzing certain *principal* differences due to a change in durability, the essence of the matter can often be brought out by using some of the simple formulas mentioned above, even if it means making rather drastic assumptions. We shall have to rely on such possibilities in what follows, in order to keep the analytical apparatus on a manageable level.

III. The Question of Maintenance and Repair

Should one consider mantenance and repair as a separate kind of capital cost, in addition to depreciation? This is a controversial issue. In what follows we shall assume that depreciation also covers maintenance and repair. There are reasons why this may be bad theory. But there are also reasons why it may not be too bad.

The main reason for singling out maintenance and repair as a separate variable would seem to be this: It is a technologically known fact that some maintenance and repair work yields a very high return in terms of preventing wear and tear of capital equipment. That is, a little oiling and cleaning may mean that a machine lasts for years instead of breaking down after a few hours or days. The same applies to replacement of parts, which may not in themselves be very costly. Thus, it may be very unrealistic to make assumptions regarding durability of capital unless one assumes some kind of normal maintenance activity. In fact, it may be possible to argue that one could dispense with the notion of depreciation all together and talk only about maintenance and repair.[1]

But there are also good reasons why one should put the main emphasis on the concept of depreciation, and, as an approximation, simply neglect maintenance and repair. First of all, one could argue that the distinction between depreciation and maintenance is largely conventional. One could therefore, perhaps, define maintenance in such a way that it would represent only a small cost item. Second, one could in part take account of the maintenance factor by assuming that the employment of labor includes maintenance and repair work, with a corresponding reduction in the net marginal productivity of labor. A third possibility of an approximation would be to assume that maintenance is roughly proportional to the amount of capital and that, therefore, maintenance could be regarded *as if* it were a part of depreciation. On somewhat more philosophical grounds one could argue that it is actually impossible to distinguish between maintenance and repair work and the efforts of workers and management toward careful use of machinery and equipment. For example, a more skilled, and therefore more expensive, worker could be worth his extra pay not because he produces more output but because he causes less wear on the capital equipment.

On these grounds I do not think that a separate consideration of the variable maintenance and repair is really essential on the level of abstraction at which this study operates.

1. This point of view has been strongly emphasized by F. Knight (cf. references, p. 40).

24

Optimal Durability of Capital Equipment

Consider a planned community which is at the beginning of a planning period as discussed in chapters xxi and xxii. As we have observed before, the community has a choice, not only concerning how high a rate of savings it wants to maintain, but also with regard to how *durable* it wants to make the physical capital which it accumulates. It is fairly easy to see, intuitively, the nature of economic considerations that could influence choice in these two respects.

At the beginning of the planning period there will be a certain amount of productive capital in existence. By some kind of full-employment assumption it may be justified to regard the future rate of depreciation of this old capital as a datum. When it comes to gross investment, however, there may be several alternatives open as far as the choice between *quantity* of new capital and its *durability*. Presumably it will take a larger amount of savings to produce a more durable than a less durable, but otherwise equivalent, unit of capital. If not, it is obvious that only the most durable kind would be chosen. The relation between the necessary accumulation of savings and the durability of a capital item may be a complicated one. But we may assume that the planners know something about this relationship. Such knowledge is fundamental to the decision concerning what kind of capital to produce.

Suppose, as an extreme case, that the capital to be accumulated can be made highly durable by spending a very large amount of savings on quality (i.e., durability) rather than on quantity. Then, at the end of a reasonably short planning period, production may not have risen very much. It may even have fallen in spite of a large, positive rate of savings, because of a gradual reduction of old capital. Even if total capital increases in value (in product units), total capital as a factor of production may decrease. The real benefit of the new and more durable capital may come only after the old capital is practically used up.

Suppose, as the opposite extreme, that the new capital is made very cheap and short-lived. Then accumulation may start having significant effects upon output very soon after the beginning of the planning period. However, as it grows, the rate of depreciation of the new kind of capital will soon become a real burden. A larger and larger part of gross investment will go to depreciation of the new kind of capital. It may also be difficult to produce effective short-lived capital very cheaply.

It is, therefore, possible that there may exist some sort of optimal degree of durability to be chosen. But the choice will evidently depend on the kind of concern that the community has for economic conditions *beyond the end point of the planning period.* A community that at a given point in time has very durable capital, i.e., a low rate of depreciation, could, if it wanted to, choose to live upon this capital for a while, by producing more short-lived capital for replacement. But the community could also live well if it had a lot of short-lived capital. However, it would have to maintain a sizable gross investment in order to keep consumption up for any length of time.

There may be other factors that counteract the advantage of having very durable capital, e.g., the possibility of unforeseen technical developments which may make the capital obsolete before it is worn out. Then some of the previous accumulation efforts may, in a sense, be a waste. Uncertainty of this kind will undoubtedly have an effect in the direction of more short-lived capital.

We want to illustrate some of the points made above by means of a much-simplified model.

I. A LINEAR MODEL

We shall use a model of the same nature as the one studied in chapters xxi and xxii.

Consider a community at the beginning of a given planning period θ. Let this point of time be $t = 0$. There will be a certain physical volume of productive capital, $K(0)$. We shall assume that this capital depreciates at a constant rate γ_0 throughout the future. This actually means that a "particle" of new capital of this kind has an average lifetime, or durability, of $1/\gamma_0$ (cf. chap. xxiii).

We now assume that for the planning period θ it is possible to *choose* the durability of the new capital that will be accumulated to replace the old capital. Let the new kind of capital be denoted by $K^*(t)$ and let γ denote its rate of depreciation. Assume that the production function for the community is

$$x(t) = A[K(t) + K^*(t)] + B, \qquad (24.1)$$

where now $x(t)$ denotes *gross output* without any deductions for depreciation. Hence A denotes *gross* marginal productivity of capital. By assumption, $K(0)$ is a datum, while $K^*(0) = 0$. As is seen from equation (24.1), we assume that both kinds of capital are equivalent when regarded as a factor of production. The only difference between them is a possible difference between γ_0 and γ.

If $c(t)$ denotes the rate of consumption, the rate of gross savings will be $x(t) - c(t)$. We now have to make an assumption concerning the technical conversion of this rate of accumulation into the rate of increase in $K^*(t)$. A very simple assumption in this respect is that the effect upon the rate of increase of $K^*(t)$ of the rate of gross savings $x(t) - c(t)$ is proportional to (γ/γ_0), that is, inversely proportional to the durability of the new capital, when the durability of the old capital is taken as a standard of comparison. We want to use this assumption. Then the net growth of $K^*(t)$ will be

$$\dot{K}^* = \frac{\gamma}{\gamma_0}[x(t) - c(t)] - \gamma K^*(t). \qquad (24.2)$$

(The net growth of total capital, $K(t) + K^*(t)$, i.e., net investment in the physical volume of total capital, will be $\dot{K}^*(t) - \gamma_0 K(0)e^{-\gamma_0 t}$.)

We assume as in chapters xxi and xxii that the plan is to have a development of consumption $c(t)$ such that

$$c(t) = at + c(0), \qquad (24.3)$$

where the coefficients a and $c(0)$ are to be chosen subject to certain constraints. From equations (24.1)–(24.3) we then get

$$\dot{K}^* = \left(\frac{\gamma}{\gamma_0}A - \gamma\right)K^*(t) + \frac{\gamma}{\gamma_0}AK(0)e^{-\gamma_0 t}$$

$$\qquad (24.4)$$

$$- \frac{\gamma}{\gamma_0}at - \frac{\gamma}{\gamma_0}c(0) + \frac{\gamma}{\gamma_0}B,$$

which leads to the solution

$$K^*(t) = \left[\frac{\frac{\gamma}{\gamma_0}AK(0)}{\gamma_0 - \gamma + \frac{\gamma}{\gamma_0}A} - \frac{c(0) - B + \frac{a\gamma_0}{\gamma(A - \gamma_0)}}{A - \gamma_0}\right]$$

$$\times e^{[(\gamma/\gamma_0)A - \gamma]t} - \frac{\frac{\gamma}{\gamma_0}AK(0)}{\gamma_0 - \gamma + \frac{\gamma}{\gamma_0}A}e^{-\gamma_0 t} + \frac{a}{A - \gamma_0}t \qquad (24.5)$$

$$+ \frac{c(0) - B + \frac{a\gamma_0}{\gamma(A - \gamma_0)}}{A - \gamma_0}.$$

From this result it is evident that, as long as $A > \gamma_0$, and we have a

$c(0)$ and a that do not make the first bracket to the right in equation (24.5) negative or zero, it is possible to make $K^*(\theta)$ as large as one pleases, by choosing γ sufficiently large. In fact, the larger γ is, the larger is it possible to choose $c(0)$ and a, for a given $K^*(\theta)$. However, it is not the size of $K^*(\theta)$ that should be of final concern, but rather the consumption it permits when enough of the gross product is set aside for replacement of worn-out capital. If $K^*(\theta)$ gets large, due to the use of short-lived capital (large γ), the depreciation charges will also become large. On the other hand, such short-lived capital can by our assumption (24.2) also be produced at low cost in terms of necessary gross savings.

We want to investigate whether there are optimal values of $c(0)$, a, and γ, under the following constraints:

$$c(0) \geqq \bar{c}(0) ; \tag{24.6}$$

$$a \geqq 0 ; \tag{24.7}$$

$$\dot{K}(\theta) + \dot{K}^*(\theta) \geqq 0 . \tag{24.8a}$$

These constraints mean that $c(0)$ should not be lower than the going rate, $\bar{c}(0)$, at the time of planning, and that consumption should never fall. At the end of the planning period θ, the society should be able at least to maintain forever its rate of consumption at the level reached.

The condition (24.8a) can be written as

$$\left(\frac{\gamma}{\gamma_0} A - \gamma\right) \left[\frac{\dfrac{\gamma}{\gamma_0} A K(0)}{\gamma_0 - \gamma + \dfrac{\gamma}{\gamma_0} A} - \frac{c(0) - B + \dfrac{a\gamma_0}{\gamma(A - \gamma_0)}}{A - \gamma_0} \right]$$

$$\times e^{[(\gamma/\gamma_0)A - \gamma]\theta} + \frac{\gamma_0 K(0)(\gamma - \gamma_0)}{\gamma_0 - \gamma + \dfrac{\gamma}{\gamma_0} A} e^{-\gamma_0\theta} + \frac{a}{A - \gamma_0} \geqq 0 . \tag{24.8b}$$

Let us first regard γ as given and consider the largest possible $c(0)$ satisfying the inequality above for $a = 0$. We find that the largest such $c(0)$ is

$$c(0)^{max} = \frac{\dfrac{\gamma}{\gamma_0}(A - \gamma_0)}{\dfrac{\gamma}{\gamma_0}(A - \gamma_0) + \gamma_0} A K(0) + B$$

$$+ \frac{\gamma_0}{\gamma} \frac{\gamma_0(\gamma - \gamma_0)}{\gamma_0 + \dfrac{\gamma}{\gamma_0}(A - \gamma_0)} K(0) e^{-[(\gamma/\gamma_0)A - \gamma + \gamma_0]\theta} . \tag{24.9}$$

We see that this expression must increase when γ increases, reaching $c(0) = AK(0) + B$ as a limit.

Furthermore, we see that, for a given γ, a can be the larger the smaller is $c(0)$. In fact, we find that the relation between a and $c(0)$ that represents the upper boundary for these two parameters, for a given value of γ, is linear and of the following form:

$$c\,(0) = -\frac{\gamma_0}{\gamma\,(A - \gamma_0)}\,[1 - e^{-(\gamma/\gamma_0)(A-\gamma_0)\theta}]\,a + c\,(0)^{\,max}, \qquad (24.10)$$

where $c(0)^{max}$ is given by equation (24.9). We see that the straight-line boundary of $c(0)$ and a is downward-sloping and that a can be the larger the larger is γ, for any given admissible $c(0)$. We also see that the slope of the boundary is not as steep as $-\theta$, which means that the a which maximizes $c(\theta) = c(0) + a\theta$ is the a obtained from equation (24.10) by setting $c(0) = \bar{c}(0)$.

The conclusions concerning γ are rather interesting: If it is as cheap to produce more short-lived capital as assumed by equation (24.2), it will pay for the community to start producing a new kind of capital, K^*, which has as low a durability as technologically possible. The point is, of course, that it is in fact not technologically possible to have a relation of the form (24.2) for very large values of γ. The production of capital with a very high γ will in practice be more expensive. The same may be true if the problem was to make γ as small as possible.

We meet here the fundamental idea of the old Austrian school of economics in a new version: The production of durable goods must, in some sense, be relatively cheaper than the production of less durable goods, in order to make the waiting for its fruits worthwhile. And, presumably, no kind of capital can be produced so cheaply in relation to its durability that it is worth waiting forever for a physical volume of it sufficient to produce any real increase in output.

25

Imports and Exports of Capital

THE difference between a closed and an open economy varies in importance according to what part of economic theory we are talking about. In the theory of capital and investment the difference is profound. Opening up the economy to trade with the outside not only introduces more degrees of freedom, but actually changes completely the kind of systematic connection between capital and its rate of growth which exists for a centralized, closed sector. The essential difference is this: In a closed economy physical stocks of goods and equipment can only change gradually, the existence of *their derivative* with respect to time has a natural explanation (disregarding earthquakes and the like). In an open economy the natural constraints on the rate of growth of physical stocks cease to exist. Finite volumes of stock can cross the borders without time being an essential, limiting factor. Of course, if we were to consider repercussions for the world as a whole, we should be back with the case of a closed economy again. Even if the particular sector considered is a very large part of the total world economy, the difference between the sector being closed and being open is profound, at any rate as long as we assume that the sector behaves as if it did not take account of repercussions of its own actions.

In addition to the possibility of almost instantaneous transfer of physical stocks between connected sectors, there is the important possibility of transferring financial income flows and the accumulation of financial assets. This, too, tends to break up the relationship that must exist in a closed economy between the rate of savings and rate of growth of physical capital reckoned in value terms. Actually, the theory of a centralized open economy becomes formally similar to a theory of the firm, except perhaps for differences in economic objectives and in the legal or institutional framework.

I. The Case of Perfect Mobility and Perfectly Homogeneous Capital

In order to bring out the essential difference between a closed and an open economy, let us consider the rather artificial case where capital can be imported and exported instantaneously at world-market prices and interest rates and where capital is a homogeneous mass of goods for which age and other quality differences can be neglected. We shall assume that this capital depreciates at a constant percentage rate, γ, per unit of time. Let us assume that the sector has an aggregate gross output, $x(t)$, per unit of time and that this output is given by an aggregate production function

$$x(t) = \Phi[K(t), N(t)], \qquad (25.1)$$

where $K(t)$ is the stock of capital and $N(t)$ the level of employment. For simplicity we shall neglect possible cost of imported raw materials or, alternatively, assume that the use of raw materials is proportional to net domestic output $x(t)$. We shall assume that $N(t)$ is a constant $= \bar{N}$, independent of time, e.g., some full-employment level in a constant population. Let the world market price of $x(t)$ be $p(t)$ and let the world market price of capital be $q(t)$. Let the rate of interest in the world market be equal to $\rho(t)$.

The assumptions of perfect mobility and a perfectly open market across the borders mean that whatever wealth, real or financial, that the sector has will earn interest at the rate $\rho(t)$, regardless of whether it consists of capital used at home or assets abroad. At any given point of time the net interest revenues of the sector is a datum that can only be changed by savings as far as possible action of the sector itself is concerned. When it comes to deciding how much physical capital should be used in the production function (25.1), we may, therefore, regard interest charges as an expense to be paid out of the sector. Depreciation is an expense to "Nature" and must also be deducted as not accruing to anybody in the sector.

Let $W(t)$ denote the interest-bearing wealth of the sector at time t. And let us assume that by some general device of a "world price deflator" this variable as well as all other money values in this model can be regarded as constant-dollar values. There the net income, $r(t)$, of the sector at point of time t can be defined as

$$r(t) = p(t)x(t) + \rho(t)W(t) - \rho(t)q(t)K(t) - \gamma q(t)K(t) \quad (25.2)$$

(remembering that x is defined net of any imported raw materials). Suppose that the sector wants to maximize $r(t)$, with $p(t)$, $\rho(t)$, $q(t)$, $W(t)$ taken as given parameters. This leads, of course, to the classical necessary condition

$$\frac{\partial \Phi}{\partial K} = [\rho(t) + \gamma] \frac{q(t)}{p(t)}. \quad (25.3)$$

From this it is evident that, unless the parameters which are regarded as data from the point of view of the sector change over time, the quantity of capital, $K(t)$, will be a constant, independent of time, once it satisfies equation (25.3). The rate of savings, $s(t)$, whatever it is, is defined as

$$s(t) = \dot{W}(t). \quad (25.4)$$

This rate of savings has no direct relation to a possible rate of capital accumulation $K(t)$. But the two variables may be indirectly related by way of effects of price changes upon both.

This model, though in most respects very far from realistic, serves to focus attention on some obvious, but absolutely fundamental, problems that we meet in trying to establish a rational theory of why there should "normally" be a tendency towards a positive $\dot{K}(t)$. Let us look briefly at some of the puzzling questions that arise.

1. The process of adjusting $K(t)$ to the equation (25.3) in order to get maximum return cannot be used to explain a *maintained level* of $\dot{K}(t)$ different from zero.

2. In an open sector the rate of savings has no direct bearing upon the rate of capital accumulation.

3. The amount of capital $K(t)$ cannot change unless the *data* involved in equation (25.3) change (e.g., a change in the relative price of capital).

4. The rate of change of capital $\dot{K}(t)$, will not in general exist as a finite derivative with respect to time unless the "datum parameters" involved possess such derivatives.

A consequence of 4 is that the question of a *"demand for investment,"* in the sense of demand for increase of $K(t)$ per unit of time, is a *nonsensical question*. In order to construct a rational notion of "demand for $\dot{K}(t)$," the behavior of the sector in regard to capital as a factor of production must contain the following two essential elements: (*a*) The sector must simultaneously consider its desire for capital at *at least two different points in time* and (*b*) the sector must have reasons for, or a desire for, a *gradual transition* from one amount of capital to another. The reason behind such preferences may be some gradually changing external conditions, some general tendency toward a certain slowness of reaction, or technological constraints upon the possible speed of reaction.

We cannot simply say that the sector demands investment because it wants to increase production. It may demand *capital* for this purpose, but why this should make $\dot{K}(t)$ a finite derivative is a far more subtle and difficult problem.

II. The Case of Perfect Mobility and a Fixed Lifetime of Capital Equipment

The previous model served to illustrate the loose connection, if any, that exists between the rate of savings and the rate of physical capital accumulation in an open economy. We shall now consider a model that illustrates the equally loose connection which we may find between the amount of *physical capital*, $K(t)$, and its *money value*.

Consider a model similar to the one above, but assume now that each capital unit has a fixed lifetime, or durability, *n* years.

Assume further that there is a perfect market, in newly constructed capital as well as in used capital. By assumption "used" capital means simply capital of a certain age but otherwise technologically equivalent to new capital.

Let us first consider a discrete model. Let $K_0(t)$ denote the amount of capital of zero age, $K_1(t)$ capital one year old, etc., up to $K_{n-1}(t)$, while

$K_n(t) = 0$. Assume that $N(t)$ is constant, so that we can write the production function (25.1) as

$$x(t) = \Phi^*[K_0(t) + K_1(t) + \ldots + K_{n-1}(t)]. \qquad (25.1b)$$

The assumption that we can sum the various types of capital into one factor is a way of expressing the technological equivalence of capital regardless of age.

It is evident that, if equation (25.1b) is the production function, the sector would use the type of capital, $K_i(t)$, that would cause the least expenditure per unit. Therefore, if there is capital of all age groups in the market and in use, and there is perfect mobility, the prices of the various kinds of capital have to be such as to make it quite indifferent whether new or old capital is applied. If this law of indifference is fulfilled in the world market, the price $q_i(t)$ of $K_i(t)$ must bear a certain definite relation to the price $q_0(t)$ of new capital and to the rate of interest $\rho(t)$.

Consider a production plan for one year t to $t + 1$ based on the assumption that the same prices and the same interest rate will prevail at the end of the year as at the beginning and that in fact no change is expected in the future. At the end of the year a certain amount of interest charges and a certain amount of depreciation will have accrued. Remembering this and that all the variables and parameters below refer to $t + 1$, let us for simplicity omit the reference to this common point in time. For the sum of interest and depreciation we shall then have, at $t + 1$,

$$\rho \sum_0^{n-1} q_i K_i + \left(\sum_0^{n-1} q_i K_i - \sum_0^{n-2} q_{i+1} K_i \right). \qquad (25.5a)$$

The prices q_i must evidently be such as to make this expression invariant to changes in the K's, subject to the condition that the sum of the K's remains a constant. Using this condition we find that we must have

$$(1 + \rho)q_i - q_{i+1} = (1 + \rho)q_0 - q_1, \quad i = 1, 2, \ldots, n - 1,$$
$$q_n = 0. \qquad (25.6)$$

Solving this difference equation, we find that we must have

$$q_i = \frac{(1 + \rho)^i [(1 + \rho)^{n-i} - 1]}{(1 + \rho)^n - 1} q_0. \qquad (25.7)$$

Inserting these results into (25.5a), we find that the expressions $(1 + \rho)q_i - q_{i+1}$ are independent of i, and that the expression (25.5a) can be written

$$\frac{\rho (1 + \rho)^n}{(1 + \rho)^n - 1} q_0 \sum_0^{n-1} K_i. \qquad (25.5b)$$

In order to maximize net income, our sector must choose the amount of capital for which we have

$$\frac{\partial \Phi^*}{\partial K_i} = \frac{\rho (1 + \rho)^n}{(1 + \rho)^n - 1} q_0, \qquad i = 0, 1, \ldots, n - 1. \quad (25.8a)$$

The expression (25.5b) can also be written as

$$\rho q_0 \sum_{0}^{n-1} \frac{(1 + \rho)^i [(1 + \rho)^{n-i} - 1]}{(1 + \rho)^n - 1} K_i$$

$$+ \rho q_0 \sum_{1}^{n-1} \frac{(1 + \rho)^i}{(1 + \rho)^n - 1} K_i, \quad (25.9)$$

where the first part represents "pure interest," and where the second part is depreciation.

The same model can also be expressed in a continuous form, to avoid the artificial planning period of one year. If we let ρ represent the "force of interest," and q_τ the price of τ years old capital K_τ, the expression corresponding to (25.5a) is

$$\rho \int_0^\theta q_\tau K_\tau d\tau - \int_0^\theta \frac{dq_\tau}{d\tau} K_\tau d\tau, \quad (25.10a)$$

where θ represent the (constant) maximum age of a capital item. This has to be equal to a constant regardless of the form of K_τ, provided the integral over K_τ, that is, the total volume of capital, stays constant. This can only be the case if

$$\frac{dq_\tau}{d\tau} - \rho q_\tau = \text{const}. \quad (25.11)$$

The solution of this differential equation has the form

$$q_\tau = A + B e^{\rho\tau}.$$

But we must have $q_\theta = 0$, and q_0 is a datum; which determines A and B, so that we get

$$q_\tau = \frac{1 - e^{-\rho(\theta - \tau)}}{1 - e^{-\rho\theta}} q_0. \quad (25.12)$$

Inserting this into (25.10a), we find that this expression becomes

$$\frac{\rho q_0}{1 - e^{-\rho\theta}} \int_0^\theta K_\tau d\tau. \quad (25.10b)$$

If the sector wants to maximize its net income, it must use an amount of capital such that the marginal productivity of capital satisfies the relation

$$\frac{d\Phi^*}{dK} = \frac{\rho}{1 - e^{-\rho\theta}} \frac{q_0}{p}, \qquad \text{where} \qquad K = \int_0^\theta K_\tau d\tau. \quad (25.8\,b)$$

Both these formulations show an obvious, but nevertheless very important, fact: From the point of view of the producing sector *it is quite immaterial whether it uses new or old capital*, so long as the prices satisfy the laws of indifference described above. What this means is that *the value* of the total capital used in production may vary between what it would cost all new, and practically zero, without affecting the rate of output! This in sharp contrast to Böhm-Bawerk's ideas which would seem to imply that prices of the various kinds of capital in regard to durability would determine the kind of capital actually used. The reason for the difference is that capital which has a long life ahead, in the Austrian way of reasoning, was assumed to be "more productive" than the short-lived type. Some optimal durability would be chosen. In order to get a corresponding result, we should have to assume that capital plays a different role in the production function according to both its quantity and its age. But this would take us away from the main "classical" argument which has been that the choice of durability as such is held to be a function of the rate of interest. This is apparently not the case according to the models studied above. *The rate of interest determines the volume of capital used, but not its composition* or, what amounts to the same, its total value.

In order to determine the value of capital used, we should have to have prices q_τ that are out of line in relation to the law of indifference discussed above.

III. Effects of Price Expectations

In the preceding model price expectations play no role. There will be instantaneous adjustment to the current prices and the current interest rate. If at t there is a sudden change in these parameters, the corresponding gain or loss in the total value of capital will be written off and will in itself not affect future behavior in regard to production. The variable W will absorb the gains or losses instantaneously. If, however, such changes are anticipated in one way or another, the effects are quite different.

Let us first consider, in a formal way, the effects of spontaneous changes in prices and the interest rate, if anticipations play no role.

Suppose, first, that $q_0(t)$ is changed in the world market. How will this affect $q_\tau(t)$ if the law of indifference is to prevail after the change? If we restrict ourselves to the continuous formulation (25.12), we see that $q_\tau(t)$ will change by a certain fraction of the change in $q_0(t)$. This fraction is the smaller the larger is τ. The *percentage* change in $q_\tau(t)$ will, however, obviously be the *same for all* τ. This means that the absolute loss of wealth due to a fall in capital values will be the smaller the older is the capital employed. It is, therefore, in a way less risky to use old equipment in production than to use new and more expensive equipment.

Suppose, next, that the rate of interest $\rho(t)$ is spontaneously changed, while $q_0(t)$ stays unchanged. How will this affect $q_\tau(t)$ if the law of indifference is to prevail? We find, from equation (25.12),

$$\frac{\partial q_\tau}{\partial \rho} = \frac{(\theta - \tau)\, e^{-\rho(\theta - \tau)} - e^{-\rho\theta}\, [\,\theta - \tau e^{-\rho(\theta - \tau)}\,]}{(1 - e^{-\rho\theta})^{\,2}}\, q_0. \quad (25.13)$$

This expression is zero for $\tau = 0$, and $\tau = \theta$, and is otherwise *positive*. This means that old capital will increase in value relatively to $q_0(t)$ if the rate of interest is increased. The reason is, of course, that older equipment does not have as much future yield to be discounted as the newer equipment. This means that if the price of new capital is expected to stay constant, while the rate of interest may be subject to increase, it is in a sense an advantage to hold old capital.

Under both these kinds of changes the amount of capital used in the production function of our sector will in general be changed, as is seen from equation (25.8b). We could now ask the question, how must $q_0(t)$ change in response to a change in $\rho(t)$ at t if production is *not* to be affected? From equation (25.8b) we see immediately that to get this result we must have

$$\frac{\partial q_0\,(t)}{\partial \rho\,(t)}\, \frac{\rho\,(t)}{q_0\,(t)} = -\left(1 - \frac{\rho\,\theta\, e^{-\rho\theta}}{1 - e^{-\rho\theta}}\right). \quad (25.14)$$

This formula shows, first, the well-known phenomenon that the effect of an increase in the rate of interest upon the price of new capital, *if* production is to remain unchanged, is negative and the larger the larger is the durability θ. It is also the larger, the larger is the level of interest at which the change takes place. In addition we find that all the prices $q_\tau(t)$ have to fall, but relatively less so the larger is τ (cf. equation (25.13)).

We must remember that even if production remains unchanged as a result of an increase in $\rho(t)$ and a fall in capital prices according to equation (25.14), there is a capital loss involved which affects $W(t)$. This loss is the smaller, in absolute terms, the older is the capital equipment used.

Note that while more durable equipment (larger θ) would mean a relatively larger price reaction than in the case of less durable equipment, the fact that capital is nearer the end of its useful life, whatever it is, means in itself that the price of this kind of capital is less sensitive to interest changes than when new. This conclusion refers, it must be remembered, to the case *where the current cost of using capital stays constant.*

Let us now consider some possible effects of anticipations concerning the development of the prices of capital $q_\tau(t)$. We shall assume that capital prices in the world market always satisfy the law of indifference discussed above, regardless of whether or not they actually change over time. And we shall assume that our sector reckons with this kind of consistent capital prices. This means that any actual or anticipated change of $q_\tau(t)$ over time will bear a definite relation to the change in $q_0(t)$, as is seen from equation (25.12).

Suppose, under these assumptions, that our particular sector at t anticipates a rate of change $\dot{q}_0(t)$ per unit of time at t, and it expects this rate to continue for some time. The rate of interest is assumed to remain constant. How will this affect the marginal cost of using capital? Consider first total cost of using a certain composite amount of capital. This will now no longer be equal to the expression (25.10a). For the capital will change its value while in use, due to the anticipated change in capital prices. It is seen that instead of (25.10a) we must now have

$$\rho\,(t) \int_0^\theta q_\tau\,(t)\,K_\tau\,(t)\,d\,\tau - \int_0^\theta \left[\frac{\partial\,q_\tau\,(t)}{\partial\,\tau} + \dot{q}_\tau\,(t)\,\right]K_\tau\,(t)\,d\,\tau,\quad(25.15)$$

where $\dot{q}_\tau(t)$ denotes the expected rate of change of $q_\tau(t)$ per unit of time (for constant τ). Using equation (25.12), which still defines constant ratios between all capital prices at any given point in time and remembering (25.10a) and (25.10b), we can write (25.15) as

$$\frac{\rho\,(t)\,q_0\,(t)}{1 - e^{-\rho(t)\theta}} \int_0^\theta K_\tau\,(t)\,d\,\tau - \int_0^\theta \dot{q}_\tau\,(t)\,K_\tau\,(t)\,d\,\tau$$

$$= q_0\,(t) \int_0^\theta \frac{\rho\,(t) - \dfrac{\dot{q}_0\,(t)}{q_0\,(t)}\,[1 - e^{-\rho(t)(\theta-\tau)}]}{1 - e^{-\rho(t)\theta}}\,K_\tau\,(t)\,d\,\tau.\quad(25.16)$$

The important feature of this result is that the fraction in the last of these integrals is *not* independent of τ. This means that the effect upon anticipated cost of using capital will now *depend on the composition of total capital.* From this result it is clear that when there is an anticipated increase in capital prices, the marginal cost of all types of capital will be momentarily reduced, which presumably means that, at least to start with, *more capital* can be used in production. Also, the reduction in marginal cost due to anticipated gains in capital values will obviously be the larger the newer is the capital equipment used. It would in fact pay to sell all old capital and buy the whole stock brand new. This indicates that there may be violent fluctuations in the *value* of total capital used, as a result of expected price changes. The change in the total physical volume of capital as it appears in the production function may, however, show only moderate changes.

Suppose, as an alternative, that a certain increase in the rate of interest is anticipated, while $q_0(t)$ is expected to remain constant for some time. We have seen that if this happens and the capital prices $q_\tau(t)$ are to continue to satisfy the law of indifference, all prices $q_\tau(t)$ for $\tau \neq 0$ must increase. That is, if $\rho(t)$ is anticipated to increase gradually at the rate $\dot\rho(t)$, we must have $\dot q_\tau(t) \geqq 0$, where the equality holds only for $\tau = 0$. The effect can be evaluated by using (25.13) and (25.15), since the only current effect will be upon $\dot q_\tau(t)$.

These results are very hard-boiled and unrealistic. But they can, nevertheless, serve to indicate how intricate is the question of an optimal use of capital in production when there are possibilities of changes in capital prices or in the rate of interest. One has only to think of the case where the law of indifference of capital prices either actually does not hold at time t or is not expected to continue to hold. Then the speculative element in regard to the composition of capital may defy all attempts at a rational explanation.

IV. Effects of Immobility

The idea that both new and old capital should be perfectly mobile across the sector borders is, of course, highly unrealistic. There may be several kinds of immobility.

First, there is the general phenomenon of delay in action concerning import and export of capital, even if mobility is technologically perfect. This may be one reason why the amount of capital may not be perfectly adjusted to current world prices of capital and products.

Second, there is the element of time involved in actually moving the physical capital. Transport takes time. But what is more important is that often the capital items imported will be only parts of a larger capital unit to be completed by the sector's own productive efforts. In Part II we have analyzed the various reasons why such construction work must be time consuming to be economically feasible. Thus, for example, if the sector considered wants to build a hydroelectric power plant, it may be able to buy the machinery in the world market on relatively short notice, but it cannot import the dams and other ground constructions. (It can, however, import consumer goods in order to divert a larger part of its manpower and resources to more intensive construction work.)

Third, there are all kinds of organizational constraints, especially those preventing unlimited credit abroad. Suppose, for example, that no foreign credit is available. Then sudden changes in the quantity of capital in the sector could only take place if the sector traded newer, more expensive capital equipment for older, less expensive equipment. Otherwise, capital could only be imported at a certain *rate* per annum, depending on the rate of export revenues. In fact, if no credit is available, the sector considered will be in almost the same economic position as if it were closed, except for the advantages of substitution between exported and imported goods.

Fourth, there is the asymmetry between the import of capital and the export of capital. That is, the capital once imported can often not be re-exported without prohibitive losses, because it has become technologically attached to local conditions. This means, e.g., that if our sector wants to buy more capital equipment, it may be able to do so rather quickly, whereas if it wants to reduce the amount of capital because the amount has become over-optimal, the sector may have to wait for the equipment to depreciate. In this respect there is apparently considerable advantage in using equipment of low durability.

The immobility of capital makes it, in general, more difficult for the sector to guard itself against losses of wealth due to unfavorable changes in prices of capital equipment. If losses and gains due to a change in capital prices are counted as part of net income, the definition of savings as the rate of change in wealth will remain valid. But the relation between the rate of savings and the physical volume of capital in the sector may be even looser when capital is immobile than when it can be bought and sold instantaneously. It is, e.g., perfectly possible that the physical volume of capital in the sector's production function stays constant, while the rate of savings is highly negative even if no foreign credit is involved. This merely re-emphasizes a point that has been repeatedly mentioned, viz., the importance of a clear distinction between the value of capital and its volume as a factor of production.

V. The High Volatility of the Rate of Accumulation in an Open Sector

Already the study of a closed economy showed us *the* fundamental problem in the theory of investment, the problem how to explain a more or less steady rate of growth of capital. In a closed sector it is relatively easy to give the reason. It is a resultant of two forces: The insatiable wish for more capital and the constraints upon the rate at which capital can be acquired. In a closed planned sector, or a Robinson Crusoe economy, it is, so to speak, the "same brain" that considers both these forces. Therefore, the simple fact that capital cannot be changed instantaneously is a constraint which is reckoned with by the planning sector.

In an open sector the situation is quite different. True, there are constraints upon the amount of capital that it is economical to use at any time. The prices of capital and products, and the rate of interest in the world market represent such constraints. But what are the constraints upon the rate of change per unit of time of capital when a spontaneous change occurs in the world market prices or the interest rate? If there is a perfect credit market and perfect mobility there are theoretically no constraints upon the rate of change of capital as far as *demand* is concerned. It may, so to speak, vary between plus infinity and minus infinity. It is of no use to try to explain this rate by pointing to a desire for more capital or less capital.

It is obvious that if a finite rate of change in the amount of capital is to be explained it cannot be explained by *preferences* in regard to the amount of capital. It must be explained by the possible actual *constraints* upon the rate of growth of capital. There is perhaps one necessary qualification to this statement. It is conceivable that people may have some sort of preference pattern concerning growth itself. That is, they may find a pleasure in the fact that the amount of capital is growing, in addition to their wish for a certain amount of capital at a given point in time. There is, in any case, probably not much hope that such a preference for growth would remain stable over time, from an econometric point of view.

The *constraints* are, however, many and easy to name, even in an open sector. The trouble with them, from the point of view of investment theory, is that these constraints are, in a sense, of "secondary quality" as far as good, solid economic theory is concerned. They are due to such things as immobility, slowness of reaction and institutional, man-made rules or habits, risk of trying too much at once, etc. If we want a hard-boiled theory of "rational behavior," we shall not be able to rely on these constraints as somethig really stable and permanent. Then we have one thing to fall back upon, namely, a given rate of growth in one or more of the *parameters* that determine the optimal amount of capital at any time. Growth of population may be one such important parameter. Gradual changes in relative prices due to technological progress may represent other growth factors. But the fundamental conclusion is that something has to change, and change gradually, over time, something upon which the optimal amount of capital depends, in order to explain a finite rate of change in the volume of capital, within the framework of classical profit maximization.

26

Comments on the Effects of Technological Change

O<small>UR</small> excursion into this formidable subject will be brief and sketchy. One reason for this is that we are not here really interested in the general theory of economic growth,[1] but only in the more direct effects upon the rate of capital accumulation. Another, and much more important, reason is that, unfortunately, very little is as yet known about how to deal with technological development in theoretical models of economic growth. The only thing we shall try to do here is to indicate, roughly, how some of our conclusions in the preceding chapters may be affected by the element of technological change.

I. PRODUCTION FUNCTIONS IN A CHANGING TECHNOLOGY

The problem of merely describing what we mean by technological change is already quite a task. Suppose we start from some given production function involving only labor and capital. We could perhaps say that the "form" of the production function describes the state of technology at the start. We could visualize many kinds of changes in this production function. We may not wish to call every such change a change in technology. But most of us probably think of a change in technology as a change in the form of the production function, or more specifically, a change in some of its parameters. Sometimes it may be natural to think of "technology" as a separate *input* element, an extra variable in the production function.

Suppose we have a change that could be described, roughly, as an increase in the productivity of labor. This could mean that there has been a change in certain conditions upon which the productive effect of a certain specified standard input of labor depends. But it could also mean that the units of labor have changed their quality in a way which is not reflected in the kind of measure we use for labor input. The same could be true for the input of capital.

A problem of the "optimal degree of aggregation" arises in this connection. Suppose new kinds of capital which are in some sense better than the old capital become available. In certain cases it may be quite simple to think of improved quality as practically equivalent to an increase in the

---

1. Cf. the author's monograph, *A Study in the Theory of Economic Evolution* (North Holland Publishing Co., 1954).

quantity of capital. In those cases we may be able to add up various kinds of capital into a simple quantity index by using appropriate weights. In other cases, however, such an index might have to be so strange and unwieldy that it would be simpler and more adequate to introduce various kinds of capital as separate variables in the production function (cf. chap. xviii on this point). If we want to have a fixed, and not very large, number of variables representing capital in the production function, each of these will in practice necessarily have to be a more or less complicated aggregate.

The meaning of a question such as: "What is the effect upon the amount of capital of a change in technology?" obviously depends very much upon how we have defined our production function. A change in technology could simply be *the same thing as* a change in the amount of a certain kind of capital, or even the same as a change in the total amount of capital, defined by some index. But it could also mean a change in the way in which a certain kind of capital is *used*.

If we have a closed economy, the quantity and composition of physical capital will be a datum at any given moment or over any sufficiently short interval of time. A spontaneous change in technology could then only affect the way in which existing capital is being used (its rate of physical depreciation). Changes in the kind of capital used would be a time-requiring process. A change in technology which would permit a larger output on the basis of existing resources would mean a larger potential of capital accumulation. But even if this means that the rate of net savings or rate of increase in the *value* of capital of all kinds would increase, the question of what would happen to the physical amount of capital relevant to the production function is still very complicated.

This difficulty is due to the possibility of varying the durability of capital equipment. It has generally been thought that the richer a community gets, the more it will expand the volume of long-range capital projects relative to short-range projects. This is really a rather doubtful proposition, even under conditions of constant technique, and, if there is technological progress, the opposite tendency may well be more true. It is in itself no advantage that capital cannot be used up except over a long period, with corresponding low annual gross yield. A change in technology may mean that it becomes possible to make and to use efficient capital of short durability. If this is so, the volume of capital, relevant as a factor of production, may grow at a faster rate than the total value of capital. If we look at the situation from the point of view of savings, an advancement in technology may mean that it becomes possible to maintain a certain rate of growth of net output with a lower amount of annual savings.

I think it is a fair guess that modern industries during the last few decades have learned relatively much more about how to produce efficient tools and equipment that live a "short and hectic life" than they have learned about the production of monumental capital installations. This development can, in part, serve as a substitute for savings, that is, for the accumulation of capital values. However, this does not mean a corresponding release of output for consumption purposes, if consumption is counted in the narrow sense in which we usually think of it. There is another kind of accumulation that must take place in order to sustain rapid growth: the accumulation of knowledge and technical skill.

II. THE ACCUMULATION OF KNOWLEDGE

Why should we not simply include some kind of measure of educational level and technical know-how as a part of capital defined in a wide sense? There is, of course, the somewhat obscure question of measurement. But there would seem to be many points of similarity between these two kinds of productive agents. They are both essentially stored-up things. They are both produced by human activity rather than being natural resources. However, there are also some striking differences. Thus, while the rate of depreciation of physical capital must be thought of as larger than or equal to zero, it is quite possible that skill and know-how (for society as a whole) have a tendency to appreciate, to grow upon themselves. While the growth of physical capital requires that a part of output is saved *instead* of being consumed, the process of learning can be both consumption and accumulation, or learning can in fact be a result of activities usually reckoned as "consumption."

If we wanted to include know-how as part of capital, we should, therefore, definitely have to give up the idea of dividing total net output into a "saved" part and a "consumed" part, regarded as mutually exclusive uses. One could try to single out that part of the education and learning processes which seem clearly to represent investment in the future and add this part to the ordinary bookkeeping concept of savings. But such a subdivision of the process of education may become rather arbitrary or artificial.

It is, probably, a more promising approach to operate with the level of know-how as a separate factor of production. It is quite possible that, in modern societies, the accumulation of this "productive agent," may serve in part as a replacement for "savings" as defined in current national accounting. If this be the case, the rate of savings in the orthodox sense may become more and more inadequate as a single index of economic growth.

PART IV

Investment Behavior in a Market Economy

In the introduction to the preceding part of this study we said that the model of a centralized economy could be used either to discuss an economy that is in fact centralized or as an artificial device for studying certain features of an economy, even if it is not centrally planned. What we want to do in this part of our study is, therefore, not so much to discuss a different kind of economy, as to analyze the particular problems that are due, essentially, to the economy being decentralized. Some of the approximations that we have discussed earlier can be used in both cases, others become impermissible when we deal with a multisector economy. It is hardly necessary to add that our analytical models will still be a long way off from a full explanation of the working of a market economy.

We cannot claim any great novelty for the models used. But it may sometimes be interesting and fruitful to give old theses a new twist. Many of the ideas to be discussed are so much in the nature of common economic knowledge that it would be rather useless to fill pages with footnotes of references. We shall, therefore, confine ourselves to such references as may be of special help to the reader.[1]

27

The Institutional Framework of a Market Economy

THE subject suggested by the heading of this chapter is much more comprehensive than what we aim to take up here. What we are thinking of is merely a brief survey of the kinds of facts we have to deal with and the kinds of questions we have to ask if our goal is to explain the process of capital accumulation in a market economy. We think it is instructive and fruitful to regard a market economy not as identical with the whole subject matter of investment theory, but as *a particular organizational form* in which the accumulation process may take place.

1. One of the most comprehensive bibliographies on the subject of investment ever published is contained in a recent work by Pierre Dieterlen, *L'Investissement*, a volume in the series "Bilans de la connaissance Économique" (Paris, 1957). For books dealing more generally with investment theory in a market economy, the reader is referred to F. and V. Lutz, *The Theory of Investment of the Firm* (Princeton, 1951); and E. Schneider, *Investering og Rente* (Copenhagen, 1944).

I. Characteristic Features of a Decentralized Economy

The all-important fact in a decentralized economy is that, usually, the individual decision units have different preferences and objectives and, also, different ideas concerning how to go about satisfying human wants. But even more important, from the point of view of economic theory, is the unavoidable *interdependence* between the activities of the individual decision units. An individual in a modern society can accomplish practically nothing in the economic field except in co-operation with his fellow citizens. Some of this co-operation he creates voluntarily by his own positive actions, but most of it is there whether he likes it or not. In fact, he is often not aware of the many ways in which he is automatically tied to the economic activities of others. He may not fully realize the extent to which his own economic success depends on the preferences of his customers or competitors. When, in economic theory, we often rely on the assumption that the individual decision-maker acts *as if* he were independent, we do not do so because we think that this is how things really are. Quite the contrary, we rely on this "as-if" attitude precisely in order to show how it leads to a particular pattern of interconnection between the economic activities of all the decision-makers in the society.

The fact that the decision-makers are different does not, of course, mean that there is anything wrong about considering such variables as aggregate investment for society as a whole. It only means that this aggregate usually will be different from the one which any one of the decision-makers would have chosen if he were to direct the whole economy. The problem of summation becomes serious only if we want to use the sum to measure and compare the performance of *different kinds of organizational structures*. Thus, in studying macroeconomic models, we must remember that there is a great deal of difference between using the trick of reasoning *as if* the whole society does this or that and the assumption that the imaginary central directorate does what is "best" in the way of allocating resources, etc.

If we use some kind of centralized economy as a standard of comparison, we shall find that one of the most characteristic features of a market economy is the incompleteness of *communication* between the decision-makers. This is due, partly, to the fact that it is too formidable a task for the individual, or the small unit, to "know the whole market." But, in part, it is also due to the circumstance that the individual decision-makers may not want to reveal information about their plans of production or their price strategies. Nevertheless, some individuals will have more information than others. This will affect the meaning of such things as profit maximization. Lack of information may mean that the individual producers do not fully know their own production functions or the constraints they really ought to take into account in their adaptation.

The element of competition is fundamental. What is usually thought of in this connection is that the pressure of competition will force the producers to economize. But it also costs to compete, and it may pay for the individual producers to use resources to fight for a larger share of the market. It may even pay, from the individual's point of view, to spend resources in order to prevent others from producing efficiently. The legal framework of the market is, therefore, of decisive importance to the actual performance of a market economy.

If our task is to derive a theory of investment behavior of the firm, the possibilities of almost instantaneous *transfers* of capital bring a highly volatile element into our models. For a closed sector we have the stabilizing element that total capital can only be changed gradually. For the individual firm the "natural" constraint upon the time derivative of the stock of capital may be wholly absent. We may have to look for peculiar elements of inertia or particular institutional constraints in order to justify that investment of the firm should have the dimension of a continuous flow.

Finally, there is the problem to what extent the firm-structure of a society is a technological datum and to what extent it is a consequence of some kind of distribution of personal abilities among actual or potential entrepreneurs. The problem of the size distribution of firms is a field where economists do not know very much and where we may look hopefully to the sociologists for help.[1]

II. The Role of Money and Credit

We need not here dwell on the absolute necessity of money as a medium of exchange. But there are other functions of money that have a decisive influence on the process of capital accumulation.

The most obvious of these other functions is the use of money as a store of wealth. Unless paper money is counted as a liability of the issuing institution, the growth of money in circulation becomes a part of total savings, but not a part of the value of capital accumulation. The distinction is more than a conventional one. If people feel richer by the amount of money they hold, this may have a real influence on the rate of consump-

1. See, however, the recent interesting article by Herbert A. Simon and Charles P. Bonini, "The Size Distribution of Business Firms," *American Economic Review*, XLVIII, No. 4 (1958), 607–17.

tion and, therefore, on the rate of capital accumulation in society as a whole.

The possibility of using money as a store of wealth may affect, to some extent, the number and kind of people who become engaged directly in business, as entrepreneurs or as owners of productive capital.

This statement about money is certainly even more true when applied to credit. The modern credit mechanism tends greatly to loosen up the connection between ownership and entrepreneurial activity. In fact, if it were not for the possibilities of loans and credit, we should have, even in a market economy, a very strong constraint upon the growth of capital within the single firm.

The institution of contracts in money terms may introduce a new kind of income element in the calculations of the entrepreneur, the possible gains or losses due to the change in the money value of capital. This means that capital may be held for speculative purposes at the same time as it serves as a factor of production.

It is essential to realize that these effects cannot be "deflated away" by reckoning in constant dollars, or the like. Actual or prospective changes in the money value of capital enter in a very real way into investment decisions and may affect the volume, as well as the structure, of capital accumulation.

III. The Rate of Interest

We recall that in dealing with the closed, centralized economy we did not need to introduce the rate of interest explicitly. If the rate of interest is regarded as an expression of time preference, this element was hidden in the preference pattern through which the future is compared directly with the present. This phenomenon has been pointed out by other writers.[2] On this point one could raise a somewhat philosophical question: Consider three points in time, the present time t_0 and two future points in time t_1 and $t_2 > t_1$. Suppose that income or consumption at t_1 and t_2 are to be evaluated and compared *as seen from* t_0. For this purpose there does not seem to be need for any explicit rate of interest. But suppose a statement is to be made at t_0 concerning how the decision-makers think that they will evaluate and compare the situations of t_1 and t_2 when the time t_1 has been reached! For this purpose it is certainly not obvious that an explicit rate of interest would be a redundant variable.

Be this as it may, there is no question that in a market economy the organizational setting is such as to make the rate of interest a funda-

2. See T. Koopmans, *Three Essays on the State of Economic Science* (New York, 1957), pp. 113–14.

mental auxiliary parameter in the calculus of yields and profit. A positive rate of interest could be said to serve the purpose of preventing a something-for-nothing possibility that could otherwise appear through the process of borrowing money and buying income-yielding real capital. The idea that the rate of interest is a purely monetary phenomenon was certainly wiped out once and for all by Wicksell in his analysis of the cumulative process.

Perhaps no subject in the field of investment theory has been more debated than the role of the rate of interest. It will be one of our major objectives in what follows to try to clarify in what respect a direct relation between investment and the rate of interest can be assumed to exist.

IV. The Structure of Production

The idea that production is subject to rather definite technological constraints is one of the fundamental assumptions used in economic theory. And this assumption is undoubtedly sound enough. But there is a long chain of reasoning involved in transforming this general idea into the assumption of given production functions for the various kinds of commodities. The thread gets even thinner when we stretch the original idea into an assumption that each firm has its own, technologically given production function. In fact we know that, if this assumption were to be taken literally, it is a rather ridiculous one. There is, first, the obvious complication that practically no firm produces just one perfectly homogeneous commodity. Here we meet the ever-present problem of aggregation again. But there is a much deeper problem involved, namely, whether technological production functions can be assumed to make sense as something which would be independent of who is the manager. Can the assumption of a given technology be interpreted simply as a vast collection of actual or potential production functions? Does the action of establishing a firm simply mean picking a particular one of these functions? Such an assumption seems drastic, to say the least. And yet, this must come very close to our way of thinking in standard theories of the behavior of the firm, in the analysis of the "free-entry" problem, and in classical theories of general equilibrium.

Recent development in activity analysis and programing has made it possible to transform the assumptions of "given production functions" into something that is less drastic. Here the firm is faced with a large variety of activities which it can combine in various ways. There is no definite relation between inputs and outputs except in the form of certain *boundaries*. It is up to the firm to choose the combination of activities and the most efficient way of using available resources. That is, the firm must in a sense construct its own production function rather than just pick it up as a datum.

This more general theoretical framework, important as it is to have found it, does not alter the basic idea that there exists something like an impersonal, technological structure facing the entrepreneurs as a datum. Obviously this cannot be strictly correct. The coexistence of large and small firms, the difference in success of similar firms—are facts that cannot be denied. It is true that such differences may sometimes be quite natural—that they can be explained by differences in the constraints facing each firm. But in that case the constraints are certainly not of a purely technological nature. They are in part man-made, organizational, or perhaps of a purely personal nature. The assumption of adjustment to given constraints becomes rather sterile if we have to stretch it too far. We may be left with the rather trivial conclusion that an entrepreneur does what he does for some unknown reason.

What we have said above is not meant to discredit the general idea that firms act under given constraints and that their action is rational in some specific sense. In fact, we have to use this idea for everything that we do in the following analysis. We have to assume that there is a structure of firms, each with a given production function or set of technological constraints. But it is important to realize that, when we use such assumptions, this is a short-cut way of describing, implicitly, a very complicated organizational setting, a milieu in which what we are discussing takes place. Therefore, when we discuss effects of specific structural changes or changes in the "data" of the firm, we must judge carefully whether or not such changes would violate the very basis which we use as our framework of analysis.

On the other hand, a certain amount of boldness in making assumptions about the firm structure is needed in order that our analysis should not bog down in a hopeless maze of details. Suppose, for example, that a firm will buy its capital equipment from other firms if the price is below a certain level but will engage in its own production of such equipment if the price is higher. How should such a firm be classified, if we want to talk about a consumer goods industry and a producer goods industry? There are at least two ways out. Neither is perfect, but they may serve as approximations with variable success. One way is to split up the firm, artificially, into two separate firms. Another way is to assume that, in practice, there are not many such cases and that we can neglect them.

The problem of what kind of production structure a firm has is, of course, intimately tied up with the degree of integration that exists in any particular industry. The degree of integration affects the list of *input factors* that it is necessary to specify, in order to operate with the notion of a production function of the firm. The main problem here is how to treat inputs of raw materials, semimanufactured goods, and auxiliary non-durable means of production. In all that follows we shall consider only two kinds of inputs, capital and labor. This simplification can be interpreted in various ways. One interpretation is that enough vertical integration is assumed to make inputs from other sectors unimportant. Another interpretation is that the inputs of raw materials, etc. are necessarily proportional to output and, therefore, not subject to substitutional choice on the part of the firm's decision-makers. That is, such inputs could be considered as having constant cost per unit of output and could be subtracted from the unit price of output. The main reason why I feel justified in neglecting these problems in what follows is that I do not believe the inclusion of more details in this direction would really change the nature of the conclusions that we are trying to establish.

In trying to define a market structure we meet innumerable problems of this kind. Perhaps the best answer to many of them is that we should give thought to them, but not too much thought, lest we get confused.

V. What Is an "Investor"?

A theory of investment behavior must build on fairly definite ideas concerning the persons or institutions who are supposed to represent the decision-makers in this field. In the economic literature the notions of "investor" and "investment" have been used with a great many different meanings. Often "investment" means simply buying something for money whether it be a physical object, a security, or a promise of repayment. Then nearly everybody would be an investor, to some extent. It is certainly quite common to call the purchase of bonds or shares an act of investment and to call those who do this "investors."

We have previously used "investment" in a much more narrow sense, and we shall continue to do so. We define investment as acquisition of capital goods for productive purposes and investors as those who make decisions in this respect. That is, we think of the investor only as a person or decision unit who is responsible for the use of capital and for what happens to it. In fact, the investor will have to be a producer of some kind. We have no use for the idea of "investing money" unless the action involved can be identified with putting physical capital into some production process. Such things as the transfer of shares from one shareholder to another fall outside our notion of investment.

It may sometimes be difficult to say exactly who is the investor in a particular enterprise. If a firm borrows money from a bank to purchase machinery and if the firm has no other assets of its own, it is somewhat problematic whether we should say that the borrower is the investor or that the bank is. In most cases the person or institution who lends money to a producer will require, and get, some additional assurance of repayment and profit, apart from the value of the capital items that the borrower acquires for the borrowed money.

The structure of decision-makers in regard to acts of investment is indeed very complex, in particular if we are asked to identify the *persons* involved. The way we usually get around this difficulty is to use a great many overlapping cross-classifications of existing persons and institutions, one for each kind of economic decision-making, and to count those who make decisions of a particular kind as a group regardless of what other activities they engage in. Thus, in our case, we describe what we mean by investment and say that an investor is anybody making investment decisions.

Very complicated problems would arise in this connection if we were to go into the process of compromise decisions by a group of people with diverse opinions, unequal power, and unequal information. We shall not be able to make any effort of supplementing theory in this direction, although it might well be fundamental in the particular field of invest- ment behavior.

VI. Producers' Strategies

The behavior of producers will be influenced by two sets of circum- stances, their objectives, and the constraints under which the efforts to reach the objectives have to take place.

We shall, generally, assume that the objective of producers is to maximize profits under given prices of factors and product. This statement is, however, rather empty until one can specify more precisely how profit is defined. It is necessary to define what kind of elements go into profit calculations. It is also important to specify the length of the time interval over which profit calculations are extended. In general, it must be assumed that it is not only total profit, discounted in some way, that matters, but also its distribution over the period considered. We shall pay at least some attention to this problem in the following chapters.

We have already mentioned the problems of technological constraints. But there are the organizational constraints and, among these, the posi- tion of the producer in the market as far as his influence on prices is concerned. Here we have the situation that there are two kinds of constraints, viz., the factual ones and those conjectured by the producers. It is the conjectured ones that really matter. That is, what matters is what the producer *thinks* his influence on prices is. There may be quite a difference between these conjectured effects and the actual ones. But the producer may learn to change his conjectures in the light of facts. On the other hand, there is obviously, in many cases, a close connection between what actually happens and what the producer thinks will happen, because of the fact that conjectures determine actions.

Strictly speaking, an assumption of "many producers" is not sufficient to insure that their behavior would be based on the assumption that the influence on prices is negligible. If they happened to think, simultaneously, that this would not be so, their experience might confirm their conjectures. However, if the producers reason partially, the assumption that they would behave as "quantity adapters" is probably a sound one. We shall use this assumption as the basis of our analysis. We shall neglect problems of monopolies or monopolistic competition, not because these cases are not of fundamental importance, but because we think that the problems before us are quite big enough even without these complications. Also, it can probably be argued that in the capital market there are, in fact, many buyers and sellers and a good deal of competition. And it is the functioning of this market which is the main objective of our analysis in what follows.

28

The Individual Producer's Demand for Capital

IN Part II we found that capital in the sense of a stock of goods could enter into a production process in several different ways. We now want to study how a producer adjusts the amounts used of capital, of various types, when he is faced with given prices, or price expectations, and wants to maximize his net return.

I. CAPITAL FOR DIFFERENT PURPOSES

Essentially there will be two kinds of capital involved in any productive enterprise, namely, working capital and instruments of production. We have found that the relation between output and the amount of working capital may be complicated, due to variable "production starting" (cf. chaps. xi and xii). The amount of working capital may also be affected by such things as interest charges and maintenance cost, to the extent that it is technologically possible to economize with the amount of working capital in relation to the average rate of output.

However, in many—perhaps most—cases, it may be sufficiently accurate, as a first approximation, to regard the amount of working capital as roughly proportional to the volume of output. If this is the case, the operating cost of maintaining working capital will be a constant unit cost. For the purpose of studying the behavior of the producer we may then regard this cost as deducted from the unit price of his product. However, we must remember that working capital is still a part of total capital employed. An increase in output may require some investment in working capital, and this must be counted as part of total investment in the economy. The adjustment of stocks of working capital to a finite change in output may be the cause of violent fluctuations in the *rate* of investment.

Concerning instruments of production, it is a question to what extent such capital can be regarded as subject to marginal adjustment. First, there is the problem of indivisibility. Thus, it may be difficult to consider factory buildings as marginally adjusted. On the other hand, the producer can usually add to, or reduce, such fixed equipment. And he can choose between a great variety of tools and machinery. We do not think that the problem of indivisibility is as serious as it may seem, at any rate not when what we are looking for is only some approximate idea of producers' behavior. But there is also the difference between possible adjustments in the short run as against such possibilities in the long run. The problem of short-run immobility is certainly important, if we are looking for short-run effects of changes in prices and interest rates. Neglecting this difference may be interpreted in two ways: As an analysis of what *would* happen under greater mobility than we have in practice or as an analysis of what would happen over a sufficiently long period of adjustment. The latter interpretation is the more dubious one in a dynamic framework, because here the point may be precisely that things never settle down and that the basis for adjustments considered change while each adjustment is taking place. We must try to keep these things in mind in judging the degree of realism of the results to be derived below.

II. THE CASE OF A PERFECT CAPITAL MARKET

We shall begin by considering a pattern of producers' behavior which is absolutely drastic in its simplifying assumptions, but which, nevertheless, is well suited to throw sharp light upon what we regard as the fundamental problem of investment theory.

For this purpose, consider a producer who uses a particular kind of capital and no other variable factors of production. Let this product be x_t per unit of time, p_t the net price he assumes per unit of product, K_t the amount of capital employed, q_t the price per unit of capital, and ρ_t the (continuous) rate of interest under which he has to operate. Let us assume, as an illustration, that his production function is

$$x_t = \Phi(K_t). \tag{28.1}$$

For the sake of simplicity—in order not to blur the main point—we shall here assume that K depreciates at a constant rate γ per year. The current rate of profit, π_t, to be maximized can then be defined as

$$\pi_t = p_t x_t - \rho_t q_t K_t - \gamma q_t K_t. \tag{28.2}$$

We assume that the producer believes that the price- and interest-situation at the time of planning, t_0, is going to be the same for as long a period ahead as he is concerned about. For simplicity we omit the subscripts t_0 for prices and the interest rate. Suppose that the producer's "horizon" is $= \theta$. He wants to maximize discounted profit from t_0 to $t_0 + \theta$, that is

$$\int_{t_0}^{t_0+\theta} e^{-\rho(\tau-t_0)} \pi_\tau d\tau$$
$$= \int_{t_0}^{t_0+\theta} e^{-\rho(\tau-t_0)} [p\Phi(K_\tau) - q(\rho+\gamma)K_\tau] d\tau. \tag{28.3}$$

Since each part of this sum is independent of any other part, it is evident that we must have, as a necessary condition for maximum, that

$$p \frac{d\Phi}{dK} - q(\rho+\gamma) = 0 \qquad t_0 \leqq \tau \leqq t_0 + \theta. \tag{28.4}$$

(This can also be proved by ordinary calculus of variation.) Hence we find that if capital is perfectly mobile, it will be adjusted instantaneously at t_0, and *kept constant over the whole horizon θ.*

There is absolutely no room for any non-zero dK/dt in this structure, (except a possible discontinuous jump in K at $t = t_0$). No finite change in the amount of capital is demanded for any finite period after $t = t_0$ unless there is a change in the *data*, i.e., in prices and interest rates. However, is it certain that the entrepreneur absolutely will refuse to receive a stream of investment goods offered to him at the price q_{t_0}? This is the crucial point. Consider the following argument:

Suppose that the producer at time $t_0 + \Delta t$ would buy an amount of capital $k\Delta t$, in addition to the K which is optimal according to (28.4).

Let the K satisfying (28.4) be $\bar{K}$. Then we should have that his discounted profit would be

$$\int_{t_0}^{t_0+\Delta t} e^{-\rho(\tau-t_0)} \left[p\Phi(\bar{K}) - q(\rho+\gamma)\bar{K} \right] d\tau$$

$$+ \int_{t_0+\Delta t}^{t_0+\theta} e^{-\rho(\tau-t_0)} \left[p\Phi\bar{K} + k\Delta t \right) - q(\rho+\gamma)(\bar{K}+k\Delta t) \right] d\tau . \tag{28.5}$$

It is evident that this expression can be brought as close as we please to the profit of using $\bar{K}$ instead of $\bar{K} + k\Delta t$, by making Δt sufficiently small. But the limit of $(k\Delta t)/\Delta t$, which is capital added per unit of time, or *net investment* at t_0, is equal to k, which is assumed to be a constant. Hence, it is in a sense *quite arbitrary what the rate of investment is at* t_0, provided it does not last for any length of time.

The question now is how this can be interpreted in a more practical sense. If the producer is able to find the accurate value of $\bar{K}$ at t_0, and if all prices and the interest rate are going to stay constant, he will obviously not want to acquire any finite amount of additional capital after t_0 (except, of course, necessary replacement to keep $\bar{K}$ constant). Therefore, for all practical purposes, the conditions above determine a zero rate of net investment for this producer. On the other hand, it is possible to argue that if there is the slightest degree of arbitrariness, or uncertainty, about $\bar{K}$, then it is possible that $\dot{K}$ for short periods may be very large and fluctuate violently.

In fact, there would seem to be three typical cases that could occur with regard to the rate of investment at any given point in time: (1) It could be zero, (2) it could be large positive or negative, or (3) it could be indeterminate between plus and minus "infinity."

Suppose, for example, that the producer is of the cautious type, using somewhat less capital than what might conceivably be advantageous because he does not quite know what $\bar{K}$ should be. Then it might, e.g., be possible for a seller of investment goods to talk him into gradually buying a little more. However, in spite of such or similar possibilities, it is clear that any systematic positive "demand for net investment" over θ is out of the question if the conditions are as assumed. It is not meaningful within the "classical" framework above to say, as is done in many textbooks, that the producer may have a higher or a lower "demand for investment," depending on his profit. This could only be meaningful *before* equation (28.4) is fulfilled. But then the producer would not be investing because his profit is high, but because he is ignorant about the amount of capital that would give him the most profit. We would get some kind of trial-and-error investment, but it would be difficult to justify any systematic growth of capital. If such growth is in a sense the normal thing, it will have to be explained by some other kind of behavior pattern or other constraints.

III. THE DURABILITY PROBLEM

Suppose that our producer uses capital that has essentially a fixed lifetime. Then his depreciation expenditures will be different from what was assumed above. However, if we assume that he is operating in a perfect capital market, with perfect mobility of capital, his scheme of production adjustment will be similar to the one discussed for an open sector in chapter xxv. It will be quite irrelevant to his net profit whether he uses capital of long durability or short durability or whether he uses new or old equipment, as long as there is no difference in technical productivity of the various kinds of capital.

If the prices of the various categories of capital satisfy the law of indifference described in chapter xxv, the *value* of capital held by the producer will be quite arbitrary, and will have to be decided upon on other grounds than those related to maximizing net profit in the production process. If there is any kind of capital which is cheaper than it ought to be under the law of indifference, the producer will choose to operate with this particular kind only.

The situation is far more complicated if the producer can vary the intensity of use of the capital and thus influence its length of life. To illustrate the kind of problem that one gets into under such circumstances consider the following scheme.

Suppose that the producer is at time t_0 and plans for an indefinite future. He assumes that all prices and the interest rate will remain fixed indefinitely. We shall assume that he has a plan of *constant* factor inputs, and thus constant output, from t_0 on, in order not to have to deal with any proof that this would, under proper conditions, be the best he can do. Let his production function be

$$x = \Phi(K, N), \qquad (28.6)$$

where x is the rate of output, K the physical amount of capital and N labor. The price of x is p, the wage rate w.

Regarding K we shall suppose that the situation is as follows: The producer can buy only brand-new capital at any time. However, he can buy capital of varying durability. But once he decides on a particular kind in this respect, he must, by assumption, stick to this kind "forever." Let θ denote the durability property of a capital item. That is, θ is assumed to be a quality index, or "normal" life, of the item. But the property θ is not assumed to affect in any way the functioning of K

in equation (28.6). All capital is assumed to be equally good while it lasts. We assume that the producer is faced with a given *price curve* of capital, $q(\theta)$. It is reasonable to assume that $q(\theta)$ increases with θ.

The producer has two kinds of choices with regard to his use of capital. He can choose θ and he can decide on how fast he will actually wear out his capital. Let the actual wearing-out time he chooses be ω. It will depend on θ, but also on the amount of labor he puts into each unit of capital. In general, let us assume that ω is a function of the following kind:

$$\omega = \omega\,(K,\,N,\,\theta)\,, \qquad (28.7)$$

where, presumably, $\partial\omega/\partial K > 0$, $\partial\omega/\partial N < 0$, $\partial\omega/\partial\theta > 0$.

Finally, let ρ be the rate of interest. The discounted profit for all future will then be

$$\int_{t_0}^{\infty} e^{-\rho(\tau-t_0)}\,[p\Phi\,(K,\,N)\,-wN]\,d\,\tau - \Big[\sum_{0}^{\infty}{}_{i}\,q\,(\theta)\,e^{-\rho i\omega}\Big]K\,, \quad (28.8)$$

where the last term represents all present and future discounted capital expenditures. The producer can choose three things at t_0, viz., K, N, and θ. Once chosen, they will, by assumption, have to remain constant.

As necessary conditions for maximum of expression (28.8) we get

$$\frac{1}{\rho}\Big(p\,\frac{\partial\Phi}{\partial N}-w\Big)+\Big[\sum_{0}^{\infty}{}_{i}\,q\,(\theta)\,\rho i\,e^{-\rho i\omega}\Big]\frac{\partial\omega}{\partial N}\,K = 0 \qquad (28.9)$$

$$\frac{1}{\rho}\,p\,\frac{\partial\Phi}{\partial K}-\Big[\sum_{0}^{\infty}{}_{i}\,q\,(\theta)\,e^{-\rho i\omega}\Big]$$

$$\qquad\qquad\qquad\qquad\qquad\qquad\qquad\qquad (28.10)$$

$$+\Big[\sum_{0}^{\infty}{}_{i}\,q\,(\theta)\,\rho i\,e^{-\rho i\omega}\Big]\frac{\partial\omega}{\partial K}\,K = 0\,,$$

$$-\Big(\sum_{0}^{\infty}{}_{i}\,e^{-\rho i\omega}\Big)\frac{d\,q}{a\,\theta}\,K+\Big[\sum_{0}^{\infty}{}_{i}\,q\,(\theta)\,\rho i\,e^{-\rho i\omega}\Big]\frac{\partial\omega}{\partial\theta}\,K = 0\,. \quad (28.11)$$

Carrying out the summations, we can write these expressions as

$$p\,\frac{\partial\Phi}{\partial N}-w+\frac{q\,(\theta)\,\rho^2\,e^{\rho\omega}}{(e^{\rho\omega}-1)^2}\,K\,\frac{\partial\omega}{\partial N} = 0\,, \qquad (28.9\,a)$$

$$p\,\frac{\partial\Phi}{\partial K}-\frac{\rho q\,(\theta)}{1-e^{-\rho\omega}}+\frac{q\,(\theta)\,\rho^2\,e^{\rho\omega}}{(e^{\rho\omega}-1)^2}\,K\,\frac{\partial\omega}{\partial K} = 0\,, \qquad (28.10\,a)$$

$$\frac{d\,q}{d\,\theta}-\frac{\rho q\,(\theta)}{(e^{\rho\omega}-1)}\,\frac{\partial\omega}{\partial\theta} = 0\,. \qquad (28.11\,a)$$

Assuming that stability conditions are fulfilled, these results can be interpreted as follows:

In the equation (28.9a) the last member to the left is the marginal "tooling cost" of labor. It is an addition to the wage cost w. In equation (28.10a) the last member to the left represents "saving of machine strain" by using capital more liberally. The last equation shows that if it is possible to increase ω considerably for given amounts of N and K by spending more on θ, the price curve $q(\theta)$ has to rise sufficiently sharply to stop the extension of ω. It is seen that the producer will have to select K, N, and θ such that the eleasticity of the $q(\theta)$ curve is smaller than the partial elasticity of ω with respect to θ.

The conclusion that can be drawn from the model above is that even if the $q(\theta)$-curve satisfies some sort of law of indifference, as far as all capital users are concerned, the ω-function particular to our producer may lead him to a unique value of θ as his best choice. This shows that the formal law of indifference, which has been used so much in capital theory, becomes very problematic if durability is not a datum but a parameter of choice of the individual producer. This may be a stabilizing factor, as far as the *value* of capital used by each producer is concerned.

IV. The Producer's Response to Changes in the Rate of Interest

In chapter xxv we studied the fairly complicated relations that may exist between the rate of interest and the marginal productivity of capital. The results derived can be applied to a single firm, as well as to a large, but open, economy. It is, therefore, not necessary to repeat these results here. But some comments may be added regarding the effects of changes in the rate of interest in the simple model of producers' behavior discussed earlier in this chapter.

The meaning of the expression "sensitivity to the rate of interest" is not obvious. One could think of a reduction in the amount of capital used due to an increase in the interest rate. But one could also think of a reduction in net profit, or one could think of a fall in the value of capital in the hands of the producer. These effects are connected but could give different impressions of sensitivity, depending on the structure of the production process and on the kind of capital employed.

Consider the effects of alternative levels of the rate of interest, ρ, at l_0, assuming prices of capital and of the final product to remain the same. The effects can be studied from equation (28.4). We see here that, if ρ is increased, K will, presumably, be reduced to some extent, but less so the larger is $d^2\Phi/dK^2$, in absolute value. But K will be reduced the more the higher is its price in relation to the price of the product. Profits will fall all the more the larger is the amount of capital used before the increase in the rate of interest.

Suppose that we ask, by how much the price of capital, q, would have to fall, in order that the producer should use exactly the same amount of capital as before, at the higher rate of interest. For this to be the case the expression $q(\rho + \gamma)$ would have to remain constant. This would be the case if q were a function of ρ such that

$$\frac{dq}{d\rho}\frac{\rho}{q} = -\frac{\rho}{\rho + \gamma}. \qquad (28.12)$$

Thus, the price of capital would have to fall by a larger percentage the smaller is γ, i.e., the more durable is the capital employed. If the producer had the capital and had no way of getting rid of it, he would have to take the capital loss, and keep on producing as much as before. If the market price fell according to equation (28.12), he could replace his capital gradually at a lower price.

Effects of immobility will certainly be important. They could be studied in the same way as was done in chapter xxv.

V. Speculative Elements in the Holding of Capital

A producer must pay attention, not only to the price of capital in relation to its productivity and its interest cost, but also to the possibility of price *changes* over his planning period. There is, of course, a great difference in this respect between the case of perfectly mobile capital in a perfect capital market and the case where the producer has to tie himself to immobile—and practically unsellable—capital. But it is not so that a producer can free himself from losses due to price falls even in a perfect capital market. This he could do only if he knew *the time* at which the price will change. Otherwise, it is always possible that the price might fall while he is holding the capital.

In the case of immobile capital, the producer cannot avoid the loss even if he knows the time when capital prices will fall, and by how much. His adjustment process may then be rather complicated. He may choose to delay replacement and gradually use less capital until the time when the price of capital will fall and then adjust the total stock of capital upward again by a lump purchase at the reduced price.

Let us consider in some detail the simpler case of a perfect capital market with mobile capital. And consider the producer whose behavior was described by equations (28.4) in the case of stationary prices. Suppose that, at t_0, the price of capital, q, is rising at the rate $\dot{q}/q$ per unit of time, and that the producer feels certain that this rise is going to continue indefinitely. Then the immediate effect upon his use of capital will obviously be as if he were faced with a lower rate of interest, $\rho - (\dot{q}/q)$. He will, therefore, adjust his stock of capital according to

$$p \frac{d\Phi}{dK} - \left(\rho - \frac{\dot{q}}{q} + \gamma\right)q = 0 . \qquad (28.4a)$$

He will then presumably be led to start out with a larger K than if $\dot{q}$ were zero. But he is going to reduce his employment of capital gradually as it becomes more expensive. It is assumed here that he will calculate interest charges according to the current value of all his capital.

It might here look as if the relative rate of increase in capital prices at t_0 could even be larger than ρ, as long as it is not larger than $\rho + \gamma$. However, if the price increase outweighs ρ, something else is going to happen. If capital could be stored with little or no depreciation, the producer may turn into a pure speculator, holding capital for the purpose of reselling it with profit. There would have to be a restriction on his credit, or some other constraint, in order to limit his amount of capital.

Suppose that at t_0 the producer could also choose γ, i.e., the durability of his capital. Let us assume that capital prices are "constant" in the sense that, if $q_t(\gamma)$ is the price of capital with a rate of depreciation equal to γ, we must have, at any time,

$$(\rho + \gamma)\, q_t(\gamma) = A_t = \text{a constant at } t . \qquad (28.13)$$

Let the expected rate of increase in capital prices be $\dot{q}_t(\gamma)/q_t(\gamma)$ which then will be independent of γ. Assume that the increase $\dot{q}_t(\gamma)/q_t(\gamma)$ is expected to be constant $= \beta$. Then the expected marginal cost of the producer will be

$$(\rho + \gamma - \beta)\, q_t(\gamma) = A_{t_0} \frac{\rho + \gamma - \beta}{\rho + \gamma}\, e^{\beta(t - t_0)} . \qquad (28.14)$$

We see that this marginal cost will be the lower the more durable is the capital equipment chosen. Thus the producer would choose as durable equipment as possible, or the most durable equipment available at consistent prices.

If a constantly falling price level for capital were expected, we should have exactly the opposite conclusion, i.e., γ would be chosen as large as possible.

Consider next the case where the producer, planning at t_0, believes firmly that there is going to be a sudden fall in capital prices sometime in the future, but he does not know *when*. He is then faced with the possibility of a sudden capital loss. If he has no idea whatsoever concerning the point of time that this might take place, he obviously would not start holding any capital at t_0 at all. Because, no matter how high his current rate of profits as a producer might be, if the finite drop in capital prices comes sufficiently soon, he is going to lose out. On the other hand, if he thinks he is safe for a certain period after t_0, he will proceed as if nothing would happen and stop the production process in time to avoid the loss.

We see from these considerations that there may be some risk in employing capital in a productive process—even in the most perfect capital market.

The situation is quite different in regard to a possible future drop in the product price p, provided this drop does not at the same time lead to a drop in q. If and when the product price falls, the producer can just reduce output by selling off capital. His loss will be that of not being able to continue earning as much as before.

This is just one of many possible examples of the fundamental difference between the economic problems of stocks as compared to those of flows.

29

Investment Behavior of the Firm

F ROM the preceding analysis it is clear that there is no particular reason for any continuous demand for investment by a producer, unless there is a gradual change in the *data* underlying his decisions or a gradual change in his own behavior pattern.

Let us first look at certain changes in the producer's data which could lead him to have a lasting, positive or negative, flow of investment.

I. INVESTMENT AS A RESULT OF
CHANGING CONDITIONS

An obvious cause of gradual changes in the optimal amount of capital could be a more or less continuous change in the production function itself. Technological progress could make it profitable to use more capital (but the effect could also be in the direction of less capital). In this connection it is essential that the producer does not know everything far into the future, otherwise he might want to make a once and for all adjustment of the amount of capital to the "best" future technique. Of course, there is no need for the theorist to worry about such a possibility.

But it is certainly not obvious that technological progress would lead to a desire for more capital. The result could, for example, be the use of less durable capital, or a more intensive utilization of capital. However, the case of capital remaining at a constant volume as an optimum is probably unlikely—i.e., it is unlikely that we should have a steady zero rate of investment.

More interesting, from an analytical point of view, is the effect of gradually falling prices of capital. Here we must distinguish between the case where the producer anticipates such a development and the case where he always projects current prices whatever they are.

In the last case the result is simple. Consider the equilibrium condition (28.4). Suppose that q is a function of time, $q(t)$, while p and ρ remain constant. Assume further that the producer pays no attention to $\dot{q}(t)$. Then we find from (28.4) that the rate of change of capital will be

$$\frac{dK}{dt} = \frac{(\rho + \gamma)\, \dot{q}\,(t)}{p\, \dfrac{d^2\Phi}{dK^2}}. \tag{29.1}$$

If we could show reasons why $\dot{q}(t)$ should remain negative, this could be an investment theory "explaining" a positive rate of investment (assuming $d^2\Phi/dK^2 < 0$). As it stands, it is just a formal relation between investment and the price of capital.

The case where the producer would anticipate the changes in q is more complicated. He may anticipate a falling $q(t)$, but he may not anticipate it correctly. Suppose, for example, that he behaves according to equation (28.4a), readjusting his plan continuously, but always on the basis of the current $\dot{q}(t)$. Then we should have, from equation (28.4a)

$$\frac{dK}{dt} = \frac{(\rho + \gamma)\, \dot{q}\,(t) - \ddot{q}\,(t)}{p\, \dfrac{d^2\Phi}{dK^2}}. \tag{29.2}$$

Thus, if the price of capital would fall, investment would be positive, provided the price did not fall with a too accelerated speed.

In the economic literature there has been much concern about the relation between the rate of interest and the demand for investment. In the case where the producer can adjust his production process instantaneously in a perfect capital market, there is obviously no room for any relation between the rate of interest and the demand for investment.

When the rate of interest and the other data are constant, the demand for additional capital is zero (or perhaps somewhat indefinite) *regardless of what the level of interest is.* If there is any relation between investment and the interest rate, it must be the *rate of change* in the interest rate that matters.

Thus, from (28.4), we get (provided the producer looks only at the current situation and does not speculate in future price or interest changes),

$$\frac{dK}{dt} = \frac{(\rho + \gamma)\,\dot{q} + \dot{\rho}q - \dfrac{d\Phi}{dK}\,\dot{p}}{p\,\dfrac{d^2\Phi}{dK^2}}. \tag{29.3}$$

Equation (29.3) describes what might gradually happen to the amount of capital if the producer is always adjusting his production process according to (28.4). Since the denominator to the right in equation (29.3) is assumed to be negative, we see that both $\dot{q}$ and $\dot{\rho}$ have a negative effect upon the rate of capital accumulation while $\dot{p}$, of course, has a positive effect.

As has been shown before, these effects will be somewhat different if the changes in the data are anticipated by the producer.

II. The General Idea of "Delayed Adjustment"

The basis of this idea is the assumption that, even if the producer would like to have such optimum conditions as (28.4) fulfilled, he may be slow in carrying out adjustments, for a variety of reasons. One reason is that it requires some time simply to make a decision and to take action. Another reason may be that the producer is not quite sure about the form of his own production function and that he seeks the optimum by trial and error. A third reason, and an important one, may be that it involves higher cost to make quick adjustments than slow adjustments. One fact is important about such adjustment hypotheses, if they be tenable: *They will not, in general, imply any sustained rate of capital accumulation,* unless the difference between actual and "desired" amount of capital gets a new "push" now and then, by spontaneous changes in prices or in the rate of interest.

It is of no use to say that there may be "increasing" return, i.e., that $d^2\Phi/dK^2$ in (28.4) may be positive or zero, because equation (28.4) does not make sense as an optimum condition in this unstable case.

Of course, there is always the question of changing technology. The producer may be chasing this by means of investment without even catching up with the optimal amount of capital.

There is, on the whole, something rather dubious about adjustment equations, from the point of view of strict economic theory. We must remember that such equilibrium conditions as (28.4) are derived on the basis of a certain pattern of behavior of the producer. When we introduce adjustment equations, we do in fact assume that the producer has a different behavior pattern or that he is faced with different constraints. Clearly, if we want an adjustment equation to make sense, we must make sure that the behavior it describes is not in any fundamental contradiction to the meaning of the goal (like (28.4)) at which the adjustments are aimed.

In the case where the firm uses absolutely immobile and unsellable capital, it is, however, possible to give rather definite meaning to a pattern of delayed adjustment. Suppose there is a shift in prices, or in the interest rate, after which the producer would want a different amount of capital. Let us, first, assume that, as a result of the shift, the condition (28.4) would require more capital. Suppose that this can only be obtained by new capital being *produced*. In Part II we have seen that the production of any finite amount of capital is necessarily time-consuming, and that the cost of production may vary with the time spent on producing a given volume. It may then be that our producer, who wants more capital, is faced with a price curve for the additional amount of capital, such that the price depends on the time of delivery. It may be very expensive to get a speedy delivery, less so if he is willing to wait. But he is losing profits in the meantime. It is easy to visualize that there may be an optimal period of delivery, that is, an optimal delay of adjustment. Such a model could be formalized, but we see no particular gain in doing this here.

Suppose, next, that the desire is for a reduction of the amount of capital. This can, under the assumptions made, only be achieved by waiting for the capital to *depreciate*. If the producer can vary the rate of depreciation, the process may become very complicated, from an analytical point of view. But the general idea is simple enough. The nature of the adjustment process may depend on whether it is set in motion by a rise in the price of capital or by a fall in the product price. In the first case, he may want to use more labor than before, and thus perhaps be able to wear out his capital faster. In the second case he may want to reduce the amount of labor employed in order to produce less, but this may slow down the most economical rate of depreciation.

Such adjustment processes as these may be important in the explanation of short-run investment demand, but they cannot, it seems, serve to explain any systematic growth process, unless we can justify that "something will happen" all the time to make the adjustment processes a normal thing. We shall see in chapter xxxi that a sustained accumulation process can, in fact, be explained in a different, and, I think, more fundamental way. Our purpose in the present and the following chapter is just to clarify the role of the individual investor as a decision-maker in the whole machinery of a dynamic market equilibrium.

III. THE DEMAND FOR REPLACEMENT

The process of replacement is often regarded as simpler to explain than the process of net investment. Replacement is thought of as something automatic: Capital "must" be maintained. I think that this, somewhat arbitrary, distinction stems from a confusion of two things; on the one hand, that depreciation charges "must" be deducted from revenues in order to get net *income* and, on the other hand, the question of the decision to employ a certain amount of capital in a production process. It does not follow that a producer "must" replace his capital as it wears out. The fundamental decision is what the future time series of the volume of capital should be as seen from a certain point in time when plans are made. The rate at which the capital will depreciate, both in value and as a factor of production, plays a role in decisions concerning the amount of capital to be used at any time. Capital must be replaced if it is to remain constant, but it is equally true and trivial that capital must be more than replaced in order to grow!

However, if the rate of depreciation is technically given, one could, perhaps, make a point of the fact that depreciation is a datum for the producer. It is an interesting datum because it is a *flow* term related to the holding of a certain stock of capital. One important practical aspect of this is that, even under stationary conditions with regard to the amount of capital, the existence of a firm employing capital means some constant employment for firms producing capital goods.

This is not saying that decisions to replace and decisions to change the volume of capital may not often be regarded by the producer as somewhat different things. Probably he makes decisions to change the amount of capital less often than decisions to replace, the latter being regarded more as a routine matter. However, we cannot escape the conclusion that, if replacement is a routine matter, this is due to the fact that a decision has been made, and is maintained, to hold capital constant.

IV. LIMITED CREDIT AS A CONSTRAINT UPON THE USE OF CAPITAL

One important assumption in the foregoing analysis has been that the producer is always able to buy capital if he wants to, whether or not he himself has any liquid assets. That is, we have assumed unlimited possi-

bilities of obtaining credit. In practice there are, of course, some constraints upon his ability to borrow. These constraints may be in the form
of a higher "personal" interest rate charged to particular borrowers.
Or there may be particular, strict conditions upon the rate of repayment
of a loan.

To illustrate the possible effects of such constraints, consider a producer
who has the production function (28.1), and is about to start production
at $t = t_0$ by buying capital. Suppose that his optimal behavior would
be described by (28.4), if there were no credit constraints. Assume that
he has to borrow all the money required to buy his initial capital. Assume
further that he only has to pay the market rate of interest ρ but that there
is a required repayment plan, including interest. Suppose that according
to this plan he has to pay out a flow of expenses from t_0 to t_1, equal
to $u(\tau)\ qK(t_0) +$ current interest on the remainder, such that at t_1
he has no more debt. And assume that he has no other means available
for this process, or for any other purchases, than his own revenues.
Assume also that he cannot sell capital. Suppose that he has an "infinite"
horizon and that he expects prices and interest rates to remain constant.
This means that he has to maximize his discounted net profit defined by

$$\int_{t_0}^{\infty} e^{-\rho(\tau - t_0)} \{ p\Phi[K(\tau)] - (\rho + \gamma)\, qK(\tau) \}\, d\tau, \quad (29.4)$$

subject to the constraints

$$\dot{K}(t) \geqq -\gamma K(t) \quad (29.5)$$

and

$$\int_{t_0}^{t} e^{\rho(t-\tau)} \left(p\Phi[K(\tau)] - qK(t_0) \left\{ u(\tau) \right. \right.$$

$$\left. \left. + \rho \left[1 - \int_{t_0}^{\tau} u(s)\, ds \right] \right\} - q[\gamma K(\tau) + \dot{K}(\tau)] \right) d\tau \geqq 0 \quad (29.6)$$

for every $t \geqq t_0$.

We have here assumed that he can earn interest by lending any accumulated revenue. If $u(\tau)$ is "liberal," the constraint (29.6) may be redundant.
Then he will buy capital according to (28.4). Otherwise he may not be
able to make this optimal adjustment at once (i.e., at t_0). It is fairly obvious how he has to proceed in this latter case. He will want current
profit always to be as high as possible at any time. At each point in time,
including t_0, he has to choose his capital as close to the optimal amount
as possible, but looking ahead to see that he can meet constraint (29.6),

remembering (29.5). As a special case, the repayment plan may be pro-hibitive. That would be the case if, for no value of $K(t_0)$, he could meet the first instalment on his loan, or more generally if there is no feasible series, $K(\tau)$, such that (29.6) is fulfilled. On the other hand, if there is an admissible series, $K(\tau)$, during the period t_0 to t_1, it will, in general, be possible for the producer to work up toward the optimal amount of capital.

Another example of this kind might be the case where the producer starts out having no assets of his own, and, therefore, perhaps, having to face a higher rate of interest. If he accumulates part of his profits, and thus perhaps becomes a better risk, his interest charges may go down (or he may repay part of his high interest loan). This may induce him to increase his capital gradually, because his marginal cost goes down.

Such constraints could obviously lead to a particular pattern of investment behavior of the firm. And such cases may be important, al-though, perhaps, less interesting from the point of view of producers' behavior.

30

The Supply of Investment Goods

In the general, neoclassical framework of market theories the sector of investment-goods *producers* seems, somehow, to have been lost or forgotten. We have static theories, like that of the Austrian school, showing alternative equilibrium levels of the amount and composition of capital. But there is not much theory to be found on the *sustained activity* of the investment-goods producers. It is as if these producers pop up for the purpose of changing the amount of capital, in a not too well-described dynamic process, and then disappear again.

Now, there is no reason in the world why there should be any mystery about the continued existence of firms producing investment goods and trying to sell these goods. It is probably the hard-boiled theory of the roundabout method of production which is to blame for the asymmetry in dealing with consumer goods industries as compared to the investment goods industries. The idea of roundaboutness leads to the natural conclusion that there is, actually, only one kind of production, the output of finished consumer goods, and that the production of capital goods is only an internal part of the process.

This idea of the roundabout process may give a good deal of insight into the production mechanism as a whole. But in a market theory, once we operate with the notions of firms, there is no reason why we should treat the firms producing investment goods as essentially different from those producing consumer goods. Nor is there any mystery about the selling of such goods. The idea of "derived" demand is only an invention of economic theory, for the purpose of understanding the economic process of a community. To producers, there is only the buying, the processing, and the selling of goods no matter what these goods are for.

It is true that the explanation of the demand for investment goods is an exceedingly complex problem. But there is no problem about the existence of a capital goods market where such goods can be sold, at certain prices. The real problem is to explain why there tends to be a sustained demand for investment goods. There is no problem about the existence of firms that produce such goods at the market price, if this price is not lower than the cost involved.

The question of what *strategic type* the firms in the capital goods industries belong to is, however, a very important one. For many firms in this sector, it would probably be all right to assume that they behave like quantity adapters, producing to maximize their profit at given market prices. This means that they have to take part in competitive selling of their goods, *after* the goods are produced, so to speak. In capital-goods industries producing large and costly units, requiring considerable time for completion, the usual procedure is, probably, to produce to order, rather than the strategy of trying to sell in the market. However, there may not be any great difference between the actual output of such firms and the optimal volume of output of firms which simply produce for the market, as long as there is no lack of orders. The formal difference may be that firms producing to order can only decide their maximum output at given prices, not their actual output. As long as their output is below that which would maximize profit, their supply is in a sense a datum parameter in their behavior pattern.

This structure of somewhat passive capital-goods producers may, however, become greatly modified by the existence of *buffer stocks* of capital goods, held either by the producers themselves or by separate middle men or speculators.

I. The Supply of Investment Goods in a
Perfect Capital Market

There is one particular feature of the investment-goods industry which is somewhat different from that of the consumer-goods industry: the fact that the price of *product* in the former happens to be the same as the price of one of the *input factors*. It is true that the individual investment-goods producer usually produces only particular kinds of capital goods and that he may be using quite different kinds of capital as a factor of production. But this does not alter the basic fact that, on the average, the product price and the factor price are prices of the same kind of things. Of course, there is also a connection between the price of consumer goods and wages. But this connection is the result of an adjustment process in the market. The connection is not as direct as between the price of investment goods and the price of capital used in producing these goods.

Consider a capital-goods producer whose rate of instantaneous output is k, as given by

$$k = \Psi(K, N), \qquad (30.1)$$

where N is his level of employment and K his capital. (Since the process here is assumed to be instantaneous we omit reference to time.) We assume that Ψ has general properties of decreasing return. Suppose that wages are constant and equal to w; while q, also constant, is the price of capital; ρ, the rate of interest; and γ, the (constant) rate of depreciation. If the capital producer maximizes current profit, $qk - wN - \rho qK - \gamma qK$, behaving as a quantity-adapter, the necessary conditions become

$$\frac{\partial \Psi}{\partial N} = \frac{w}{q}; \qquad (30.2)$$

$$\frac{\partial \Psi}{\partial K} = \rho + \gamma. \qquad (30.3)$$

We shall assume that ordinary stability conditions are fulfilled. Thus, the marginal productivity of capital, in equilibrium, will not depend on the price q. The amount of capital employed will, however, in general depend on q, by equation (30.2).

The situation becomes different if the producer takes account of expectations concerning the price of capital. His current profit function may then be $qk - wN - \rho qK - \gamma qK + \dot{q}K$, so that, instead of equation (30.3), we get

$$\frac{\partial \Psi}{\partial K} = \left(\rho + \gamma - \frac{\dot{q}}{q}\right). \qquad (30.4)$$

(The reason why the rate of change of prices does not affect "real marginal revenue" [the left-hand side of equation (30.4)] is that we have assumed no lag between inputs and output, and that k is a *flow* term, while K is a *stock* term.)

If the producer operates in a perfect capital market, he is faced with consistent capital prices as previously defined (cf. chap. xxviii). This means that, if no price expectations are involved, he will be indifferent to the age- and durability-composition of his capital. In this respect his position will be of the same nature as that of a producer of consumer goods.

However, the producer of capital goods may have considerable choice concerning the durability properties of his *output k*. Even if he is faced with a perfect capital market, both as far as his product and his employed capital are concerned, this does not mean that he is indifferent to what kind of capital he *produces*. His production function will probably be such that the cost of producing one degree of durability will differ from that of producing another degree of durability. And these costs may differ in a way which is not the same as the difference between consistent prices in the capital market. Let ω denote a measure of durability of new capital equipment, while k measures simply number of units of output. We assume that all units are equally good, as a factor of production, while they last. It may be that our capital goods producer has a particular production function of the form

$$k = \Psi(K, N, \omega).$$ 	(30.5)

Suppose that consistent unit prices of new capital in the perfect capital market are given by $q(\omega)$. Then the producer may find that his profit varies with ω. Regarding the function $q(\omega)$ as a datum, he will want to maximize his profit also with regard to ω. Clearly, if the market data change over time, output, k, as well as its durability property, may change.

II. Lag in the Production Function for Capital Goods

The production of any finite amount of output is necessarily time-consuming, as pointed out in Part II. In the capital-goods industries this is, of course, particularly important. Actually, the average time lag between inputs and output will depend, not only on the volume of output, but also on its variations over time. This connection may be quite complicated, as shown in Part II. Therefore, if we say that there is a *constant* average lag between the input of factors N and K and the output k, this will, at best, be only a rough approximation. In the capital-goods industries this is, nevertheless, undoubtedly better than to consider inputs and outputs as simultaneous. If, for example, the production function is like (30.5), but with lags, we could have, as an approximation,

$$k_{t+\theta} = \Psi\left(K_{t+\theta_1},\, N_{t+\theta_2},\, \omega_{t+\theta}\right), \qquad (30.5a)$$

where θ, θ_1, and θ_2 represent average lags. The dating of ω as $t + \theta$ refers the durability property to the finished capital goods it applies to. The *decision* concerning ω would usually have to take place at t, on the basis of existing prices, wages, and interest rate—or expectations concerning these data over the period θ.

If the production function is of the type (30.5a), an additional cost element comes into the picture, viz., interest charges and, possibly, depreciation charges on goods in process. The value of goods in process will depend on the cost of raw materials (which in the foregoing we have implicitly assumed to be proportional to output). There will also be the value of incorporated labor cost and incorporated capital cost. In connection with these cost elements there may also be speculative gains or losses due to price- and interest-charges. Any bookkeeper will know that it is extremely difficult to allocate these various charges to the items of finite output to which they properly belong. In fact, it is almost certain that, in the capital-goods industries, the maximization of profit will have to be made on some average basis. It may be more important for a capital producer to be relatively sure that he will have *some* profits over a certain period of time than to try to find the exact profit maximum.

This behavior could be taken into account by assuming some kind of formal profit maximization under given prices, but using "cautious" levels for these prices as data rather than simply current prices or loosely expected prices.

If the capital producer works on the basis of orders, he may know his future gross revenues (assuming agreed prices). But he may still not know his costs. If he also is able to contract for the inputs, he may succeed in safeguarding himself, but in return he will probably have to forego some possible gains.

All this would take us deep into the theory of risk and uncertainty. I do not feel that I could have much to offer in that direction. But what has already been said is sufficient for one conclusion that is very important for the following: There may obviously be a rather loose connection between the current level of capital prices and the *starting* of productive activity in the capital-producing industries. The time lags in the production functions of these industries are absolutely essential in this connection. Even if current prices in the capital market would pay for a considerable amount of output of capital goods, the expected future prices may be such as to make the producers of capital goods very hesitant (or very eager, as the case may be).

III. BUFFER STOCKS OF CAPITAL GOODS

Some capital items, like buildings and constructions, cannot very well be stocked. But many kinds of tools and equipment can, of course, be held in stock. If the producer of capital goods holds such stocks himself, e.g., in proportion to his average output, he can smooth his output. The cost involved will have to be added to the other costs. But the holding of such stocks means, in fact, that the average time lag between production starting and final sale becomes even longer, with an additional speculative element involved.

The same can be said about the holding of stocks of raw materials.

Our conclusion concerning the supply of capital goods will, therefore, be to emphasize something which is well known: The high vulnerability of the capital-goods producer in a world of uncertainty. In particular, if he produces large units of capital, involving a lengthy process, he has nearly all the types of risks which any market participant could have. He risks value losses on his capital. He risks losses on the stock of goods in process. He risks losses on stocks of raw materials and finished products. Of course, we could also say "gains" instead of losses in all these instances.

However, in spite of these properties of the capital-goods industries we want to maintain what was said earlier in this chapter concerning a permanent capital-goods industry. It is unreasonable, and in fact quite unrealistic, to assume that the capital producing firms are, as it were, some kind of *ad hoc* institutions. What interests us even more than the possibilities of instability in these industries is the fact that, on the average, they may be assumed to have an output which can easily exceed total depreciation of capital in the economy. It is this phenomenon which is the key to an understanding of the process of sustained capital accumulation in a market economy.

31

Investment and General Equilibrium

In the introduction to this study we pointed out the lack of a basic market theory of investment. We have theories of supply and demand in the consumer goods market which plow deep into axioms of behavior and their consequences, theories which possess considerable formal elegance. In the theory of investment, on the other hand, all sorts of loose hypotheses of behavior have been advanced, leading to assumed behavior patterns that have a sad tendency to disintegrate and to be replaced by new ones within relatively short periods of time.

This state of affairs may be due to the nature of the subject matter itself. One may feel that a formal investment theory in a perfect capital market, with a perfectly rational behavior as its base, would mean to start very far away from reality. On the other hand, it is certainly tempting to look for such a formal theory. I think that it is relatively simple to derive one. I hope to show this in the present chapter. Moreover, I shall try to show that a formal market theory of investment actually demonstrates very clearly how sensitive the rate of investment may be to disturbing elements, such as uncertain price expectations and the like. I, therefore, think that a formal theory of the "normal" investment process in a market may be a good basis for developing more realistic theories.

I. THE GENERAL LAW OF INDIFFERENCE OF CAPITAL PRICES

We have repeatedly referred to—and made use of—this "law," in various forms. It is of fundamental importance in a formal market theory of investment. We want to sum up the main conclusions that follow from this law and some useful corollaries that can be derived.

The basis of the whole idea is that capital as a factor of production is defined in physical units and that such units have a well-defined market price. Two capital units can differ in various ways. They can be different in the sense that, if their places in a production function were interchanged, the production result would be changed. In that case they are *different factors of production.* As a result of a market equilibrium mechanism certain price ratios may be established between such different factors of production. But this is *not* what we mean by the law of indifference of capital prices. The law of indifference of capital prices refers to units of capital that are *perfect substitutes* in any production function as far as the effect upon current output is concerned. Such units of capital can differ in regard to durability and cost of maintenance. And such differences can be due to the units having different durability properties "built in" when produced, or because of different in age.

The law of indifference of capital prices states that, for units of capital that are equivalent in any production function, the prices in a perfect capital market, without elements of price expectations or the like, can differ only because of differences in the durability properties. The formulas (25.7) and (25.12) express this law in special forms.

Consider, in particular, the set of consistent capital prices defined by (25.12). This formula defines the price of a capital unit of age τ in relation to the price of new capital of original durability θ. If this relation between prices of all age groups of capital is fulfilled, the marginal cost of using capital is given by the coefficient $\rho q_0/(1 - e^{-\rho\theta})$ in (25.10*b*), regardless of the age composition of capital used by any "small" producer. But this law of indifference can be extended further. Let $q_0(\theta, t)$ denote the price of *new* capital of durability θ at time t. Then the expression $\rho\, q_0\,(\theta,\, t)/(1 - e^{-\rho\theta})$ must be independent of θ. Let the price of new capital of "infinite" durability be $q_0(\infty, t)$. Then we must have

$$\frac{\rho\, q_0\,(\theta,\, t)}{1 - e^{-\rho\theta}} = \rho\, q_0\,(\infty,\, t)\,. \qquad (31.1)$$

Thus if the law of indifference of capital prices holds throughout, there will be *only one unknown price of capital to be determined by the required equality between producers' demand for capital and the available total stock of capital at any time.*

One should note carefully that this strong law of indifference is not something that must necessarily be true "by definition," as it were. It is the consequence of a formidable assumption about the actual performance of a perfect capital market with perfect mobility of capital between individual users of capital, as well as between holders of stocks of new capital equipment and ultimate users. We have already seen that if the various participants in this market have different price expectations, or different expectations concerning the rate of interest, this would be sufficient to upset the universal law of indifference (cf. chap. xxv). But for a market where expectations play no role, the law of indifference is a powerful means of simplifying a general equilibrium theory.

The formulation in equation (31.1) refers to capital items with a given lifetime. But it can easily be extended to other kinds of durability properties. Suppose, for example, that physical depreciation of capital as a factor of production is simply proportional to the amount of capital, regardless of its age. Let $q_\gamma^*(t)$ denote the price of t, of a unit of capital that depreciates at the rate of γ per unit of time. Then the expression $(\rho + \gamma)\, q_\gamma^*(t)$, which is the marginal cost of capital at t, must be independent of γ. If $q(t)$ is the price of capital of "infinite" durability (i.e., $\gamma = 0$), we must have

$$q_\gamma^* \, (t) = \frac{\rho q \, (t)}{\rho + \gamma}, \tag{31.2}$$

which determines $q_\gamma^*(t)$ for every value of γ when $q(t)$ is known.

If we have the case where the rate of depreciation—or the actual lifetime—of capital can be varied by the producer using the capital, the situation becomes more complicated. The parameters θ and γ will no longer be fixed properties of the various physical capital units as such. Then there can be no law of indifference of capital prices which is independent of the set of production functions where the capital may be employed. However, to the extent that it is practically difficult, or uneconomical, for the users of capital to vary the rate of depreciation very much, the law of indifference, as stated above, may still be a fair approximation. It may also be possible to deal with this problem by assuming that, in order to have really different durabilities, the capital units must be different in some technological sense. They could perhaps be regarded as different factors of production, each with a constant durability. Then the law of indifference could hold within each category of capital, while there would be as many capital prices to be determined by equating supply to demand as there were kinds of capital regarded as different factors of production.

II. A Simple Model of "Dynamic Equilibrium"

We shall present a greatly simplified determinate market model which, nevertheless, will serve to bring out the essential features of a general equilibrium theory where investment is involved.

For this purpose we shall use the simplifying device of an aggregative formulation of those parts of the theory which we are not particularly interested in for our purpose here. We shall assume that there is a number, n, of producers of consumer goods, each using capital and labor. It is assumed that consumer goods can be regarded as a single, uniform commodity. We also assume that there is a number, m, of producers of capital goods, each using capital and labor. It is sufficient for our purpose to consider the case where there is only one kind of capital, which, however, can have various properties of durability. But we shall consider these durability properties as fixed properties of each unit of capital. We shall leave out all monetary factors, except money as a pure *numéraire*. We disregard, for the time being, all speculative elements, such as price expectations. We shall also assume that each firm is vertically integrated in the sense that there is no purchase of raw materials or half-finished products. We do this to simplify the cost functions of the firms. We shall also disregard the existence of commercial stocks.

We shall make use of the rigid law of indifference of capital prices as described above.

It is convenient to being with a complete list of variables to be considered in this model. Until otherwise stated, the symbols below will have the following meanings:

$x(t)$ = total output of consumer goods
$x_i(t)$ = output of consumer goods by firm i
$p(t)$ = price of consumer goods
$N_i'(t)$ = labor employed by consumer-goods producer i
$K_i'(t)$ = capital employed by consumer-goods producer i
$q(t)$ = price of capital of "infinite" durability
$q_\tau(\theta, t)$ = price of capital of durability θ, and age τ
$k_i(t)$ = output of physical capital units by capital-goods producer i
$N_i''(t)$ = labor employed by capital-goods producer i
$K_i''(t)$ = capital employed by capital-goods producer i
$\theta_i(t)$ = durability of capital produced by capital-goods producer i, at t
$\rho(t)$ = the rate of interest
$w(t)$ = wage rate
$N(t)$ = total supply of labor
$K(t)$ = total physical amount of capital in existence at t
$W(t)$ = total value of capital at t

(We omit reference to time t where the omission can do no harm and is convenient for typographical reasons.)

Consider, first, the behavior of producers in the consumer-goods industries. Let their production functions be

$$x_i(t) = \Phi_i [K_i'(t), N_i'(t)] , \qquad (31.3)$$

assuming the input-output relation to be instantaneous. If they maximize current profit as quantity adapters and if we can assume that such maxima actually exist, we must have

$$\frac{\partial \Phi_i}{\partial N_i'} = \frac{w(t)}{p(t)} ; \qquad (31.4)$$

$$\frac{\partial \Phi_i}{\Phi K_i'} = \rho(t) \, \frac{q(t)}{p(t)} . \qquad (31.5)$$

The right-hand side of equation (31.5) is a result of assuming that the law of indifference of capital prices is fulfilled.

Consider next the sector of capital-goods producers. Suppose, as the simplest case, that "lags" in their production functions can be neglected. But assume that the capital-goods producers can choose to produce capital of different durabilities, $\theta_i(t)$. We assume here that $\theta_i(t)$ means simply "number of years." Let the production functions of the m capital producers be

$$k_i(t) = \Psi_i [K''_{ii}(t), N''_i(t), \theta_i(t)] . \tag{31.6}$$

Here $\theta_i(t)$ is a *parameter*, affecting the physical volume of output $k_i(t)$.

The current rate of profit of capital-goods producer i will be $q_0(\theta_i, t)$ $k_i(t) - w(t) N''_i(t) - \rho(t) q(t) K''_i(t)$. We get the following necessary conditions for maximum, assuming that all prices are regarded as given,

$$q_0 (\theta_i, t) \frac{\partial \Psi_i}{\partial K''_i} = \rho (t) q (t) ; \tag{31.7}$$

$$q_0 (\theta_i, t) \frac{\partial \Psi_i}{\partial N''_i} = w (t) ; \tag{31.8}$$

$$\frac{\partial q_0 (\theta_i, t)}{\partial \theta_i} \Psi_i + q_0 (\theta_i, t) \frac{\partial \Psi_i}{\partial \theta_i} = 0 . \tag{31.9}$$

Obviously $q_0(\theta_i, t)$ will have to be an increasing function of θ_i. We shall assume that the usual stability conditions are fulfilled.

Because of the law of indifference of capital prices, we must have

$$q_0(\theta_i, t)_0 = q(t) (1 - e^{-\rho\theta_i}). \tag{31.10}$$

If there were lags in the production function (31.6), as in (30.5b), and if we assume that the producers make firm decisions on the basis of *current prices*, we should have the same equations (31.7)–(31.10) with prices dated at t, but with capital, employment, and durability dated with the appropriate lags for each producer. There is no need to reproduce all the formulas for this case here.

To the equations above, we can add three bookkeeping relations, viz.,

$$\sum_1^n K'_i + \sum_1^m K''_i = K ; \tag{31.11}$$

$$\sum_1^n N'_i + \sum_1^m N''_i = N ; \tag{31.12}$$

$$\sum_1^n x_i = x . \tag{31.13}$$

We are not specifically interested in studying the *supply of labor* in this connection, but it is, nevertheless, of importance to the solution of the model what kind of assumptions we make about this supply. Two alternatives may be of particular interest here, namely, the following:

$$N(t) = N\left[\frac{w(t)}{p(t)}\right];\qquad\qquad (31.14\,a)$$

$$\frac{w(t)}{p(t)} = \text{constant}.\qquad\qquad (31.14\,b)$$

These alternatives have played an important role in the economic theories of employment.

We also need to make an assumption concerning the total demand for consumer goods. This is, of course, by itself a whole chapter of economic theory. For example, to what extent should capital losses and gains be included as motivating consumers' spending? How about the rate of interest? How about the level of wealth? The essential thing for our purpose is, however, only to recognize in one way or another that consumers' demand is a constraint upon the rate of capital accumulation. It is sufficient here if we write

$$x(t) = F \text{ (income, interest, etc.)}\qquad\qquad (31.15)$$

where the arguments of F are restricted to functions of variables already defined in our system.

Because of the system being homogeneous of degree zero in all absolute price variables, we may choose, conventionally,

$$p(t) = 1, \text{ or some arbitrary number, for all } t.\qquad (31.16)$$

It will be seen that the system (or rather the alternative systems) above can be made *closed and formally determinate in two ways.*

One way is to consider it as a requirement of short-run equilibrium, or equilibrium *at t.* Then $K(t)$ is a datum, and so is its internal composition with regard to age and durability. The value of $K(t)$ can then be expressed as a function of $q(t)$ and the rate of interest $\rho(t)$ by means of

$$q_\tau(\theta, t) = [1 - e^{-\rho(\theta-\tau)}]\, q(t).\qquad\qquad (31.17)$$

The other way—and the one that has to be chosen to describe the time development of the system—is to take account of the relation between the output of capital goods and the rate of growth of total capital. This requires the knowledge of certain *initial conditions,* viz., the volume and the internal composition of K at a given point in time, say t_0. If this is known, we can calculate the development of $K(t)$, its internal composition, and its total market value. This can be seen as follows: For a given size and distribution of $K(t)$, the rate of output of capital goods and the current durabilities $\theta_i(t)$ of this output are given. And so is the *value* of $K(t)$ which may play a role in equation (31.15). The rate of physical depreciation can be computed, and also its value. Therefore, we shall know $K(t + \Delta t)$ and its composition for a small Δt, and so on. It is, therefore, possible to derive $K(t)$, its value, and the rates of change of these two variables at any time t.

Consider $K(t)$ at $t = t_0$. Let its distribution-density function over the variables θ and τ be $K_{\theta,\tau}(t_0)$, such that the integral over θ and τ is equal to $K(t_0)$. We have, first, to find out how much of this stock will disappear per unit of time at t_0, because of overage. Assume that $K_{\theta,\tau}(t_0)$ is so defined that it *includes all capital of age* $\tau \leqq \theta$. Then the rate of depreciation per unit of time at t_0 is evidently

$$\int_{\theta_1}^{\theta_2} K_{\theta,\,\theta}(t_0)\, d\theta = \text{rate of physical depreciation of } K(t_0), \quad (31.18)$$

where θ_1 and θ_2 denote minimum and maximum durability, respectively. We then have

$$\dot{K}(t_0) = -\int_{\theta_1}^{\theta_2} K_{\theta,\,\theta}(t_0)\, d\theta + \sum_{1}^{m} k_i(t_0). \quad (31.19)$$

Let us now find the *value* of $K(t_0)$. This value is obviously

$$W(t_0) = q(t_0) \int_{\theta_1}^{\theta_2} \int_{0}^{\theta} K_{\theta,\,\tau}(t_0) [1 - e^{-\rho(\theta-\tau)}]\, d\tau d\theta. \quad (31.20)$$

Since the units that reach the age θ already have the value zero, the rate of change of $W(t_0)$ is obviously the total stock at t_0 times the rate of change of the value of each item due to time or age plus the value of newly produced capital. Hence

$$\dot{W}(t_0) = \dot{q}(t_0) \int_{\theta_1}^{\theta_2} \int_{0}^{\theta} K_{\theta,\,\tau}(t_0) [1 - e^{-\rho(\theta-\tau)}]\, d\tau d\theta$$

$$+ q(t_0) \int_{\theta_1}^{\theta_2} \int_{0}^{\theta} K_{\theta,\,\tau}(t_0)\, e^{-\rho(\theta-\tau)} [\dot{\rho}(\theta-\tau) - \rho]\, d\tau d\theta \quad (31.21)$$

$$+ \sum_{1}^{m} q_0(\theta_i, t_0)\, k_i(t_0).$$

Here the first member to the right is changes in value due to changes in the level of capital prices. The second term is the value of depreciation, including the effects of a changing rate of interest upon capital prices. And the third term is the value of current gross investment.

One will notice that, because of the composition of gross investment in the past, there may be "holes" and strange peaks in the surface $K_{\theta,\tau}(t_0)$. And its development may also become very complicated from t_0 on, depending on the choice of the most profitable durabilities $\theta_i(t)$ by the various capital-goods producers.

From the formulas (31.20) and (31.21) one can easily check the following well-known result: Under stationary conditions the annual interest revenues ρW is equal to the interest that the capital would have carried if infinitely durable minus the annual depreciation charges of capital as it actually is.

III. INTERPRETATION OF THE SYSTEM ABOVE

Consider the system at a given point in time. Then $K(t)$ and its composition are data. All the variables of our system can be expressed as a function of $K(t)$ and its composition. We shall assume that this solution is unique, which will be the case, I think, under quite reasonable assumptions. The system, regarded *at a given point in time*, has all the usual properties of a classical static model of instantaneous adjustments. The first and the most fundamental conclusion which we want to draw is this:

There is no special reason why we should have $\dot{K}(t)$ equal to zero.

This means that even in the absence of uncertainty, speculative elements, new techniques, or any other special flow of investment opportunities it would be "quite normal" to have a positive rate of growth of the volume of capital. This would be particularly true if the amount of capital had been growing in the past at a rate and with such composition as to make the rate of depreciation moderate as compared to the rate of gross investment. The rate of gross investment depends fundamentally on the production structure in the capital-goods industries and the profitability of *producing* capital goods.

One may now ask: What is the "demand" for net investment? Who asks for $\dot{K}(t)$? There are several ways of explaining this. One way is simply to restate what the system says, that the rate of interest, the price of capital and other variables must perforce move in such a way that room is made for $\dot{K}(t)$ among the producers maximizing current profit. A tempting explanation is that both the rate of interest and capital prices must gradually fall, and perhaps also the rate of net investment. But these conclusions are not safe. The answer depends upon the form of the demand for consumer goods, among other things. We can, however, say this:

If the marginal productivities of capital in the various production structures depend only on the amount of capital used, then ρ or q, or both, must be falling at time t if $\dot{K}(t)$ is to be positive.

The next fundamental conclusion that can be drawn is this:

We cannot infer from a positive $\dot{K}(t)$ that $\dot{W}(t)$ will be positive. And, conversely, we cannot infer from a positive $\dot{W}(t)$ that $\dot{K}(t)$ will be positive.

This statement does not, of course, make any sense if we look at the explicit, dynamic solutions of the system, because then there will be a definite relationship between $\dot{K}(t)$ and $\dot{W}(t)$. But if we imagine a change in some initial conditions at t this change could evidently affect $\dot{K}(t)$ and $\dot{W}(t)$ very differently.

The third fundamental conclusion that can be drawn is this:

It is meaningless to say that the "demand for investment" is determined by the rate of interest.

The rate of interest is, first of all, not a free variable, it gets determined by the requirements of the system. And even if we try to reason partially upon the behavior of the producers, the statement is based on confusion. Demand for investment could be said to be a function of $\dot{\rho}(t)$, but not of $\rho(t)$, except to the extent that the *effect of $\dot{\rho}(t)$* is influenced by what $\rho(t)$ is. But we see, in any case, that if the producers were faced with constant prices, their demand for investment would be zero except if $\dot{\rho}(t)$ is not zero.

A fourth and last conclusion of considerable interest is this:

The composition of capital with respect to durability is determined on the supply side rather than on the demand side.

It is immaterial to the producers how their own capital is composed. It is the varying profitability of *producing* capital durability that determines how capital will be composed. Of course, this conclusion is reached under the strict assumption of fixed lifetime of each capital unit produced, regardless of use.

IV. The Question of Stability of the System

We must now try to answer a question which we have so far left open and which may have been bothering the reader while we drew conclusions from the system: How about stability?

If this question refers to the mathematical properties of the system as we have described it, it is an important and interesting problem. The question is then whether in the long run we get growth, stagnation, or ruin. I think further information on the functions involved is required to answer this question. I only want to say this: It is certainly no particular virtue or sign of realism of our system as stated if it leads to stagnation.

But the question of stability may refer to something like the short-run properties of the system or, more precisely, whether the behavior described actually would lead to uniquely determined quantities and prices at a given point of time. To this I will say that the question has no meaning without further specification, and it is not a mathematical question that could be answered by analyzing the system as it stands.

There seems to be some confusion among economists concerning the meaning of a "stable market." I shall, therefore, offer a few comments in general, before studying what could be done in connection with the particular system above.

Roughly speaking, what economists apparently have in mind if they ask about the short-run stability of a system, such as the one above, is not related to that system as such, but to *some other system* of which the one we have is a simplified version. More specifically, consider a more complicated dynamic system with a whole network of short-run adjustment equations embroidered upon a system as outlined above. What is meant by short-run stability of the system above is then evidently whether this more complicated system would have components all of which would be heavily damped except for those that the system above may possess.

This is an interesting question, but it is not a question of our system as it stands but of another, enlarged dynamic system. And how to define this enlarged system is not a question to be solved by mathematics. It is a question of making assumptions concerning the functioning of the economy.

Therefore, the question of short-run stability of our particular system above is not a question of mathematical properties of that system, but a question of what I, or the reader, would consider a good economic theory of short-run adjustment behavior, e.g., certain assumptions of a finite speed of reaction of producers in maximizing profit.

My own impression of the "long-run" system described above is that it might be quite reasonable to add such assumptions concerning the short-run adjustment processes that the system could become *highly unstable, at least in the small.* I think this is an important and realistic aspect of the system outlined. In other words, it is important that we do *not* have to make any "queer" assumptions in order to get *in*stability. There is no question that our system can be realistically unstable if we make it sufficiently dynamic. Our a priori worry here should not be about instability, but rather about our theory yielding a too smooth behavior of investment as compared to observed facts.

By generalizing our system with an "embroidery" of short-run dynamics with changing structural characteristics, we could reproduce almost any equilibristic jumps ever observed in statistics of the rate of investment.

To illustrate the possible short-run instability because of dynamic aspects that actually might belong in our system, consider the following highly simplified case.

Take the equations (31.5) and (31.7), and let us assume that—over a short period of time from t on—the following simplifications hold as good approximations: (1) The marginal productivities of capital are approximately constant for a relatively wide range around the actual amounts of capital used at t, and also approximately independent of employment. (2) The quantities θ_i are all *large* and constant. (3) Total capital in society can change very slowly. (4) The equations (31.5) and (31.7) are not all fulfilled, because for some reason, the quantities $q(t)$ and $\rho(t)$ are out of equilibrium.

Suppose now that the producers try to reach optimum profit by adjusting their capital expenditures and that they go about this with rather great speeds which, however, may differ from one producer to the next. Their short-run adjustment equations, which then would take the place of equations (31.5) and (31.7), could be

$$\frac{1}{q\,(t)\,K_i'\,(t)}\,\frac{d}{dt}\,[\,q\,(t)\,K'\,(t)\,] = a_i\,[\,A_i - \rho\,(t)\,q\,(t)\,] , \tag{31.5a}$$

$$A_i > 0 , \qquad a_i \geqq 0 ;$$

$$\frac{1}{q\,(t)\,K_i'\,(t)}\,\frac{d}{dt}\,[\,q\,(t)\,K_i''\,(t)\,] = b_i\,[\,B_i - \rho\,(t)\,]\,q\,(t) , \tag{31.7a}$$

$$B_i > 0 , \qquad b_i \geqq 0$$

where A_i, B_i, a_i, b_i are constants. Carrying out the derivations on the left-hand side of these equations and assuming that the *average percentage change* in the volume of capital over short periods is negligible in either sector, we obtain by summation the following approximate short-run adjustment equations:

$$\frac{\dot{q}\,(t)}{q\,(t)} = A - \bar{a}\,\rho\,(t)\,q\,(t) ; \tag{31.22}$$

$$\frac{\dot{q}\,(t)}{q\,(t)} = B\,q\,(t) - \bar{b}\,\rho\,(t)\,q\,(t) , \tag{31.23}$$

where the constants A, B, $\bar{a}$, $\bar{b}$ are functions of the constants A_i, B_i, a_i, b_i above. These equations can be interpreted as describing a short-run process of underbidding, or overbidding, in the capital market.

From equations (31.22) and (31.23) we obtain

$$\frac{\dot{q}(t)}{q(t)} = \frac{\bar{b}\,A - \bar{a}B\,q(t)}{\bar{b} - \bar{a}}. \tag{31.24}$$

We see at once that the question of stability depends on the sign of the *difference in the average speeds of reaction in the two sectors*. We can get both a stable and an unstable development of the level of capital prices. In the stable case both $q(t)$ and $\rho(t)$ will tend toward positive levels. This short-run adjustment assumes, of course, that both $\rho(t)$ and $q(t)$ are extremely flexible in the capital market. We have also made the highly unrealistic assumption that variations in the relative prices of capital of different durability do not really matter very much. But the model may nevertheless serve to illustrate the point that the question of short-run stability is a question of *economic assumptions*, and not a question of the mathematical properties of the reduced, semistationary system.

It is obvious that the introduction of expectational elements in the "equilibrium model" that has been discussed in this chapter could make it more realistic and capable of reproducing almost any known development of an accumulation process. The trouble with these expectational elements, from an econometric point of view, is that it is very hard to find their invariant properties, if any.

32

Macroeconomic Models

THE reader who has stayed with us through the preceding chapters of this study may already feel himself torn between two reasons for despair: On the one hand, we have cut almost to the bone, as far as making simplifying assumptions is concerned. We have probably made hundreds of such assumptions, some even rather fantastic. On the other hand, I think that the reader will agree that an exhaustive analysis of what remains after all the drastic simplifications is still quite a formidable task. We have left innumerable aspects of our simplified schemes untouched, or have just skimmed the surface.

Could we take very much more in the way of simplifications? The reader may well deny this. May we then remind him—if this is any comfort—that there is more, and worse, to come in the way of simplifications if we want to arrive at the kind of simple macro models that have filled our economic textbooks for the last two or three decades. We do not want to deny the usefulness of such models. But it is hoped that the analysis we have gone through in the preceding chapters may have served, at least, to emphasize how drastic the simplified macro models of the textbooks really are.

We shall consider a couple of versions of such models which may be said to belong at the end of a thread which we have now spun long and thin.

I. A Macro Model of "Classical" Theory

The model described below can be regarded as a condensed, and slightly modified, version of the more general model in the preceding chapter. We assume that the technological relations and the behavior relations of all the producers can be aggregated. The method of aggregation used here is based on what could be termed "the method of analogy." That is, we consider the producers as if they were one single sector but assume that the sector keeps the behavior patterns of the small producer in a large economy. A similar reasoning is used to get aggregate consumers' demand, etc. For the sake of simplicity we shall assume that physical depreciation is proportional to the amount of physical capital, the "remainder" being, technologically, "good as new."

We use notations corresponding to those in the previous chapter, but they can now be simplified to some extent. We shall now use the following symbols:

$x(t)$ = total output of consumer goods
$k(t)$ = total output of capital goods
$N(t)$ = total employment
$K(t)$ = total volume of physical capital
$R(t)$ = total national income
$w(t)$ = wage rate
$p(t)$ = price of consumer goods
$q(t)$ = price of capital goods with depreciation coefficient = $\bar{\gamma}$ (i.e., price of capital goods of "standard durability")
$\rho(t)$ = rate of interest

We shall first assume that the rate of depreciation is a *constant* proportion, $\bar{\gamma}$, of total capital. Under this assumption we shall suppose, somewhat artificially, that the output of consumer goods and the output of capital goods can be measured in the *same physical units*. On this basis we write the global production function as

$$x(t) + k(t) = \Phi\,[K(t),\,N(t)]\,. \qquad (32.1)$$

By way of analogy we now assume that the behavior of producers can be represented by the following two conditions, obtained from maximizing the profit $p\Phi - wN - (\rho + \bar{\gamma})\,qK$,

$$p\,(t)\,\frac{\partial \Phi}{\partial N} = w\,(t)\,; \qquad (32.2)$$

$$p\,(t)\,\frac{\partial \Phi}{\partial K} = [\rho\,(t) + \bar{\gamma}]\,q\,(t)\,. \qquad (32.3)$$

We shall assume that Φ is such that equations (32.2) and (32.3) lead to a unique profit maximum.

The definition of national income is

$$R(t) = p(t)\,x\,(t) + q(t)\,k(t) - \bar{\gamma}\,q(t)\,K(t)\,. \qquad (32.4)$$

Let consumers' demand be represented by

$$x\,(t) = f\!\left[\frac{R\,(t)}{p\,(t)},\,\rho\,(t),\,\frac{q\,(t)\,K\,(t)}{p\,(t)}\right], \qquad (32.5)$$

assuming that total wealth plays a role in this function and, possibly, also the rate of interest, in addition to total income.

The supply of labor, written in classical style, is

$$N\,(t) = g\!\left[\frac{w\,(t)}{p\,(t)}\right], \qquad (32.6)$$

where g denotes a given function.

We have the definition

$$\dot{K}(t) = k(t) - \bar{\gamma}\,K(t)\,. \qquad (32.7)$$

The system is assumed to be homogeneous of degree zero in prices and the wage rate. We can, therefore, write, by convention,

$$p(t) = 1,\ \text{for all}\ t\,, \qquad (32.8)$$

or we can regard the price $p(t)$ as an *arbitrary constant*.

Because of the way in which we measure physical capital, we can also write

$$q(t) = p(t) \equiv \text{an arbitrary constant}\,. \qquad (32.9)$$

Here it should be noted that $q(t) = (pt)$ is an equilibrium *condition* for $q(t)$, not a definition.

The formally determinate system above represents the "harmonious-family" type system of long-range economic development. (Of course, the family may not be entirely happy, in spite of all the equations being nicely fulfilled.) What consumers do not want flows smoothly into the stock of capital. Under reasonable assumptions, the amount of employment will rise gradually as long as $k - \bar{\gamma}K$ is positive. The rate of interest will then have to fall gradually in order that $k - \bar{\gamma}K$ be absorbed by the users of capital. If the consumers do not want to accumulate wealth at interest below a certain level, their only alternative is to consume the whole national income.

It should be noted that producers are indifferent as between x and k as long as $p = q$. The system is *highly unstable* with respect to disturbances upon this condition.

Actually, the investment theory implicit in the model above is not as "un-Keynesian" as one might think. If producers would try to increase the amount of capital in the short run, capital prices would increase, because of the assumed form of Φ. In the long run, the marginal productivity of capital must fall as long as $k - \bar{\gamma}K > 0$. Compare this with the following passage from *The General Theory:*

If there is an increased investment in any given type of capital during any period of time, the marginal efficiency of that type of capital will diminish as investment in it is increased, partly because the prospective yield will fall as the supply of that type of capital is increased, and partly because, as a rule, pressure on the facilities for producing that type of capital will cause its supply price to increase; the second of these factors being usually the more important in producing equilibrium in the short run, but the longer the period in view the more does the first factor take its place.[1]

In other words, the rate of investment is determined by a conjunction of the cost of producing capital goods and the yield from its use as a factor of production. Note that it is, actually, not the users of capital who "demand" investment, it is the producers of capital goods who determine how much they want to produce at the current price of capital. The demand for investment is, directly, a function of $\dot{\rho}(t)$, rather than of $\rho(t)$ itself.

I believe that Keynes has often been misinterpreted on this point, due to an unfortunate slip on page 136 of the *General Theory*, where he talks about the "demand for investment" instead of what he actually means, namely, an equation resulting from a *conjunction* of the supply of investment goods and the marginal efficiency of capital.

---

1. Lord Keynes, *The General Theory of Employment, Interest and Money* (1936), p. 136.

It is seen from the system above that there is no particular reason why the system should be stationary, i. e., $k - \bar{\gamma} K = 0$ for all t. This would be a very particular case. But must not the system tend toward a stationary level? That depends on consumers' behavior and on the supply of labor. What has often been forgotten by the advocates of the stagnation thesis is that, as society tends toward some kind of saturation of wealth, it also gets an increasing income out of which to save. The way these two forces balance each other may vary from one society to another.

II. Effects of Variable Durability of Capital

In the system above, the *value* of total capital is at any time simply $q(t) \ K(t) = K(t)$. That is so because the existing capital is assumed to be composed of units that depreciate in quantity at the same rate, age being no cause of technical inferiority. The effect of assuming that capital can be *produced* with varying degrees of durability can be brought into the system in a simple way. Assume that the capital price $q(t)$ above applies to capital goods with standard depreciation coefficient $\bar{\gamma}$. A simple hypothesis would be that $\bar{\gamma}$ does not enter the production function Φ, but that the output of capital goods with depreciation coefficient $\bar{\gamma}$ could be converted into less quantity and more durability according to a simple conversion relationship. However, in that case producers' behavior would be quite unstable, because there might be one or more values for γ for which it would pay to produce capital goods rather than consumer goods. Then the producers would choose $x = $ zero which, of course, is an impermissible result. If different γ's could be chosen for $k(t)$, the coefficient $\gamma(t)$ would have to be in the production function in such a way that, taking account of the relation between prices of capital of different durabilities, both consumer goods and capital goods could be produced with a stable maximum profit.

Let us, therefore, write the production function as

$$x(t) = \Phi^* \left[K(t), N(t), k(t), \gamma(t) \right], \qquad (32.10)$$

where now $K(t)$ could be composed of capital of different durability properties but consisting of technologically equivalent units. Here $\gamma(t)$ denotes the depreciation coefficient for new capital produced at t. Using the law of indifference of capital prices and setting the price of capital with a durability coefficient of a fixed $\gamma = \bar{\gamma}$ equal to 1, producers would maximize

$$x(t) + \frac{\rho(t) + \bar{\gamma}}{\rho(t) + \gamma(t)} \, k_\gamma(t) - w(t) \, N(t) - [\rho(t) + \bar{\gamma}] \, K(t) \qquad (32.11)$$

subject to the constraint (32.10); $k_\gamma(t)$ denotes output of capital with durability coefficient equal to $\gamma(t)$. We obtain, as necessary conditions of maximum, the following equations:

$$\frac{\rho(t) + \tilde{\gamma}}{o(t) + \gamma(t)} = -\frac{\partial \Phi^*}{\partial k_\gamma};\qquad (32.12)$$

$$k_\gamma(t)\,\frac{\rho(t) + \tilde{\gamma}}{[\rho(t) + \gamma(t)]^2} = \frac{\partial \Phi^*}{\partial \gamma},\qquad (32.13)$$

We also have, in addition, the equations (32.2) and (32.3) with Φ replaced by Φ^*.

But here an interesting thing happens: If we try to combine these results with the other equations above, the system becomes, in general, *over-determinate*. That is, it is not permissible to make the assumption that the price of a certain kind of capital is equal to one, if the production function is (32.10). If we drop equation (32.9), however, we obtain a formally determinate system where now also γ becomes a function of time. And so does the price of capital of standard durability.

If γ is variable, the stock of capital $K(t)$ may be composed of capital units with different γ's. At a given point in time, say t_0, let there be a given distribution, $K_\gamma(t_0)$, of capital according to "built-in" durability. Age does not matter here. Then we have

$$K(t_0) = \int_0^\infty K_\gamma(t_0)\,d\gamma,\qquad (32.14)$$

and

$$\dot{K}(t_0) = -\int_0^\infty \gamma K_\gamma(t_0)\,d\gamma + k_\gamma(t_0).\qquad (32.15)$$

For the value of capital, $W(t_0)$, we get

$$W(t_0) = q_{\tilde{\gamma}}(t_0)\,[\rho(t_0) + \tilde{\gamma}]\int_0^\infty \frac{1}{\rho(t_0) + \gamma}\,K_\gamma(t_0)\,d\gamma,\qquad (32.16)$$

and

$$\dot{W}(t_0) = q_{\gamma}(t_0)\,[\rho(t_0) + \tilde{\gamma}]\left[\frac{1}{\rho(t_0) + \gamma(t_0)}\,k_\gamma(t_0)\right.$$

$$\left. -\int_0^\infty \frac{\gamma}{\rho(t_0) + \gamma}\,K_\gamma(t_0)\,d\gamma\right] + q_{\tilde{\gamma}}(t_0)\,\dot{\rho}(t_0)\qquad (32.17)$$

$$\times \int_0^\infty \frac{\gamma - \tilde{\gamma}}{[\rho(t_0) + \gamma]^2}\,K_\gamma(t_0)\,d\gamma + \frac{\dot{q}_{\tilde{\gamma}}(t_0)}{q_{\tilde{\gamma}}(t_0)}\,W(t_0).$$

Here the first term to the right is the value of *net investment*, not corrected for effects of price and interest changes. The second term is the effect of changes in relative capital prices according to their property γ. The third term is pure value-changes, due to development of the level of capital prices.

One should note that there is no simple relation between the value of net investment and the physical volume of net investment (cf. chap. xxxi and formula (31.21)). For example, if the γ of gross investment at t_0 is large as compared with the average γ in $K(t_0)$, $\dot{W}(t_0)$ may be negative, while $\dot{K}(t_0)$ is positive. It is not possible to get rid of this discrepancy by any simple "deflating." Thus, $W(t_0)$ is already reckoned in "constant dollars," so that this is no solution.

Of course, $\dot{W}(t_0)$ is the rate of savings in the economy, if income is properly computed. It is interesting to note that it is quite possible for the economy to get along very well as far as growth of consumption is concerned by having a growth in γ over time such that $W(t)$ grows less rapidly than $K(t)$. This means to consume wealth, which, in the short run at least, is not necessarily the same as consuming productive power.

Of course, what we have discussed above is a *dynamic* phenomenon. Under stationary conditions with regard to γ, the possible differences discussed above disappear.

It should be emphasized that the model above, including equation (32.17), does not make any allowance for price expectations. The rates of change of prices in equation (37.17) are the results of a natural "course of events." They are price effects *ex post*. By assumption, the entrepreneurs *expect* unchanged prices all the time. If they started to anticipate price changes, the definition of $\dot{W}(t)$ could become far more complicated than the expression in equation (32.17) (cf. chap. xxv).

33

Investment, Money, and Employment

In the models we have studied so far, money has been merely an automatically supplied "oil in the machinery." The various behavior patterns considered were not influenced by any concern about money for its own sake. Many economists would argue that, if we omit this essential element, the explanatory power of what remains is almost nil. Perhaps no field of economics has been as extensively dealt with as precisely the role of money in modifying the classical economic mechanism of general equilibrium. The opinions in this literature vary between extremes. Many blame "money illusions" for most of the trouble in the economic system. Others emphasize how essential a well-developed money market is for the process of production, savings, and capital accumulation. Both these ideas may be right. To reconcile them is the objective of monetary theory and monetary policy.

I do not know whether one can say that recognition of the influence of money is more important when we try to understand the behavior of investment than when we deal with other economic variables. Strictly speaking, such a view is probably rather meaningless. It violates one of the fundamentals of economics, which is that "everything depends on everything else." But it makes sense to ask how alternative monetary structures may affect particular economic variables—in our case, investment. However, in order to do this, it is necessary to bring the alternatives concerning money into a complete system. This is the reason why the models we consider must necessarily bring in a lot of things that are not directly part of our subject matter.

I. A Fundamental Overdeterminacy

An essential feature of the models we have studied in the preceding five chapters is that the rate of interest is one of the *endogenous* variables. To the extent that our models have a unique solution, the rate of interest must have a particular value at any point in time, in order that the economy should function as assumed. This characteristic feature is far more general than what our particular models may suggest. It has little to do with the degree of aggregation or disaggregation we use. It applies even if capital is perfectly mobile and all prices perfectly flexible. One might, e.g., think that a variable price of capital in relation to the price of consumer goods could be sufficient to equate producers' demand for capital to the existing stock of capital. But that is not so. The main reason is that the price of capital goods produced cannot be independent of the price of existing capital.

If, under these circumstances, we put additional constraints upon the rate of interest, a fundamental overdeterminacy emerges. Logically, such an overdeterminacy simply means that there is no solution satisfying the requirements of the model. It is obvious what an actual economy does under such circumstances: It operates under a different model that does have a solution. Why, then, should we take even the slightest interest in an overdetermined model? If we do, the only acceptable reason would seem to be that we believe that, somehow, the economy first "tries out" the hopeless model, and then *derives* a practicable alternative *in a way which could be predicted by studying the overdetermined model.*

Additional constraints upon the rate of interest can come about directly, through an autonomous interest policy of the monetary authorities. More indirectly we can get constraints upon the rate of interest through the existence of a "liquidity preference function" coupled with a monetary policy that implies some constraint upon the *real* amount of money.[1] For our purpose here it does not really matter much whether the autonomous setting of the rate of interest takes place directly or indirectly. But to make sure that there be no confusion on this much discussed point, consider the effect of adding a liquidity preference function to any one of the models discussed in chapters xxxi and xxxii.

Such a liquidity preference function could be formulated in a great many ways. One formulation, which will cover a lot of ground in modern macroeconomic literature, is

$$\rho\,(t) = L\left[\frac{M\,(t)}{p\,(t)}, \frac{R\,(t)}{p\,(t)}, \frac{q\,(t)\,K\,(t)}{p\,(t)}\right], \qquad (33.1)$$

where $\rho(t)$ is the rate of interest for lending money, $M(t)$ the absolute amount of money, $p(t)$ the price of consumer goods, $R(t)$ income (or "volume of transactions"), $q(t)$ the price of capital, and $K(t)$ total capital, or "physical wealth." The usual interpretation of the function L is that it will be the smaller the larger is $[M(t)/p(t)]$, and that L will be the larger the larger is $[R(t)/p(t)]$. Presumably, the partial effect of $[q(t)\,K(t)/p(t)]$ is also positive.

The introduction of equation (33.1) means by itself no new constraint upon variables in the models previously discussed, at least as far as the number of degrees of freedom is concerned. Equation (33.1) is an additional equation, but it also introduces an additional variable, M. (We have not introduced M in any of the systems discussed so far. This may be somewhat unrealistic, but it does not matter too much for the argument which we are about to present.) In fact, it is even permissible to put a direct additional constraint upon M, the absolute amount of money, without logical difficulties, as long as absolute prices and wages are otherwise arbitrary (cf. equation (31.16) or (32.8)). The solution of the system would then exhibit the so-called Pigou-effect whereby the liquidity preference function determines the absolute level of prices.

On the other hand, if monetary policy is such as to imply a fixed value (or a fixed time function) for the *real* amount of money, M/p,

1. On this point cf. Don Patinkin, *Money, Interest and Prices* (Evanston, Ill.: Row, Peterson & Co., 1956), in particular, chaps. ii–iii.

regardless of the value of p, the inclusion of equation (33.1) will, in general, lead to overdeterminacy. For all the other, "real," variables in equation (33.1) are already determined by our models as they appear before introducing (33.1). If, under these circumstances, the rate of interest for borrowing money must satisfy equation (33.1), this rate of interest will, in general, not be equal to the rate of interest which would be consistent with the models of chapters xxxi and xxxii. Thus, if equation (33.1) holds, it is seen that control of M/p has the same effect as a direct control of the rate of interest ρ, as far as the number of degrees of freedom is concerned.

Consider, therefore, a monetary policy which implies

$$\rho(t) = \rho^*(t) = \text{a given time function autonomously determined} \atop \text{by the monetary authorities.} \quad (32.2)$$

(Then equation (33.1) will determine the amount of money M which it is necessary to supply, for given values of the other variables involved.)

If equation (33.2) means an effective additional constraint upon the variables in the models we are considering, and if this does not mean that the whole system is thrown into chaos, we must look for ways of possible reconciliation. The processes of reconciliation that have been discussed in economic literature belong essentially in one or the other of the following two groups: (1) the "breakdown" of one or more classical behavior patterns to make room for equation (33.2), or (2) some dynamic scheme in which the economy is constantly chasing fulfilment of *all* the equations without, of course, actually reaching this goal.

In the first of these two categories we have the theories of the breakdown of the demand function for labor[2] (when ρ^* is "too large") or the breakdown of the equilibrium between supply and demand for capital (when ρ^* is "too small").

In the second category we have a great many dynamic models, of which perhaps the most famous is the Wicksellian cumulative process.

Both these theoretical frameworks have a particularly close relation to the behavior of investment. It may, therefore, not be out of place to review them there.

II. Money Interest and the Demand for Labor

In the classical models discussed in chapters xxxi and xxxii it is, as we have seen, quite meaningless to ask what happens to employment if

2. Some economists would here have said "supply function" instead of "demand function." But I think that "demand" is correct, because it is the profit maximizing procedure of producers that becomes inoperative. But, in *addition*, it is of course quite likely that the classical pattern of the *supply* of labor will also be disrupted.

the rate of interest is changed. The rate of interest is not a free parameter. Changing it would mean to change some element of structure in the models. There are innumerable such possibilities, and their effects on employment might be very different. If we want to make statements concerning such effects, we should specify the particular way in which the structure is supposed to yield ground to permit the inclusion of a constraint of the type (33.2). I think it is justified to say that much confusion has prevailed in the "unemployment literature" on this point. Here we find such ideas as this: "The supply function of labor expresses what workers want to do, but they cannot do it." Let us try to see how this confusion probably arises.

Consider the supply function of labor. Its theoretical basis is that certain preferences are maximized under *given constraints*. The question which the classical supply function of labor answers is this: "There is a given wage rate. You can work as much as you want to. How much do you choose to work?" If we formulated this question differently, the answer might be quite different, even if the preference schedules of the workers were the same. Suppose, for example, that the question to the individual worker was: "There will be a given wage rate. Only so and so many workers can be employed. What will *you* do?" I do not think the classical supply function for labor answers this question.

The general conclusion is this: If we want to derive a "breakdown" theory on the basis of an overdetermined system, we must make definite assumptions concerning some *altered conditions of choice* of one or more behavioral groups.

Consider, in the light of this general idea, what producers in our "classical" models might do if an additional constraint (33.2) made the rate of interest "too high," i.e., higher than the solution obtained for $\rho(t)$ from one of our equilibrium models, *excluding (33.2)*. The economic argument might run roughly as follows. Producers would try to sell capital to each other, thus pressing down the price of capital. This process, however, could not lead to the fulfilment of all the equations of the system, as it is, by assumption, overdetermined. (Price changes cannot help as long as the system is homogeneous of degree zero in all price variables.) What we have to take account of is a possible change in *producers' strategy* at the same time as they try to get rid of capital. Here it would seem to be a realistic hypothesis that, under conditions of falling prices, producers become afraid of not being able to sell and start producing to order, instead of producing as if selling was no problem. *This will, in general, introduce one or more new degrees of freedom in the system, making room for equation (33.2).*

As the total amount of capital in the economy at any given moment is a fixed magnitude, the new producers' strategy would have to imply—somehow—that this amount of capital is held and used by the producers (as long as use of the capital does not mean a direct loss). The form of the complete model (including equation (33.2) and possibly such additional equations as there may now be room for) will determine what values the other variables of the system must have in order that the above-mentioned condition for total capital be fulfilled. In particular, the level of real wages must be such as to satisfy this condition. Whether this would lead to realistic values for real wages under the economic conditions considered will depend in part on the assumptions made about the form of the supply function for labor.

Another way to meet the condition that total capital is a datum is to assume that producers *use what they have of capital while they are trying to sell some of it.* This strategy may mean that such dynamic elements as $\dot{q}/q$ will enter into the behavioral equations of producers. (It should be observed that if one or more equations of the original models are changed so as to include rates of changes of prices, this alteration will, in general, make room for equation (33.2) without leading to overdeterminacy, because the inclusion of such terms would, in general, remove the price-homogeneity property from the model. One could then say that there is room for equation (33.2) "as long as prices are in motion" [cf. the Wicksellian cumulation process discussed below].)[3]

Let us now try to illustrate how the argument outlined above could be formalized. Consider any producer who has a given production function and assumes that he is faced with given factor prices and price of product. Consider two different producer strategies.

Strategy of Type A.—Maximize profit with regard to the inputs by maximizing profit for any given level of output *and* choose that output which gives the largest among the relative profit maxima.

Strategy of Type B.—Maximize profit with regard to the inputs by maximizing profit for an *assumed given* volume of output (the volume to be determined by somebody else).

It is seen that strategy of Type A would generally lead to *one more constraint* than strategy of Type B. This is, of course, a well-known proposition from the classroom theory of the firm.

Now let $\bar{p}(t)$ be the solution of, e.g., the first model in chapter xxxii. Suppose that we add another variable to our system at the same time

3. Cf. also the author's article: "The Notion of Price Homogeneity," *Festskrift til Jørgen Pedersen* (Aarhus, 1951), pp. 72–79.

as we include equation (33.2), the somewhat strange variable: "Strategy."
Assume that this "variable" satisfies the following relation:

$$\text{``Strategy''} = \begin{cases} A \text{ if } \rho^*(t) = \bar{\rho}(t), \\ B \text{ if } \rho^*(t) > \bar{\rho}(t). \end{cases} \tag{33.3a}$$

In a formal way this would solve the problem of overdeterminacy for all cases where $\rho^*(t) \geqq \bar{\rho}(t)$. But for $\rho^*(t) < \bar{\rho}(t)$ the problem of overdeterminacy is still present. To solve this problem, consider what might very likely happen if money could be borrowed cheaper than the productivity rate of interest. Then, very likely, the capital-goods producers would be pressed for quick delivery of new capital goods. They would have to use some kind of rationing, some first-come–first-served principle. And the producers would try to overbid each other in the attempt to get hold of capital. Some or all of the capital users would have to give up the idea of having their conditions of maximum profit with regard to capital fulfilled. Thus the part of A that has to do with the factor capital could be replaced by

Strategy of Type C.—Use available capital and try to buy more.

This would give the required degree of freedom, because both consumer-goods producers and capital-goods producers would have one maximum condition less than under A, while the relations expressing their efforts to buy capital would bring the motion of absolute prices into the "real" part of the model. Hence, the additional variable "Strategy" that would let equation (33.2) into the system without contradictions, could be as follows:

$$\text{``Strategy''} = \begin{cases} A \text{ if } \rho^*(t) = \bar{\rho}(t), \\ B \text{ if } \rho^*(t) > \bar{\rho}(t), \\ C \text{ if } \rho^*(t) < \bar{\rho}(t). \end{cases} \tag{33.3b}$$

Let me first try to underline what I think is the important lesson of our analysis above. It is this: There is no reason why the *form* of a realistic model (the form of its equations) should be the same under all values of its variables. We must face the fact that the form of the model may have to be regarded as a function of the values of the variables involved. This will usually be the case if the values of some of the variables affect the basic conditions of choice under which the behavior equations n the model are derived. Thus, for example, it is obviously absurd to maintain a supply equation which presupposes free quantity adaptation to given prices if the actual market situation is characterized by selling difficulties. It is likewise absurd to assume profit maximization on the basis of free adaptation of capital if additional capital cannot be bought at any price.

I should, however, like to add a few qualifying remarks to the formalistic approach outlined above.

The definition of the *A-B-C*-strategies as stated represents one possibility out of many. The scheme selected serves mainly to illustrate the general principle involved. From the point of view of realism, our choice may not be the best. For one thing, the "depression" strategy *B* may give results concerning employment that are contrary to observed facts, viz., falling prices, high *real* wages, high employment, and high rate of production. This would seem to be a strange effect of a rate of interest that is "too high." The main reason for this kind of effect is the maintenance of the assumption that the supply of labor is a rising function of the real wage. Then, if capital and labor are substitutes, wages must be high to keep all capital employed, but then employment must be high! This suggests that it would be wise to examine whether the conditions that, by definition, lead to a *B*-strategy for the employers, would not also lead to a revised strategy as far as the supply of labor is concerned. Similar remarks may apply to the behavior patterns of the other participants in our market economy.

We have already suggested that the strategies *B* or *C* may involve more dynamic patterns of producers' behavior than is the case under a strategy of Type *A* (cf. the activity of bidding capital prices up or down). To get more realistic results from our models under strategies *B* or *C*, it would probably be necessary to introduce a variety of dynamic elements also in the other behavior equations of the system.

There is an intricate problem in connection with the *A-B-C*-strategies that I should like to mention, namely, the problem of explaining a *switch* from one strategy to another. It is true that our scheme above defines uniquely which strategy the producers are assumed to operate under at any given time. However, it is probably not very realistic to assume that producers compare the market rate of interest ρ^* with the rate of interest, $\bar{\rho}$, that would correspond to a strategy of Type *A*. The effect of a change in ρ^* will certainly depend on *the kind of strategy that is prevailing* at the time when the change takes place. Thus, for example, under a *B*-strategy the actual marginal efficiency of capital may be lower than it would have been, for the same amount of capital, under an *A*-strategy. If producers compare the market rate ρ^* with the actual marginal efficiency of capital, rather than with $\bar{\rho}$, we could in fact get the disturbing result that if a *B*-strategy is in operation the producers would be led to switch into a *C*-strategy and, once in the *C*-strategy, they would be led to switch back into a *B*-strategy! It could indeed be a fascinating research project to study more generally the conditions under which a given set of rules for the choice of strategy would lead to consistent and workable solutions. But we shall not follow up this idea in the present context.

The brief comments above are, of course, a mere introduction to a tremendous and difficult subject. It is tempting, however, to draw one conclusion which lies very near at hand and which concerns the use of changes in the interest rate as a policy measure for influencing investment. It seems definitely quite wrong to reason as if there is a stable, simple connection between the rate of interest and the rate of investment. A change in the rate of interest may change producers' behavior from a strategy of Type *A*, or *C*, to a strategy of Type *B*. This could mean changing the main determinants of investment from the supply side to the demand side. This again means changing the rate of investment from something which is based on capacity to produce to something which is based on preferences and behavior in regard to the desired rate of *change of the stock of capital*. Such considerations may well be the key to a better understanding of some of the wild behavior of observed rates of investment.

III. THE WICKSELLIAN CUMULATIVE PROCESS[4]

Wicksell was perhaps the first economist to see clearly the impossibility of adding a constraint of the type (33.2) to the "classical" equilibrium system without causing an inconsistency. Of course, his language was somewhat different from that of today. But if we do not stick pedantically to the particular form of expression which was in use at his time, we shall realize that he discovered a fundamental piece of economic theory which will probably live with us for a long time to come.

The Wicksellian cumulative process is a clear illustration of the truth of the following general proposition: Consider a dynamic economic system which is such that, if we *omitted* all the dynamic elements in it, we should have an overdetermined *static system*. Then the dynamic system may have a solution, but it can have *no stationary solution*. The economic meaning of this is that the time-motion of prices and quantities may serve as an outlet for the forces that press for fulfilment of the impossible conditions for stationariness.

4. Wicksell, *Lectures*, II, 190–208. See also R. Frisch's article on Wicksell in *The Development of Economic Thought: Great Economists in Perspective*, ed. Henry William Spiegel (New York: John Wiley & Sons, 1952), pp. 683–93.

The Wicksellian cumulative process can be described as follows, using our own terminology. Consider the first model described in chapter xxxii. Let $\rho^*(t)$ in equation (33.2) be an autonomously *given function of time*. This would then be the money rate of interest at t. Consider, on the other hand, the rate of interest, $\bar{\rho}(t)$, which would be the solution of the system in chapter xxxii. Suppose that we should find $\bar{\rho}(t) > \rho^*(t)$. What could happen, if money were lent at rate $\rho^*(t)$? It is not possible to say anything about this until we specify how the various participants in the model might act. In order to get the Wicksellian cumulative process we need a particular specification, which is that movement of *absolute prices* would tend to slow down the rate of desired real capital accumulation. This could be so because the spending of more and more money for each capital unit might act as a partial outlet for the efforts to acquire more capital. In the system of chapter xxxii, the absolute level of prices played no role. Therefore we could put $p(t) = q(t) = 1$, or some other arbitrary number. Let us now instead put $p(t) = q(t) = P(t)$.

Consider now equation (32.3). If $\rho^*(t)$ be substituted for $\rho(t) = \bar{\rho}(t)$ in this equation we should, under the form assumed for Φ, get a right-hand side which would be smaller than the left-hand side. Suppose that this would lead to a strategy of Type C, which could be expressed as follows:

$$\frac{d}{dt}[P(t)\,K(t)] = \beta P(t)\left\{\frac{\partial \Phi}{\partial K} - [\rho^*(t) + \bar{\gamma}]\right\}, \quad (33.4a)$$

where β represents the speed of reaction of the producers. This means that, because of equation (32.7), we should have (instead of (32.3))

$$K(t)\frac{\dot{P}(t)}{P(t)} = \beta\left\{\frac{\partial \Phi}{\partial K} - [\rho^*(t) + \bar{\gamma}]\right\} - [k(t) - \bar{\gamma}K(t)]. \quad (33.4b)$$

Wicksell considered the case where, in the short run at least, $[k(t) - \gamma K(t)]$ was approximately zero. Then it is clear that the absolute price level would rise as long as $\bar{\rho}(t) > \rho^*(t)$. To the extent that new capital would actually be forthcoming (i.e., $[k(t) - \bar{\gamma}K(t)] > 0$), this would slow down the rise in prices. However, we cannot safely conclude that, if $[k(t) - \bar{\gamma}K(t)]$ were sufficiently large, prices would fall instead of rise, because this might take us into a producer strategy of Type B, with an entirely different attitude regarding the demand for capital.

It only remains to express what the reader must already have observed, viz., the extremely close connection that exists between the "Keynesian" effects of liquidity constraints and the Wicksellian theory of the cumulative process. The main difference is perhaps that one feels a little more comfortable about the Wicksellian theory when $\rho^* < \bar{\rho}$, and a little more comfortable about the Keynesian ideas when $\rho^* > \bar{\rho}$. It is hard to tell what is the proper verdict on the case $\rho^* = \bar{\rho}$, because this case may actually be far more unstable with regard to producers' behavior than it appears from our scheme above.

34

The Number-of-Firms Problem

We have studied the process of capital accumulation in a market economy under the assumption that the number of firms was a constant. A continued positive rate of accumulation would depend on the ability of some firms to produce capital at the current market price. The output of capital goods would flow automatically into the stock of existing capital.

In the case where this means that the price of capital will have to fall gradually over time, the rate of net profit in the capital-goods–producing industries may fall, in relation to the price of consumer goods. If the capital-goods producers have unequal production functions, some of the producers may eventually reach the zero level of profit and go out of business. But we may also have the development that profits are growing in both industries (e.g., because of population growth). This may mean an incentive to start new firms. Actually, one could say that the incentive is there as long as a firm can be started that will yield a positive net profit. If the incentives are strong, we may here have a very powerful, persistent force leading to demand for capital expansion. But what is *delaying* the process of starting new firms if opportunities of positive net profits prevail? How can there be fewer firms than "desired"? These are questions which we must take very seriously if we want to build a theory of investment on the possibility of growth in the number of firms.

The number-of-firms problem is evidently extremely complicated. We need only to look at the actual size-distribution of existing firms at a given point in time to see that the complexity of the dynamic process which could lead to such a distribution must be quite overwhelming, from an analytical point of view. It may well be that the driving force in this process is something like a "supply of entrepreneurs," and that positive profit possibilities are only a necessary condition. (Actually, we are not even sure that we need the latter.)

Indeed, how should we define an "entrepreneur"? It seems that he is not just a capital-owner, or one who has the right of disposal over capital. He is not simply a manager, because as such he could be counted among the employees. He could be said to be the party who gets net profits. But for what? This is a very old subject of debate. Perhaps the best way out is to define the entrepreneur as the "owner of a production function." In this way he has some sort of exclusive right. Nobody else can use *his* production function. On the other hand, there may exist other production functions that will influence very strongly what the exclusive right of a particular producer is worth. It is, presumably, in the analysis of this influence that we could, perhaps, get some meaningful results by a strictly economic way of reasoning. But the deeper understanding of why—and how—a new firm is established is probably the task of social science in a much wider sense than economics.

I. Free Entry under Perfect Mobility
and Divisibility

Let us consider a scheme of instantaneous adjustment of the number of firms, based on the classical principle that a "something-for-nothing" situation cannot prevail. This may be a most unfair caricature of the classical theory of zero profits. But it may serve as a useful introduction to the basic ideas involved.

Suppose that, at a given point in time, there are n firms, using capital and labor as factors of production. Let their production functions be

$$x_i(t) = \Phi_i[K_i(t), N_i(t)], \qquad i = 1, 2, \ldots, n \quad (34.1)$$

where x is output, N_i labor and K_i capital. Suppose that the producers maximize current net profit under the assumptions of given wages $w(t)$ and capital costs. The latter we shall assume are proportional to the amount of capital used and equal to $[\rho(t) + \gamma] \, q(t) \, K_i(t)$, where $\rho(t)$ is the rate of interest, γ the rate of depreciation and $q(t)$ the price of capital. Let the price of product be equal to 1, by convention. Then we have

$$\frac{\partial \Phi_i}{\partial N_i} = w(t), \quad (34.2)$$

$$\frac{\partial \Phi_i}{\partial K_i} = [\rho(t) + \gamma] \, q(t). \quad (34.3)$$

At a given point of time, t, we have

$$K(t) = \text{a datum at } t. \quad (34.4)$$

Let us also assume, for the sake of simplicity, that

$$w(t) = \text{a datum at } t, \quad (34.5)$$

$$\rho(t) = \text{a datum at } t. \quad (34.6)$$

Assuming that equations (34.2) and (34.3) lead to stable profit maxima, the conditions imposed will determine employment and the price of the capital employed.

Suppose that the result at t is some net profit in all firms. And suppose that new firms could be established at once, by transfer of capital from old firms. Could we assume that n would be instantaneously increased? Apparently not, because this would depend on the profit possibilities in some collection of "latent" production functions. If there were no latent production function with a prospective, positive net profit, there would be no new firms. If, on the other hand, there were latent possibilities of new profitable firms, the result might be either increase, no increase, or decrease in the number of firms, depending on how many would come in and how many would go out.

Consider the special case where all the production functions Φ_i above are alike and equal to Φ, and that there are innumerable latent Φ's of the same kind. Then, using the artifice of regarding n as a continuous variable, we should have the equilibrium condition

$$\Phi\left[\frac{K(t)}{n(t)}, \frac{N(t)}{n(t)}\right] - w(t)\frac{N(t)}{n(t)} - [\rho(t) + \gamma]\,q(t)\frac{K(t)}{n(t)} = 0\,, \quad (34.7)$$

where

$$N(t) = \sum_{1}^{n} N_i(t)\,, \; K(t) = \sum_{1}^{n} K_i(t)\,.$$

This equation, together with the relations above, would determine $n(t)$, in addition to the other variables. This would mean a redistribution of existing capital and also a new equilibrium price of capital. No total "net investment" is involved in this instantaneous adjustment process.

One should note that the condition of zero profit in equilibrium can, in general, only be fulfilled when all the production functions considered are equal. Otherwise, there would always be the possibility of firms with special privileges. One could, of course, assume that the process of making all Φ's equal had taken place by a rule of "survival of the fittest." But then it would be somewhat problematic to consider the possibility of equation (34.7) not being fulfilled. It is really questionable whether one should consider the process of making all firms equal as, in some sense, "faster" than the process that makes profits equal to zero.

We shall try to probe a little deeper into the dynamics of these processes, in particular, the possible dynamics behind the "equilibrium condition" (34.7). Admittedly, there is not much hope of simple and clear results. Our comments will at best serve to emphasize the pressing need for research in this field.

II. Comments on the Dynamics of the
Firm Structure

It may be tempting to construct a simple, dynamic theory of the number of firms along the following lines: If the expression on the left-hand side of equation (34.7) is larger than zero, the number of firms will increase; if the expression is smaller than zero, the number of firms will decrease. The speed of adjustment could be limited by the higher cost of producing new capital at a high rate and also by various kinds of "inertia" in the *supply* of new entrepreneurs. However, there are many reasons why such a theory may be problematic, both from a logical point of view and from the point of view of realism.

First, there is the problem of the *initial conditions*. Suppose we start with a certain number of firms, all having the same production function. Then, if they are fully adjusted, the firms should all use the same amount of capital. Assume that this is the case, and that they are all making a positive net profit, after deducting wages and capital cost according to the principle of a marginal rate of return to these factors. Then there may be a positive difference between the average return on capital if used to start a new firm and the marginal return to capital added to the capital stock of old firms. Is it meaningful to assume that the old firms are fully adjusted with regard to capital while at the same time there is obvious profit to be obtained by starting a new firm? Or, putting the question differently, why should some firms have been expanded beyond the level of optimal marginal return to capital in the first place? This cannot be explained by any hardboiled theory of profit maximum with regard to alternative uses of capital. The existence of a gap as described must be due to a real difference between the operation of adding capital to old firms and the use of capital to establish a new firm.

Second, if we accept such initial conditions as suggested above, there is the question, what size of firm a new entrepreneur would aim at. Would he aim at a size such that the net marginal return to capital would be maximum? Would he start operating the firm before it reached that size, if the firm is built up gradually? There may be a loss of earnings involved in waiting for the completion of a bigger firm than for a smaller firm. Suppose that the capital already invested in existing firms is immobile, i.e., that it can only be reduced by depreciation. Then, theoretically, the flow of new capital goods would go entirely into the establishment of new firms of such a size that their discounted average net return to capital would be maximum. The speed of this process would depend on the supply of new capital, which again would depend on the maximum price for capital that could be paid by new entrepreneurs. In short, does it make sense to start from an initial condition which is clearly not optimal with regard to the size of firms and assume that, suddenly, the adaptation process becomes highly rational?

Third, there is the undeniable fact that, in reality, there is a persistent, enormous difference between the size of firms, even within sectors that produce very similar goods. We can observe that existing firms grow larger at the same time as more firms come into existence. This and other observable facts concerning the firms' structure suggest that a theory based on the requirement of a simple equality of return to capital in all uses may not go very far in explaining the process of capital expansion in a market economy. Profit calculations may still be a very important driving force, but it has to be brought into a framework which permits other factors to account for apparent, persistent "maladjustments."

One idea, near at hand, is that the production function of a firm depends on the *age* of the firm. A firm may be able to absorb more capital as it gains experience. (In some cases the opposite may be true: It finds that it can do better with less capital.) In that case a perfectly "classical" behavior of a producer at any point in time could be combined with a growth process which would exhibit no obvious tendency toward stagnation. Such a process could be concurrent with a high, as well as a low, rate of growth in the number of firms, depending on how the prospects of a new firm would look as compared with the marginal productivity of capital in old firms. It is, however, not likely that we could successfully pursue this idea very far by means of the "classical" framework that we have developed in this study. So, what we have said has to remain a suggestion for further analysis.

A study of the dynamics of the firm structure may be the key to a realistic theory of capital accumulation in a market economy. It is, however, important to realize that even the most extreme assumption of a perfect equilibrium as expressed by equation (34.7) does *not* imply a state of stagnation with zero net investment. For the possibility of a steady increase in the number of firms of optimal size is still wide open. There is no reason why there could not be a sizable net output of capital goods which would then go exclusively for the establishment of new firms. The only constraints upon this growth process would be such things as increase in wages due to a relative shortage of labor or, perhaps, a slowing-down effect due to a lack of supply of new entrepreneurs.

III. A Note on the Problem of Initial Cost of New Firms

When capital in old firms is immobile once it has been acquired, new firms can only be established by means of a flow of newly produced capital. The establishment of a new firm will, therefore, necessarily be a time-consuming process. The expected profitability of a new firm may depend, to some extent, on how quickly new capital can start earning something in a new firm. Suppose that physical capital were fairly divisible, but that it takes a certain *bulk* of it in order to put a new firm into operation.

In that case it may be that the marginal gross profit of starting a new firm may look somewhat less attractive than it actually is because the expected earnings in the new firm are more remote. This, of course, applies only when new capital in old firms can "earn as it grows," whereas in new firms it earns nothing until it suddenly starts earning a finite revenue.

To illustrate how a prospective new entrepreneur might calculate in such cases, consider the following. Suppose that, because of the number of new firms "under construction," it is estimated that it will take T units of time to get enough capital worked up for a new firm, in order that the firm may reach a size where profits including interest are at a maximum per unit of capital. And suppose that it is not possible, or not practical, to start the firm with any smaller amount of capital. Let the amount of capital required for this size of a firm be $\bar{K}$. Assume that the capital producers "accumulate" $\bar{K}$ at approximately a constant rate, per unit of time, and that, alternatively, this flow of capital could have gone into old firms as gradual addition to their operating capital. Let the current marginal earning on capital in old firms be $\rho =$ the current rate of interest, and let the prospective yield in the new firm be $\bar{\rho}$.

The difference between the discounted expected yield of a unit of capital placed in new firms and in old firms could then be written as

$$\bar{\rho} \int_T^\infty e^{-\rho\tau} d\tau - \frac{\rho}{T} \int_0^T \tau e^{-\rho\tau} d\tau - \rho \int_T^\infty e^{-\rho\tau} d\tau \equiv \frac{1}{\rho} (\bar{\rho} - \rho) \ e^{-\rho T}$$
$$- \frac{1}{\rho T} [1 - (1 + \rho T) \ e^{-\rho\tau}] . \tag{34.8}$$

In order that this difference be positive, it is obvious that we must have $\bar{\rho} > \rho$. If, for example, ρ is 5 per cent and $T = 2$ years, we find that $\bar{\rho}$ must be about $\bar{\rho} = 5.3$ per cent. If $T = 3$, we get $\bar{\rho} = 5.4$ per cent.

The critical value of the difference $(\bar{\rho} - \rho)$ appears to be small for moderate values of T and ρ. If this is the case, and if the expected $\bar{\rho}$ is much larger than ρ, the delay before a new firm gets into operation may be of lesser importance. Of course, if there is some larger risk involved in connection with $\bar{\rho}$ than with ρ, the picture may look very different. Then it is quite possible that a new firm will have to look exceptionally good, in order that a prospective entrepreneur should decide to go ahead with it.

35

Concluding Remarks

For those who are looking for "*the* investment equation" as the missing link in modern macroeconomics, our rather lengthy analysis may not have yielded much satisfaction. Our efforts have been directed toward a more modest goal. We have tried, by adoption of the most hard-boiled assumptions, to discover whether there is room for a positive rate of capital accumulation within the traditional framework of general equilibrium analysis. We have tried to show that the answer to this queston is in the affirmative. But we hope, also, to have convinced the reader that this answer is not reached simply by a traditional supply-demand scheme, equating the "demand for investment" to the supply of a flow of new capital goods. The "demand" in this case is for a *stock* of capital, whereas the supply is a flow. In this dimensional difference between the demand and the supply side lies the main problem of an equilibrium theory of investment. Here lies, perhaps, also the key to an understanding of why actual processes of investment, in the short run, may be wild and, perhaps, unpredictable.

However, even if short-run fluctuations in investment may be difficult to predict, our analysis suggests that a positive rate of capital accumulation certainly does not have to be explained solely by external factors. It is not so that we have to have new technological or other "shocks" all the time in order to have sustained growth. Even if the price of capital is such that the marginal return to the existing volume of capital makes this volume instantaneously optimal, this does *not* necessarily mean that it would not pay to *produce* capital at that price. If we want to draw a parallel to the Böhm-Bawerkian notion of roundaboutness, we could say that the existing amount of capital at any time corresponds to the desired degree of roundaboutness at the current level of *consumption*. But if the current level of consumption were equal to total net *output*, the desired degree of roundaboutness might be much higher. Hence, we should have a positive rate of capital accumulation.

I should also like to re-emphasize a negative result which I feel that we have established with some force. This is the conclusion reached concerning the dubious theoretical validity of the "investment schedule" in recent macroeconomic models. I do not, of course, mean to reject the possibility that an empirical relation may be found between the rate

215

of interest and the rate of investment. What we should reject is the naïve reasoning that there is a "demand schedule" for investment which could be derived from a classical scheme of producers' behavior in maximizing profit. The demand for *investment* cannot simply be derived from the demand for *capital*. Demand for a finite addition to the stock of capital can lead to *any rate* of investment, from almost zero to infinity, depending on the additional hypothesis we introduce regarding the speed of reaction of the capital-users. I think that the sooner this naïve, and unfounded, theory of the demand-for-investment schedule is abandoned, the sooner we shall have a chance of making some real progress in constructing more powerful theories to deal with the capricious short-run variations in the rate of private investment.

Because of the possibility of violent short-run deviations from the "normal" market behavior in the models of chapters xxxi and xxxii, these models may have only a low power of prediction for year-to-year variations in the rate of investment. What is more important, however, is the actual loss of economic welfare that may result from such violent short-run fluctuations. If the "normal" market development is regarded as in some sense optimal, then clearly any deviations from this development have to be counted as a loss. But one could, of course, question the optimality of the market development that we have termed "normal." In order to deal with this question we should have to study the performance of the "normal" market mechanism in relation to the basic purpose of capital accumulation for society as a whole.

In Part III we tried to bring out the fundamentals of capital accumulations without imposing any particular, organizational constraints upon the economy. We rediscovered some well-known, almost classical, conclusions: The willingness of an economy to hold a certain stock of capital depends on the level of consumption. The difference between total net output and the lowest rate of consumption at which the economy is willing to hold the existing stock of capital determines the instantaneous rate of accumulation. But the economy cannot make a sensible choice of current consumption except by looking into the future. The economy has to choose between the present and the future, taking into account the productivity of the amount of capital held at any moment.

Of course, the notion of an optimal choice in this case would depend on what we mean by a preference function for the "economy as a whole." If the economy is composed of many individual decision units with different preferences, and we do not accept any principle of weighting individual preferences, the notion of an optimal rate of capital accumulation makes no sense.

It is of little use in this connection to introduce the weaker notion of optimum known as the "Pareto optimum," because it is hard to conceive of any practical initial situation such that a change would not be detrimental to at least one decision-maker. If we are thinking in terms of alternative ways of organizing an economy, we cannot use the Pareto principle to decide whether any one such organization, is by itself, good or bad. For example, if we did not have progressive taxation, it may not be an improvement, in the Pareto sense, to introduce such taxation. If we do have progressive taxes, it may not be an improvement, in the Pareto sense, to abolish them.

However, every modern society does, in fact, operate with some kind of global preference function for the economy as a whole. Thus, for example, every modern society has some policy directed toward the redistribution of income. Every modern society recognizes that all its members, and not only the entrepreneurial group, have an interest in how capital accumulation and productive capacity develops. In every democratic society the political group in majority has enormous constitutional powers to change the ways in which the economy is operating. How does the economic framework of a market economy as described in chapters xxxi and xxxii fit into the observable patterns of economic, social, and political struggle in modern societies?

For one thing, it is clear that the normally high rate of capital accumulation in modern societies, based on private enterprise, expresses the desires of a vast majority, and not only the preferences of a few rich people. In all such societies the number of people with incomes below a level of almost zero savings could, by constitutional majority decisions, legalize taxes that would greatly reduce the rate of capital accumulation. But considerable voluntary restraint is shown in this respect. This leaves room for a sizable sector of capital-producing firms, within the productive capacity of the economy.

A market framework of the kind described in chapters xxxi and xxxii may function quite well even if a public policy of taxation and other fiscal measures is superimposed on it, which means a considerable redistribution of income. The system may normally be capable of operating efficiently at a low as well as a high rate of capital accumulation. It is quite possible to have a system of taxation which regulates the use of resources toward more consumer goods or less consumer goods without having the effects of unemployment or idle capacity.

But the market framework has undoubtedly some aspects which are less happy. Of these we want here to emphasize only one, namely, the way in which the system interprets the *preferences behind a demand for wage increases.* It may be argued, with considerable force I think, that the system tends to *misinterpret* these preferences as if they meant a *request from the workers to economize with labor.* The reason for this is, that the single parameter "wages" has to serve too many purposes. One important function of wages is to distribute labor among the various lines of production so as to avoid *relative malallocation.* This "message" of wage demands the market framework probably interprets in a rather satisfactory way. Another function of wages is to regulate the rate of consumption, in relation to the rate of capital accumulation. That the wage rate can serve this purpose is due to the historical and institutional fact that most of the wage bill in the economy goes to the lower income groups. Here the market systems misinterpret the "message" in a demand for wage increases as a desire for less total input of labor. If such a desire is involved, this is certainly, in most cases, only a small part of the story. A third function of the wage rate is to serve as an economic-political measure of redistribution of income. Also this "message" the market system will tend to misinterpret as a general desire in the economy to *use less labor* in production.

As a result of these "misinterpretations," an increase in wages tends to *reduce employment and, therefore, the marginal productivity of the existing amount of capital* (assuming capital and labor to be complementary factors). This effect upon the apparent marginal productivity of capital, and the resulting fall in capital prices, and in the supply of new capital goods, may not represent what labor as a group wants to achieve by a wage increase. If the market mechanism is to function properly, it would seem necessary that the economic-political struggle be fought with other instruments than the wage rate. Alternatively, one could visualize a policy of taxes and subsidies that would intercept the equality between wages and the marginal productivity of labor as a guide for entrepreneurial decisions.

Index

PRINTED IN U.S.A.